Building Wellbeing and Resilience

How to Help

Rob Long

Building Wellbeing and Resilience

Published by:
Pavilion Publishing and Media Ltd
Blue Sky Offices, 25 Cecil Pashley Way
Shoreham-by-Sea, West Sussex
BN43 5FF

Tel: 01273 434 943
Email: info@pavpub.com
Web: www.pavpub.com

Published 2021

ISBN: 978-1-912755-96-7

Pavilion Publishing and Media is a leading publisher of books, training materials and digital content in mental health, social care and allied fields. Pavilion and its imprints offer must-have knowledge and innovative learning solutions underpinned by sound research and professional values.

Author: Dr Rob Long
Cover design: Emma Dawe, Pavilion Publishing and Media Ltd
Page layout and typesetting: Emma Dawe, Pavilion Publishing and Media Ltd
Printing: CMP

Contents

Series Preface

Young people in today's society face considerable stresses. The Prince's Trust, which has monitored youth opinion for ten years, found that just under half of young people who use social media now feel more anxious about their future when they compare themselves to others on websites and apps such as Instagram, Twitter and Facebook. A similar proportion agreed that social media makes them feel 'inadequate'. The *Guardian Weekly* noted in early 2019 that more than half of young people think that social media creates 'overwhelming pressure' to succeed.

There are many issues that are likely to affect every pupil at some point during his or her time at school. How these are dealt with can be 'make or break' for some pupils, because of the crucial stages in education that can be affected. The implications are deep and broad because, understandably, the child's experience of education, and his or her success at school, can have a tremendous impact on later life chances.

The *How to Help* series covers a broad and comprehensive range of topics that will have resonance for today's parents, carers and educators. Each title is designed to make a valuable contribution in the breadth of issues that it introduces, and the realistic helping strategies that it puts forward.

Gavin Reid and Jennie Guise
Series Editors

About the Author

Dr Rob Long is a Chartered Psychologist who provides independent training to teachers and other professionals concerned with children and young adults. He also offers individual advice and support to young people and their families. Previously, Rob lectured in Psychology and Sociology before working as an Educational Psychologist for Wolverhampton and then Devon Education Authorities. During this time he managed a Primary Behaviour Support Team, and also supported secondary schools in reviewing their behaviour management policies and practice. Rob's main area of interest is supporting children who face social, emotional and mental health difficulties. He is committed to developing, through training and project work, an understanding of these children and providing solutions and practical help to school staff involved with them. He is a tutor on a distance learning course in Social, Emotional and Mental Health issues run by Oxford Brookes University and the Social, Emotional, Behavioural Difficulties Association (SEBDA). He is also an active member of SEBDA.

Author's Preface

Concerns about the wellbeing of children and young people have increased around the world. Of course adults have always expressed concern for children's welfare, but today this seems to have increased exponentially. In the past the concern was usually about problem behaviours, and the aim was simply to remove them. Schools employed counsellors, education welfare officers, educational psychologists and social workers to address this. Programmes were developed, and most schools today have policies that aim to remove problem behaviours and encourage positive ones.

Many of the problem behaviours that children and young people can exhibit seem to share common indicators. For example, there are four broad categories of socioeconomic circumstance that are closely associated with most adolescent problem behaviours: early educational failure, childhood problems, family dysfunction, and poverty. As a result, children's services have focused on designing programmes to tackle these common indicators as ways of improving outcomes.

The better wellbeing is understood, the more it becomes clear that there can be no 'quick fix'. The many difficulties that children and young people face today are the result of many complex factors interacting with each other. Some factors promote wellbeing whereas others prevent it, and it is important to understand both. To that end, this book is intended to be a resource for professionals, parents and carers, and community leaders. It is hoped that it can be as jargon-free as possible and, whenever terms are used that require more precision, definitions will be provided.

Dr Rob Long

How to Use This Book

Topics in this *How to Help* book are organised within five major sections, comprising Parts 2 to 6:

- The science of wellbeing
- Wellbeing and development
- Wellbeing at home and in school
- Resilience and mental health
- Complex difficulties and disadvantage

Within these sections, each specific topic is discussed in a separate chapter (although it should be noted that in practice there will frequently be areas of overlap), with advice for parents, carers, teachers and schools. You can read through the sections in order or go straight to what most concerns you. The topics have been chosen to represent the key issues that typically arise when seeking to parent, teach, support and understand children and young people with regard to their wellbeing and resilience.

 Whenever you see the *How to Help* icon, you can expect to find practical, ready to use suggestions and strategies for helping children and young people to build and maintain their levels of wellbeing and resilience.

We recommend that you read in full the Introduction (Part 1) and Conclusion (Part 7). The former serves as an entry point to the field of general wellbeing and resilience, whereas the latter collects and summarises the book's most important advice on *How to Help*.

To keep up to date with the *How to Help* series, bookmark:

www.pavpub.com/howtohelp

"It is easier to build strong children than to repair broken men."

Frederick Douglass

To my wife, Chris, children Jenni and Joe and their families.
Ever onward together.

Part 1: Introduction

Chapter 1: What are wellbeing and resilience?

Introducing wellbeing and resilience

Wellbeing is a term that can be hard to define. Often it is confused with mental health, or with physical wellness. In fact, wellbeing incorporates aspects of both – as well as elements of purpose, opportunity, relationships and satisfaction – into a broader concept of 'how we are'. If either our physical or mental health is poor, we'll find it hard to achieve a state of positive wellbeing; conversely, neither good physical health nor good mental health in itself ensures high wellbeing.

There are scientific definitions of wellbeing that bring in elements of the natural environment, the economy, education and much more. For us, and to begin this book, it is enough to say that personal wellbeing can be thought of as a measure of our current state of happiness, health, comfort and overall contentment with our lives. Wellbeing isn't about the moment; it reflects our relationship with ourselves at a particular stage of our lives, rather than our state of mind at a specific point in time.

Key Point

Personal wellbeing can be thought of as a measure of our current state of happiness, health, comfort and overall contentment with our lives.

Resilience is the ability to cope with adversity and bounce back. All of us will encounter negative experiences at some point in our life – whether it be health problems, job issues, financial worries or the loss of a loved one. People generally adapt surprisingly well to such situations, thanks partly to resilience. This doesn't mean that resilient people don't experience difficulty or distress; rather, it means that they find it within themselves to work through adversity, adapt, move forward and grow.

Resilience is linked directly to high levels of personal wellbeing. This is because its influence extends far beyond occasional life-changing situations; it also enables us to cope with the normal ups and downs of life and stay confident, optimistic and in control. Such skills are especially important for young people given the stresses they face during the transition through adolescence to adulthood. Most crucially of all, resilience involves behaviours, thoughts and actions that anyone can develop. It can be learned!

A brief history of psychology

From the time of the Ancient Greeks, people have tried to make sense of human behaviour. The history of how we have tried to investigate our natural and social worlds is a fascinating account of rivalries and dramatic discoveries. For the Greeks, everything could be explained by the existence of numerous gods; this changed with the rational approaches of Socrates and Plato. The Roman philosophers then explored mysticism and emphasised the importance of reason and self-control over human emotions.

We then enter the Dark Ages, a period when religion was the dominant source of knowledge and understanding, before they in turn give way to the Enlightenment of the 17th and 18th centuries. This was the beginning of the scientific approach, where enquiry began to be based on reason rather than religion. During this time God was believed to exist, but not to interact with the physical world – a world that followed laws that could be studied thorough observation and experimentation.

So successful were the natural sciences at discovering the laws of nature that the social sciences tried to emulate their approach. Psychology set out to analyse the individual, sociology set out to study society, and anthropology set out to understand human culture. During this mid-20th century period, which was described as modernity, the foremost minds believed that human behaviour could be studied scientifically to uncover the universal laws that were assumed to govern it.

This paradigm has gradually been challenged and we are now in period, popularly known as the postmodern era, which does not reject modern beliefs but rather sees a need for correction or editing of them (Elkind, 2009).[1] While accepting universality, there is also particularity. The postmodern paradigm accepts order but also disorder, and it accepts that there is no theory or discipline can single-handedly explain the overwhelming complexity of human behaviour.

This book is unashamedly biased towards a psychological perspective. Within psychology, the concepts of wellbeing and resilience are both related specifically to the field of *positive psychology*. Positive psychology is considered to have been founded as a discipline and field of study in 1998 by the American psychologist Martin Seligman, and represents a move away from psychology's traditional focus on healing mental illness and toward what enables people to have happy, fulfilling lives.

---

1   Elkind D (2009) In Scarlett W, Chin Ponte I and Singh J (2009) *Approaches To Behavior And Classroom Management: Integrating Discipline And Care*. Newbury Park, CA: Sage.

Positive psychologists are interested not in studying what is wrong with people, but in exploring what is 'right' about healthy people and how such character strengths can be defined and acquired to promote positive human development. They believe that human beings can and should be drawn by the promise of the future more than they are driven by the memories of the past – and that changing this perception of time can have a profound effect on how we think about happiness.

During the two decades since positive psychology took flight, researchers have explored a wide range of topics. Thanks to them, we now know far more about wellbeing and what leads us to be happy.

Key Point

Positive psychologists are interested not in studying what is wrong with people, but in exploring what is 'right' about healthy people.

What determines wellbeing?

In the past there would have been heated arguments as to which academic discipline wellbeing belonged to. Psychologists, sociologists and the medical profession would each have had a claim.

- **Psychologists** believe that it is the inner world of an individual that determines the life they will lead. A person's thinking style, childhood experiences and learning ability will determine the degree to which they can achieve wellbeing.
- **Sociologists** believe that it is a person's social class and economic status that matters most of all. Factors such as education level, occupational status and life expectancy will determine and/or influence a person's level of wellbeing.
- **Medical professionals** would argue that lifestyle, diet and exercise as well as inherited predispositions to certain illnesses are the determining factors.

Each of these assertions has an element of truth. We might think of the well-known parable of the blind people meeting an elephant and then returning to their village to explain what kind of animal they had encountered. For one it was like a snake, for another like a rope, for another like a pillar, for another like a wall, and so on. Each told the truth and spoke honestly about their experience. Today it is more generally accepted that a full understanding of wellbeing involves many approaches. Wellbeing is too complex to be explained from any one perspective.

For a child or young person, wellbeing will be influenced by a number of interconnecting factors:

Individual

- Physical health
- Social and emotional skills.
- Learning and development

Family

- Parental/carer physical and mental health
- Family relationships
- Financial hardship

Learning environment

- School connectedness
- Peer relationships
- Academic engagement

Community

- Neighbourhood safety
- Neighbourhood poverty
- Physical environment
- Social inclusion

The need to understand and promote wellbeing was well articulated by Robert F. Kennedy in 1968 when he said: "*But even if we act to erase material poverty, there is another greater task: it is to confront the poverty of satisfaction – purpose and dignity – that affects us all.*" Today, though, there is an even stronger justification for prioritising wellbeing when we consider the growth in the number of children and young people experiencing some form of mental health issue. The things that underpin positive wellbeing – like self-regulation, emotional literacy, problem-solving and healthy peer relationships – are believed to be the very same tools needed to combat some of the mental health problems that children and young people can experience.

Mental health and wellbeing

Wellbeing and mental health are often seen as being closely related, but are they? Can you be mentally well and have poor wellbeing, or can you have positive wellbeing but be mentally ill?

It is important to understand that, although mental health and wellbeing share similarities, there is a marked difference between them. Let us first consider mental health. If we think of mental health and illness as two ends of a spectrum, a young person is either mentally ill or mentally well, right?

If only it were that easy!

A mental illness occurs when an individual is having difficulty functioning or coping. In children and young people, symptoms show in the following areas:

■ Emotional: anxiety and depression

■ Behavioural: defiance and challenging behaviour

■ Developmental delays: in speech and communication, as well as cognitive delays

■ Relationship difficulties: observed in attachment issues such as non-trusting

Such symptoms can lead to a suitably qualified person diagnosing a specific condition. In other words, adults who know and care about a particular young person can recognise signs that all is not well, and a doctor, psychologist or other professional can then confirm whether or not a mental illness is present.

So, are we mentally healthy if we don't have a diagnosis of being mentally ill?

Not at all!

We described mental health and illness above as a spectrum. In fact, this is how conditions such as autism are classified – the exact way in which autism affects individuals is very variable, so experts describe it as a spectrum. In the same way, we are all on a mental health spectrum; for instance, most people have anxieties, perhaps towards heights or snakes, but the level of anxiety they experience is not severe enough for it to interfere with their normal activities and therefore it does not qualify for the label of a clinical phobia.

Let us now return to wellbeing. Wellbeing is not a panacea for mental health issues, nor does it even correlate directly to mental health. Children and young people can have a strong sense of wellbeing and still become mentally ill, just as eating five portions of fruit and vegetables a day is good for you but won't stop you breaking your leg (although it will help with recovery). Similarly, wellbeing can help a child or young person to cope with anxiety or depression, but it cannot prevent it.

Key Point

Wellbeing can help a child or young person to cope with anxiety or depression, but it cannot prevent it.

Wellbeing, then, is a positive aid and a valid goal, but it is not a form of inoculation against mental illness. Just because young people are taught how look after their wellbeing, this does not mean that they cannot suffer a mental illness. The key benefits of positive wellbeing lie elsewhere. It can empower children and young people to act freely and make choices; it can help them feel safe and secure in their daily lives and social relations; it can promote a sense of personal autonomy and satisfaction; and it can provide them with a sense of meaning and value in their lives.

It is a powerful force for good.

Chapter 2: Wellbeing in context

Wellbeing across societies

Having wellbeing means in essence that children and young people can do the positive things that they are expected to do given their sociocultural status and background. As the anthropologist Tom Weisner puts it: *"Wellbeing is the ability of a child to actively participate in the activities that that society thinks is important and desirable"* (Weisner, 1984).[2] This naturally means that wellbeing will vary across different societies and will change over time. So wellbeing today is not the same as wellbeing in the 1800s. It will also vary between social classes, ethnic groups and religions. At best we can find a few universal aspects of wellbeing that seem to be relatively fixed between societies and ages, but when we look more closely we should always expect to see big differences.

> ## Expert View
>
> *"The importance of keeping the context in mind needs to be brought out more strongly in how we think about kids and how we try to improve their wellbeing."*
>
> Tom Weisner

Since 2012 the United Nations has employed a 'World Happiness Report' to survey the state of global wellbeing and happiness, and since 2011 the Organisation for Economic Co-operation and Development (OECD) has maintained a set of indices that allow wellbeing to be compared across different countries. Some of the key markers of wellbeing used are health, housing, education, environment, safety, and life satisfaction.

A country that has taken wellbeing and happiness to heart is the Himalayan Kingdom of Bhutan. Initiated by King Jigme Singye Wangchuck, who popularised a statement made by Dutch politician Sicco Mansholt that *"gross national happiness is more important than gross domestic product (GDP)"*. Bhutan's drive for greater happiness among its citizens is today supported by his son Jigme Khesar Namgyel Wangchuck, who took over as King when Jigme Singye Wangchuck abdicated in 2006. Although Bhutan is a poor and underdeveloped country of some 750,000 people with problems that include youth unemployment and inequality,

---

2   Weisner T (2016) *What is the most important influence on child development?* [video]. TED Conferences.

it is also an example of a country that has taken the pursuit of happiness seriously and embraced it at a national level.

The motivation to devote a similar scale of research to 'the worthwhileness of life' as to GDP is high for many affluent Western countries. This point was made forcefully by the results of a 2007 UNICEF report, which found that all the countries it surveyed had weaknesses with respect to wellbeing for their children.[3] Both the UK and US placed in the bottom third of rankings for five of six wellbeing dimensions, and the UK occupied one of the bottom two places on 'subjective wellbeing'. This state of affairs does seem to be changing for the better though – OECD data ranked the UK 18th out of 36 OECD countries for wellbeing (2013),[4] and UNICEF data showed that 86% of children living in the UK rated their life satisfaction highly (2011).[5]

Wellbeing and socioeconomic status

Contrary to what many of us suppose is the case, there is no natural link between being poor and a person's sense of wellbeing. Wealthy people certainly do not always have high wellbeing. However, what is undoubtedly true is that there are conditions associated with poverty that have been shown clearly to impede individual wellbeing – including poor physical health, mental health problems, underachievement at school, social deprivation, feeling unsafe, stigma and bullying at school.

Poorer areas typically lack a range of neighbourhood institutions that more prosperous ones will have, such as childcare centres, after school programmes, sports facilities, and theatres (Neckerman, 2004).[6] When an area has a high turnover of residents, and when criminality/delinquency and vandalism are common, the children and young people living there are likely to have those involved in such behaviours among their peers and role models. So it is easier for deviant behaviour to become the norm.

3   UNICEF (2007) *An Overview Of Child Wellbeing In Rich Countries*. Available at: https://www.unicef.org/media/files/ChildPovertyReport.pdf [last accessed 4 February 2021]

4   Organisation for Economic Co-operation and Development (2013) OECD: *Your Better Life Index*. Available at: http://stats.oecd.org/Index.aspx?DataSetCode = BLI Index website: http://www.oecdbetterlifeindex.org/ [last accessed 15 February 2021

5   UNICEF Office of Research (2011) *Child Well-being In Rich Countries: A Comparative Review*. Available at: https://www.unicef-irc.org/publications/683-child-well-being-in-rich-countries-a-comparative-overview.html [last accessed 15 February 2021]

6   Neckerman K (2004) *Social Inequality*. New York, NY: Russell Sage Foundation.

Wellbeing across the generations

Although we've said that the formal science of positive psychology began around the turn of the millennium, its founders built on work that had been going on under other names for many years. In fact, a gradual change in thinking about mental health had been underway since World War Two. Prior to that, the overriding emphasis had been on fixing problems once they occurred; today, the focus is much more on preventing mental health problems from occurring in the first place.

Key Point

In the 1950s and 1960s, largely in response to the physical and moral destruction caused by two World Wars, individuals began to be valued for their uniqueness.

Prior to the 1950s, the science of psychology was dominated by two schools of thought known as behaviourism and psychoanalysis. Put simply, these approaches sought respectively to control human behaviour and to fix internal conflicts. In the 1950s and 1960s, largely in response to the physical and moral destruction caused by two World Wars, individuals began to be valued for their uniqueness. Psychological movements emerged that studied individual perceptions and personal meanings. Approaches that had been frowned upon became acceptable, and subjective concepts like wellbeing and resilience could finally be studied in more scientific ways.

Wellbeing as a state, as we have touched upon above, is typically thought to involve a combination of satisfying social relationships, optimal health, lifelong learning abilities, social and personal responsibility, and purposefulness (Foege, 2003).[7] Before embarking on a more detailed discussion, we should establish why wellbeing has become such a focus of current attention. The contemporary concerns are mainly on account of a dramatic rise in mental health issues among children and young people. This is made clear by the charity Young Minds in their ongoing 'Wise Up' campaign:

---

7   Foege WH (2003) Foreword. In Bornstein MH, Davidson L, Keyes CLM, Moore KA (Eds.) (2012) *Well-Being: Positive Development Across The Life Course*. Mahwah, NJ: Lawrence Erlbaum Associates.

*"There is a mental health crisis in our classrooms. Three children
in every classroom have a diagnosable mental disorder and 90%
of school leaders have reported an increase in the last five years
in the number of students experiencing anxiety, stress,
low mood or depression."* (Young Minds, 2016)[8]

Media headlines regularly highlight the mental health issues facing
today's children and young people, questioning whether they face more
stresses than previous generations. This reflects a growing awareness and
acceptance that children and young people are indeed experiencing more
mental health problems. The reasons behind this are complex. Children and
young people are growing up in a world that is very different to the one
their parents knew, and with the growth in digital media they have means
of communication far beyond the imagination of earlier generations.

To make sense of the challenges that they face, it may help if we consider
the generational changes that have taken place since the end of World
War Two. Different generations are often stereotyped by the media and
can be described as 'cohorts'. A generational cohort is defined by the year
in which people were born. There are usually key events and common
experiences that shape and influence a cohort. So by age, the generational
cohorts of the past 75 years can be classified as follows:

Baby boomers: Born 1944–1964
Current ages – 55–75
Nickname – Hippies
Shaping experiences – the Cold War, the Vietnam War

Generation X: Born 1965–1979
Current ages – 40–55
Nicknames – the latchkey generation or the MTV generation
Shaping experiences – end of The Cold War, the rise of personal computers

Generation Y: Born 1980–1994
Current ages – 25–40
Nickname – Millennials
Shaping experiences – the explosion of the Internet, social media, 9/11

---

8   Young Minds (2016) *Young Minds Annual Report* 2015–2016. Available at: https://
youngminds.org.uk/media/1233/youngminds-annual-report-15-16-final.pdf [last accessed at 4
February 2021]

Generation Z: Born 1995–2015
Current ages – 5–25
Nicknames – Post-millennials
Shaping experiences – the financial crisis of 2008, Internet available from a young age

These generational names are commonly used in marketing to identify groups with similar attitudes and motivations for consumer purposes. As individuals we don't typically see ourselves in such ways, although it does highlight that children of different times will have different experiences. And, as we shall see, the key issues of any era come to set the agenda/ issues that families and children must face.

Wellbeing in our times

None of us can escape the times we were born in, and those times will, to varying degrees, shape how we think and feel. Moreover, we are influenced not only by our own times, but also by the times that our parents grew up in and how they influenced the ways in which they went about raising us.

Parenting manuals tend to advocate one specific method of raising children – for example, filling a nursery with sounds and visual objects to keep a child stimulated. The American paediatrician Dr Benjamin Spock, whose seminal 1946 book *Baby And Child Care* is still in print, advocated that babies should be fed on demand and parents should aim to satisfy their needs at all times.[9] This permissive parenting style influenced many people's early experiences. It stands in stark contrast to, for example, the strict routine approach advocated by Gina Ford in *The Contented Little Baby Book* (1999), which suggests waking and feeding a baby by 7am and then once every four hours.[10]

Key Point

Today, more than ever, children and young people develop with a wide range of influences affecting them.

Today, more than ever, children and young people develop with a wide range of influences affecting them. Many of these are positive, but there are also those that many would consider potential risk factors. In the past, children and young people acquired the skills to manage everyday pressures from family, friends and peers. Over the course of this process

---

9   Spock B (2018) *Dr. Spock's Baby And Child Care*. London: Pocket Books.
10 Ford G (2006) *The New Contented Little Baby Book*. London: Vermilion.

they learned from each other key social skills such as problem-solving and relationship skills. Children and young people growing up in the 21st century are more often not under the watchful eye of an adult, so the spontaneous learning of how to be with other people, how to solve differences and so on is less readily available.

Conversely, more time is spent on social media, which is an individual experience. This is not to berate social media such as Instagram and Snapchat. There are many good things to be said about them. For example, children and young people can readily find others who are facing similar problems to themselves, and form support groups as well as safely exploring problems in a private way. There is a price to be paid for this, however. The World Happiness Report (2019) found that:[11]

> "In the US the amount of time children and young people spend on screen activities has increased for 17–18-year-olds to more than six hours per day, and some 45% said they were online 'almost constantly'. Today it seems that social interaction between adolescents is more often through online activities and not face-to-face."

---

11   Twenge JM (2019) The Sad State Of Happiness And The Role Of Digital Media. In Helliwell JF, Layard R & Sachs JD (Eds.) *World Happiness Report 2019*. Available at: https:// worldhappiness.report/ed/2019/the-sad-state-of-happiness-in-the-united-states-and-the-role-of-digital-media/ [accessed 4 February 2021]

Chapter 3: Wellbeing and development

Stress and its effects

Are our children and young people more stressed than ever before? Are they suffering more mental health problems? Numerous credible studies seem to suggest that children and young people today experience more stress than previous generations as indicated by the number of disorders recorded (Transforming Children

and Young People's Mental Health Provision, 2017)[12]. Specific data will be presented later; for the moment, suffice to say that one in ten young people have a diagnosable mental health disorder. That equates to a total of 850,000 children and young people in the UK alone.

People often speak of 'being stressed', but what does this really mean? Stress means that demands are being made of us that exceed our ability to cope. The demand might be emotional, cognitive or physical. And a stressor may be good or bad – for example, arranging a wedding can be stressful, but it is a very different experience from coping with unexpected redundancy.

How we react to stress involves the complex interplay of several systems and contextual factors. Stress can be understood on two basic levels, physiological and psychological. The normal physiological stress response is adaptive and short-lived. It is part of our biological inheritance. It prepares us for a 'fight or flight' response, as if we were being attacked. As a result, it increases our heart rate, muscle tone and alertness. Small amounts of stress can be positive, improving how we cope with a situation.

A key part of our stress reaction involves a hormone called cortisol, often thought of as 'the stress hormone'. Cortisol is much more than just a stress hormone, however, and its effects can be positive or negative. Our cortisol levels increase in the morning as we become

---

12 Department for Education (2017) *Transforming Children And Young People's Mental Health Provision: A Green Paper*. Available at: https://assets.publishing.service.gov.uk/government/uploads/system/uploads/attachment_data/file/664855/Transforming_children_and_young_people_s_mental_health_provision.pdf [last accessed 4 February 2021]

active, and they decrease towards the end of the day in preparation for rest. So far, so good. The main problem with cortisol occurs when we are exposed to a high level of stress for long periods of time. *"We are then in a state of fight or flight, and can be oversensitive to see threats when none exist"* (Parr, 2019).[13]

This perpetual state of heightened cortisol can be especially relevant to children and young people who are overexposed to threatening or frightening situations. Under such circumstances, young people cannot be described as school-ready; instead, they arrive like a shaken up can of Coke.

Under normal circumstances, then, stress is short-lived. A short-lived bodily state or condition like this is often referred to as 'acute', as opposed to 'chronic' conditions, which are more persistent. Homeostasis, or bodily balance, returns quickly. Being able to adapt quickly to a possible threat is a response known as allostasis, and a rapid return to a normal state of functioning makes good survival sense – being on 'red alert' for an excessive time would be counter-productive.

How does stress affect development?

Stress can be very harmful to normal development. If children and young people experience chronic stressful experiences, then their physiological ability to manage stress effectively is jeopardised. So instead of the stress being properly regulated by the body it becomes dysregulated – the normal allostasis processes are unable to return the individual to a state of balance. The response pattern becomes maladaptive, and stress-induced hormones such as cortisol remain in circulation while hormones that promote a return to balance are deficient. The young person is put in an over-alert state of readiness for potential threats, and subconsciously they will expect to encounter danger simply because they are in a physiological state that has prepared them for it. Under such circumstances, positive wellbeing is a physical and psychological impossibility.

Key Point

If children and young people experience chronic stressful experiences, then their physiological ability to manage stress effectively is jeopardised.

---

13 Parr C (2019) Cortisol: Not The Baddie You Might Have Thought. *Times Educational Supplement*, 8 March 2019. Available at: https://www.pressreader.com/uk/tes-times-education-supplement/20201120/page/92 [last accessed 4 February 2021]

There is evidence to support this. Research by Landsford et al (2012) found that children who experienced physical aggression from their parents were more likely to develop impulsive aggressive behaviours.[14] A study by Arsenio and Gold (2006) found that maltreated children with insecure attachments lacked empathy towards others and often believed that life was not fair, just or safe.[15] As one teacher explained, referring to the American psychologist Abraham Maslow's famous 'hierarchy of needs': "*For children to be able to access learning they need to be in a position where they're not stressed, where they're able to focus*" (Mellor, 2019).[16]

It would seem that the nervous systems of children and young people who are abused or mistreated develop patterns that help them make sense of the situations in which they find themselves. Having an over-aroused nervous system enables them to be hypervigilant. Because they are surrounded by unpredictability, it makes sense for them to be super-alert as a way of surviving and coping. Just as a car that is stuck in a low gear will over-rev as if it is always about to climb a hill, so a child who has adapted to circumstance in this way is constantly over-prepared for threats and dangers.

Key Point

Stress in the early formative years can have profound consequences for wellbeing in later life.

Such chronic stress is especially concerning because of the human brain's plasticity. The brain of a child or young person is still developing, and it is responsive to external factors. Exposure to chronic stressors during sensitive periods of development can cause long-lasting changes in the brain's neural system, and these can lead to changes in how a young person responds in the future. So stress in the early formative years can have profound consequences for wellbeing in later life, as maladaptive responses lead to a range of possible social, emotional and mental health problems.

The Adverse Childhood Experiences (ACE) study (Felitti et al, 1998) is one of the largest investigations of the link between childhood maltreatment

---

14 Landsford J (2012) Boys' and girls' relational and physical aggression in nine countries. *Aggress Behav* 38(4): 298–308.

15 Arsenio W, Gold J & Adam E (2006) Children's Conceptions And Displays Of Moral Emotions. In Killen M & Smetana J (Eds.) *Handbook Of Moral Development* (pp. 581–609). Mahwah, NJ: Lawrence Erlbaum Associates.

16 Mellor A (2019) Cited in Hazell W. A Matter Of Life And Death. *Times Education Supplement* 15 March 2019. Available at: https://www.kuleuven.be/thomas/algemeen/obed/item/5/44618/ [last accessed 4 February 2021]

and later health and wellbeing.[17] It began in the 1980s, when physician and researcher Dr Vincent Felitti became frustrated by high drop-out rates in his San Diego obesity clinic, despite good results. He stumbled upon a link between the development of obesity and childhood sexual abuse, and subsequently led a study involving more than 17,000 people. Participants were asked about their health history as well as their childhood experiences. Specifically, they were asked if they had been exposed to any of the following issues, grouped into three categories:

Abuse
- Psychological abuse
- Physical abuse
- Sexual abuse

Neglect
- Emotional neglect
- Physical neglect

Household dysfunction
- Family breakdowns
- Violence in the home
- Mental illness in the home
- Criminality in the home

Expert View

"Time does not heal all wounds, since humans convert traumatic emotional experiences in childhood into organic disease later in life."

Vincent Felitti

The study found that the more adverse experiences encountered in childhood, the greater the risk of the individual developing a range of problems in adulthood. Those who experienced more than four adverse childhood experiences were at the greatest risk. It concluded that if children and young people are exposed to frequent and/or prolonged stress during sensitive periods of brain development, then it can cause lasting change in how they will cope with stressors in later life. Their responses can become maladaptive and result in a range of social, emotional and mental health problems. This in turn will, clearly, have a serious impact on their resilience and ability to achieve positive wellbeing.

---

17   Felitti V, Anda F, Nordenberg D, Williamson D, Spitz A, Edwards V, Koss M & Marks J (1998) Relationship of childhood abuse and household dysfunction to many of the leading causes of death in adults: the adverse childhood experiences (ACE) Study. *Am J Prev Med* 20(2): 245–58.

An overview of child development

To better understand how we can improve the wellbeing and resilience of children and young people, we first need an understanding of the basic processes of normal child development. Historically, the study of child development began to emerge towards the end of the 19th century, linked to the advent of compulsory education and the need for young people to be literate and numerate in order to join an increasingly industrial workforce. By the early 20th century, it was of interest to researchers in disciplines such as psychology, sociology, economics and medicine – as well as, of course, education.

Key Point

The development of a young person is influenced by a diverse cocktail of factors, starting with the individual's own inherited temperament.

The development of a young person is influenced by a diverse cocktail of factors, starting with the individual's own inherited temperament. As soon as they are born, they begin to be influenced by factors that they experience in the outside world. These come mainly from their parents and carers, but broader factors such as how the economic climate of the day determines the family's lifestyle will also come into play. All these factors interact with the parenting style that the children experience.

In the early years of their development children and young people are vulnerable because their coping skills are still emerging. During this time they experience a combination of protective and risk factors operating at different levels of immediacy and distance. For example, the parenting they experience, the nursery and school they attend, and more distant socioeconomic factors may all help or hinder them when it comes to obtaining employment in later life (Bronfenbrenner, 1979).[18] So each specific individual's development and future wellbeing is affected in a unique way across a range of domains.

We will explore development and its processes in more detail in Part 3.

---

18 Bronfenbrenner U (1979) *The Ecology Of Human Development*. Cambridge, MA: Harvard University Press.

Chapter 4: Issues, evidence and definitions

The media and mental health

The media frequently display alarmist headlines concerning children and young people:

- *"Mental health issues in young people up sixfold in England since 1995"* – The Guardian, 11 September 2018
- *"UK youth suffer low 'mental wellbeing'"* – BBC News, 8 February 2017
- *"Mental health of children and young people at risk in digital age"* – The Guardian, 5 November 2014
- *"Child mental health referrals up 26% in five years, says report"* – BBC News, 7 October 2018
- *"Calls for action over UK's 'intolerable' child mental health crisis"* – The Guardian, 30 August 2018
- *"Poor mental health 'part and parcel' of childhood"* – BBC News, 19 July 2018

It is noticeable that the focus of such headlines is almost always on uncovering problems rather than celebrating success, and to some extent this is unsurprising. As we touched on in the first chapter and will explore in more detail later, psychology for much of its history aspired to be considered a 'hard science', and as such it was influenced by the growing success of the medical world. The emphasis was on 'solving' human ailments such as trauma, anxiety and depression, and the guiding principle was that life would be better if these negative emotional states could be understood and changed. So it is not hard to understand why the study of wellbeing and resilience has not figured until relatively recently in psychological research, and why it is still in the process of filtering out to the wider world.

It is worth saying that the study of negative emotional states does still have an important role to play in a holistic understanding of human mental health and wellbeing. From an evolutionary point of view, being able to predict danger has an obvious survival value. Ein-Dor (2015) found that people with insecure attachments were better at spotting danger, and clearly a pessimist is more likely to prepare adequately for a famine than an optimist.[19] So negative moods can have a functional value; but, as with any human trait, if taken to extremes they can become more of curse than a blessing.

The scale of the problem

So, what is the evidence for an increase in mental health issues among children and young people? After all, there is an inbuilt tendency for the media to sensationalise issues – 'clickbait journalism', as it is called. For example, a tragic 2019 case of suicide in a young person is presented as happening because he lost his phone. An investigation by Natasha Devon in *The Times Educational Supplement* reveals a multi-faceted narrative of a sensitive young man who hid his depression but was aware of his mental health problems and sought help that never came.[20]

With that said, it is well-documented by research evidence that there have been significant changes in the behaviour of children and young people over time. More than a quarter of a century has passed since Michael Rutter and David Smith (1995) brought together studies showing that there had been upward trends in psychosocial disorders in young people, and findings from the Nuffield Foundation's Changing Adolescence Programme of 2009 supported this.[21] In 1974, just seven per cent of parents reported behaviour problems in their fifteen- and sixteen-year-old children; by 1999 this had doubled. Further, over the same period, the number of fifteen- and sixteen-year-olds reporting feelings of depression and/or anxiety had also risen to one in five for girls and one in fifteen for boys.[22]

Towards definitions

When people use the same terms, but with different meanings, we are in danger of following Humpty Dumpty, who said a word meant *"just what I choose it to mean – neither more nor less"*. This is to be expected when terms are beginning to be adopted by people, especially if those people are

---

19   Ein-Dor T (2014) Facing danger: How do people behave in times of need? The case of adult attachment styles. *Front Psychol* 5: Article 1,452

20   Devon N (2019) *Archie Tragedy Tells Us We Can't Blame Tech For Mental Ill Health.* Available at: https://www.pressreader.com/uk/tes-times-education-supplement/20190201/page/8 [last accessed at 4 February 2021]

21   Rutter MJ & Smith DJ (1995) *Psychosoicial Disorders In Young People: Time Trends And Their Causes.* Chichester, West Sussex: John Wiley & Sons, Ltd.

22   Nuffield Foundation (2009) *Changing Adolescence Programme Briefing Paper.* Accessed at: https://www.nuffieldfoundation.org/wp-content/uploads/2019/12/Changing-Adolescence_Social-trends-and-mental-health_introducing-the-main-findings.pdf [last accessed 15 February 2021]

from different academic or professional backgrounds. So, remembering our example of the blind men and the elephant from Chapter 1, a medical practitioner may see things quite differently from a social worker, who in turn may in turn see things differently from a psychologist.

Some would argue that no one really knows what the terms below really mean in an empirical sense, because they can be viewed through different interpretative lenses and their meanings will vary accordingly. Furthermore, it doesn't really matter whose definition is 'right', what is important is how each interpretation contributes to improving and widening our overall understanding. For the purposes of this book, however, we should aim to be clear and to define them in everyday language.

Expert View

"I dislike jargon intensely and cannot stand people who think that complex ideas need to be expressed in a way that is obscure or rarefied."

Michael Craig-Martin[23]

Mental health

We all have a state of mental health, just as we have a state of physical health. Mental health for children and young people means being able to have social, emotional and moral experiences and relationships that are appropriate to the situation and developmental stage. Good mental health enables children and young people to cope with adversity and develop into well-balanced adults.

Mental disorder

This is a difficult concept to tie down, as it involves more than just having certain symptoms. Feeling anxious before an exam is normal, but if the anxiety prevents you taking the exam then it can be a mental disorder. A disorder is when a person's, thoughts, feelings and/or behaviours interfere with them being successfully accepted and included within their immediate community and culture.

Wellbeing

Wellbeing is used to describe the successful and positive integration of the different elements of a child or young person's development (e.g. physical development, cognitive development, emotional development, social development, and moral development). As we said in Chapter 1, wellbeing is a measure of a young person's current state of happiness, health, comfort and overall contentment.

23   Craig-Martin M (2015) *On Being An Artist*. UK: Art/Books.

Emotional wellbeing

Emotional wellbeing refers to possessing core skills for understanding emotional states. It means that an individual can identify and express different emotions appropriately. The skills include self-esteem, optimism, personal control and the ability to maintain mutually satisfying relationships.

Social wellbeing

Social wellbeing is concerned with the extent to which children and young people have a sense of belonging to and inclusion with different groups. They will also share values and lifestyles with group members and have the necessary skills to maintain and develop relationships.

Resilience

Resilience is the ability to cope with, recover from and adjust to adverse life experiences. It is influenced by a range of factors and influences, some specific to the individual and others drawn from the broader family and community environment. As we said in Chapter 1, resilience is the ability to work through adversity, adapt, move forward and grow.

Expert View

"The absence of pathology does not necessarily equate with psychological wellness."

Sam Goldstein and Robert Brooks[24]

Cautionary note: Absence of evidence is not evidence of absence

Many of the above concepts and definitions have been arrived at through researchers looking for specific defects in children and young people who display some kind of a symptom. The presence of symptoms shows that the child or young person has some degree of distress and is not coping; and, by the same token, children and young people who do not display symptoms have generally been assumed to be healthy. However, while mental health professionals are good at spotting symptoms indicating that a child or young person does not have the necessary skills to cope, they are less well-equipped to measure whether a child or young person *does* have those skills. Absence of evidence is not evidence of absence, and we need to be careful not to assume wellbeing and resilience simply because of a lack of clear evidence to the contrary.

---

24 Goldstein S & Brooks RB (2014) *Handbook Of Resilience in Children*. London: Springer.

Ten key things to know about wellbeing and resilience

1. Wellbeing is a measure of an individual's current state of happiness, health, comfort and overall contentment with life.

2. Wellbeing incorporates physical wellness and mental health, as well as elements of purpose, opportunity, relationships and satisfaction.

3. While psychological wellbeing and mental health have areas of overlap, there are also marked differences and it is possible to have either one without the other.

4. Wellbeing changes across countries, cultures, classes, religions and societies, as well as over time; wellbeing today is not the same as wellbeing fifty years ago.

5. There is no 'quick fix' for generating wellbeing in children and young people; high wellbeing is the result of many complex factors interacting with each other.

6. Resilience is the ability to cope with, and bounce back from, the negative experiences and adversity that we will all encounter at some point in our lives.

7. Resilience involves behaviours, thoughts and actions that anyone can learn and develop, and is linked directly to high levels of personal wellbeing.

8. Resilience is influenced by a range of factors and influences, some specific to the individual and others drawn from the broader family and community environment.

9. Resilience enables us to cope not only with one-off life-changing situations but also with the normal ups and downs of life and stay calm, confident, optimistic and in control.

10. Within psychology, the concepts of wellbeing and resilience are related to positive psychology – the science of 'what makes life most worth living' (Peterson, 2008).

Part 2:
The science of
wellbeing

Chapter 5: Evidence-based practice

The 'what works' agenda

These days, with schools under pressure to achieve success in so many areas from academic to pastoral, it is no wonder that staff look for different ways to reach these goals. The quicker, cheaper and easier the better. There are programmes that are well-marketed and packaged to be appealing, but their claims can at times be somewhat economical with the truth. As a result, evidence-based practice (EBP) is seen as a way of avoiding such misleading claims and levelling the playing field. The 'quick fix' is always tempting, but will it really do what it says on the tin?

Expert View

"Evidence-based practice involves the use of the best available evidence to bring about desirable outcomes, or conversely, to prevent undesirable outcomes."

Tone Kvernbekk[25]

The expectation today, in an environment of limited resources, is that any interventions must be justified. To this end, interventions based on research should be systematic and rigorous, and there is a strong emphasis on EBP – in other words, using tools and techniques that are proven to yield results. This is sometimes referred to as the 'what works' agenda. In addition, sciences that were once separate or even opposed to each other now work together or create new fields between the two and expand the evidence base – examples are cognitive neuropsychology and psycholinguistics.

A workable definition is that EBP in child mental health is practice that is:

"... consistently science-informed, organised around client intentions, culturally sensitive, and that continuously monitors the effectiveness of interventions through reliable measures of the child and family response, contextualised by the events and conditions that impact on treatment." (Fonagy, 2014)[25]

---

25 Fonagy P (2014) *What Works For Whom?: A Critical Review Of Treatments For Children And Adolescents*. New York, NY: Guilford Press.

How does this relate to wellbeing?

Once we have a broad understanding of wellbeing, the next step is to ask the question: how can we improve wellbeing for children and young people? Many programmes and interventions claim to enable this, so how can a school, parent or carer decide if a specific programme's claims are justified? For many educationalists, the best way to achieve sure-footed improvement is through research-informed interventions (Slavin, 2002) – in other words, by using EBPs.[26] Evidence-based practice uses evidence to support any claims. At its heart it is scientific – it believes in causality, which is the principle that observable variables can have a cause-and-effect relationship.

A key advantage of knowing that something is supported by evidence is that not only is it known to work, but the reasons why it works have been investigated (Hargreaves, 1996).[27] So any evidence-based programme should:

■ Clearly state the benefits of the programme, i.e. what it will achieve.

■ Have explicit and agreed steps and procedures (protocols) that need to be followed for successful outcomes.

■ Have been shown to be more effective than similar interventions.

■ Adhere to accepted scientific procedures.

■ Have produced similar results in other contexts, showing that it is robust enough to cope with unspecified variables.

■ Be based on Randomised Controlled Trials (RCTs) – meaning that it was given to one group or individual and the results were compared to a control group that did not receive it.

The dangers of rigid thinking

This section is intended to give a balanced view to EBP. The writer believes that there are far more gains than losses if EBP is used as a useful touchstone. However, extreme reliance on EBP can mean that the insights, experience and professional judgements of practitioners may be undervalued (Biesta, 2007).[28] Those who advocate EBP may fail to understand that school staff, parents and carers are, at an everyday level,

---

26   Slavin RE (2002) Evidence-based education policies: Transforming educational practice and research. *Educ Res* 31: 15–21.

27   Hargreaves DH (1996) *Teaching As A Research Based Profession: Possibilities And Prospects.* London: Teacher Training Agency.

28   Biesta G (2007) Why 'What Works' won't work: Evidence-based practice and the democratic deficit in educational research. *Educ Theory* 57(1):1–22.

mini-researchers in their own right. They are testing new ideas with young people all the time. There is not and never will be a 'one-size-fits-all' solution to a problem; even a parent, when a child cries, will need to explore various ideas as to what is causing the tears.

Rigid adherence to the principles of EBP can also mean that the subjective experiences of children and young people are ignored (Schmidt Neven, 2010).[29] For example, two children may both have attention deficit hyperactivity disorder (ADHD), but how they experience and cope with this condition can vary greatly. So from a distance EBP may explain the general issues common to all children and young people with ADHD, but to school staff and parents and carers it is only by knowing the individual that effective support can be implemented. Therefore as Hargreaves (1996) stated, the aim of EBP should be to build and develop professional judgement, not to replace it.

Expert View

"Judgments in education are ultimately value judgments, not simply technical judgments."

Gert Biesta

Evidence-based practice also assumes that education is similar to the natural sciences in that any causality is based on physical interactions. But education is a process based on communication and symbolically mediated interactions. This makes prediction more difficult. The natural sciences have, as a core, the aim of finding universal laws – that is, laws that will apply consistently in similar contexts. The context is decisive in determining whether a predicted outcome will occur. But in education contexts differ as no two schools or classrooms are identical and no two homes are the same, so the variables that enable a programme to be successful may exist in one context but not in another (Kvernbekk, 2017).

When a programme is developed in a specific context, it is easy to miss the fact that unseen variables will almost certainly have contributed to its success. Schools and homes are extremely complex places. These variables are known as moderator and mediator variables, and an example will show how they make the transfer of any programme to new contexts as much an art as a science.

Let's say a programme to teach children problem-solving skills to enhance their wellbeing is found to be effective at a specific primary school. The two key variables were the scores on a set of problem-solving exercises and the thinking strategies that the children were taught. A control group were taught non-related exercises. When this programme was trialled in a different primary school, the results were not found to be significant. So why the difference? The moderating variable was that the reward given to motivate the children was not the same for each school. So while the results were not replicated, it was not because of the programme itself but because of other variables.

A moderating variable is one that can affect the strength of the relationship between two variables. In the example above the reward is the variable that moderates the strength of the relationship between the problem-solving intervention and the children's existing skills. So making a programme effective in different contexts involves much more than naively expecting a straight transfer to work. In a new context, by understanding the variables at play, it is possible that a hybrid programme could be developed. This does not mean that the programme protocols have been violated, but that EBP takes place in the real world, not in laboratories where total control is easily achieved.

 ## How to help – wellbeing programme checklist

☞ Below is a user-friendly checklist to use when considering the pros and cons of any suggested programme or intervention.

WELLBEING PROGRAMME CHECKLIST All questions must be answered YES or NO		
1	Are the benefits clearly stated?	YES/NO
2	Does the programme have a fully explained manual?	YES/NO
3	Is there clear evidence as to how effective it is?	YES/NO
4	Does the programme claim to be evidence-based?	YES/NO
5	Has it worked in different contexts?	YES/NO
6	Are contact details of other users given?	YES/NO
7	Is there a support service provided?	YES/NO
8	Are you asked for feedback after use?	YES/NO
9	Does the programme involve pre-training?	YES/NO
10	Do you collect data to decide effectiveness?	YES/NO
Scoring: 4–6 YES: promising; 6-8 YES: excellent; 8 YES and above: worth trying.		

Chapter 6: Measuring wellbeing

Intrinsic and extrinsic outcomes

The fact that a UNICEF multinational report of 2007 looking at the wellbeing of children and young people ranked the US and UK 17th and 18th of 21 countries respectively demonstrates very clearly that the economic wealth of a country is no indicator of success in this area.[3] Yet, given the importance of wellbeing in young people, it's surprising to find a shortage of reliable measurements. Without good data it is hard to determine how effective the social policies of a country are in promoting wellbeing.

Wellbeing is a psychological construct. In other words, it is a hypothetical concept created by human beings, albeit one that impacts the real world, and measuring such constructs is a challenge. Wellbeing is not an entity in its own right; it is an umbrella term that encompasses many aspects of development. The benefits that an individual experiences when they have a good sense of wellbeing are that they feel happy, they feel confident, and they have a positive sense of self-esteem. These are *intrinsic outcomes*, and they are vitally important to the individual concerned. However, the only way to measure them is to interview and collect data from that individual.

Outcomes that can be measured, and that enable comparisons of one person versus another to be made, tend to be valued by people who are external to the individual. Examples are educational achievement, literacy, numeracy and good health. These are referred to as *extrinsic outcomes*. At the broadest level, the consequence of doing well in these areas is usually that the individual is more likely to be in work and less likely to need healthcare or other forms of support, so there are benefits to society as a whole. Intrinsic outcomes matter more to the individual. However, with the rising number of children and young people with mental health issues, it is becoming increasingly clear that intrinsic outcomes such as wellbeing also carry tangible cost implications for society.

The need to be able to measure wellbeing is important if programmes designed to make improvements are to be evaluated. Negative outcomes such as substance abuse, school exclusion and teenage pregnancy are all measurable. It is the positive outcomes associated with wellbeing – outcomes such as empathy and positive character traits – that are much more difficult to quantify. The difficulties are further complicated by the cultural diversity that exists within societies as well as between countries. Can measures developed and validated in the UK or US be simply and validly applied in, for example, China? Given that China has a more collectivistic philosophy as opposed to individualistic Western countries with capitalist economies, it seems clear that questions linked to constructs such as leadership and teamwork would be interpreted differently by citizens.

Key Point

The need to be able to measure wellbeing is important if programmes designed to make improvements are to be evaluated.

Part of the problem is that wellbeing is not in itself a single, unitary thing. It is believed to be made up of a range of components. Martin Seligman, a key proponent of wellbeing, believes that it involves several core elements that we will explored in detail shortly. So, to date, no standardised test of wellbeing exists. Neither is there any agreement between researchers as to how the relationships between the developmental systems in children and young people are to be studied. How can problem-solving skills be meaningfully compared between a six-year-old and a teenager?

Intrinsic measurement

Given that it is a subjective concept, wellbeing can be measured using self-reporting. The use of self-reporting is fundamentally different from using more objective measures such as household income, unemployment levels and neighbourhood crime. All these metrics are often used to assess wellbeing, but only young people themselves have first-hand insight into whether they are feeling good or not. This is complicated, however, by the fact that while children are believed to be able to introspect and provide feedback on their thoughts from the age of about seven or eight (New Economics Foundation, 2009), their evaluation of the quality of their life and their actual experience of positive emotions may not be the same.[30] So a young person could be very happy with their life, but not report having many happy emotions.

---

30 New Economics Foundation (2009) *A Guide to Measuring Children's Well-Being.* Available at: https://neweconomics.org/2009/09/guide-measuring-childrens-wellbeing [last accessed 4 February 2021]

A possible solution may be to ask parents and carers who know a young person very well to evaluate their perceived degree of wellbeing. However, a child or young person's self-evaluation and that of an adult who knows them have been found in research to only moderately correlate, so this still leaves room for error. A further issue is that children and young people typically have a natural desire to please adults. Clearly, then, measuring wellbeing in children and young people via self-reporting is far from easy. To be effective self-reporters, children will need to have achieved a certain degree of cognitive development, to be able to understand such concepts as what a good or bad life means, and to possess the necessary skills to communicate the results in a meaningful way.

What level of wellbeing should be measured? There are three approaches:

- **Global** – This style of explores how children and young people rate their satisfaction with life in very general terms. For example: "My life is going well."
- **Specific** – This approach explores a specific aspect of a child or young person's life: for example, school, family or friends. A set of questions will be specific to the area being investigated. Then the scores from each domain area are totalled to give an overall score.
- **Multidimensional** – This approach is similar to the global approach, but it provides a profile of a child or young person's wellbeing for each unique area. With this approach a range of different assessment tools can be used for each domain being studied.

The advantage of each of these approaches is that rather than inferring a child or young person's wellbeing from pathological conditions, they are designed to tap into their own subjective evaluation of how they rate themselves with respect to wellbeing.

An ongoing challenge

Below we will present a range of scales, questionnaires and other instruments that can be helpful for measuring wellbeing. Before doing so, however, it seems appropriate to stress again that the accurate measurement of wellbeing in children and young people remains something of a Holy Grail. Some of the issues yet to be resolved are:

- Does wellbeing at one age translate/evolve into wellbeing at another age?
- If wellbeing is situated not in the individual but in the quality of the interactions within a person and the multiple contexts around them, can solely person-related questionnaires reveal much?

- Is wellbeing stable or unstable? Are some features of wellbeing more unstable than others?

- If cultural context helps to define wellbeing, can tools make cross cultural comparisons valid?

Issues such as these highlight the complexity of the ongoing challenges faced by researchers, policy-makers and those actually supporting children and young people in practice.

H2h How to help – measuring wellbeing

There are many instruments, scales and assessments that set out to measure some or all aspects of a child or young person's wellbeing. Some of the best-known examples are described below.

☞ The Good Childhood Index

This is a single item measure designed by the Children's Society to measure the subjective wellbeing of children over the age of eight. It looks at ten aspects of a child's life, including family, school, friends, health, appearance and their future.

☞ The Warwick Edinburgh Mental Wellbeing Scale (WEMWBS)

Developed in Scotland for use with young people over the age of thirteen, and used internationally to monitor and evaluate projects concerned with children and young people's mental wellbeing, the WEMWBS consists of two scales of fourteen items and one of seven. Areas covered include sense of meaning and fulfilment to life (eudaimonic wellbeing) and personal satisfaction (hedonic wellbeing).

☞ Huebner's Student Life Satisfaction Scale

This was developed in the US and used extensively by The Children's Society. The scale has seven questions that are easily read by younger children. The scale uses simple statement questions such as "my life is going well", "my life is just right" and "I would like to change many things in my life".

Health Behaviour in School-Aged Children

This measure was one of the first international studies of adolescent health. It is a classroom-administered questionnaire, used in some forty countries, that provides a range of data for use by national and international agencies. The data include a global measure of a young person's wellbeing.

The assessment uses the Cantril Scale, which involves asking respondents to rate their life on a ladder. The top of the ladder (10) represents the best possible life, and the bottom of the ladder (0) represents the worst. Respondents are asked where they think they are on the ladder right now.

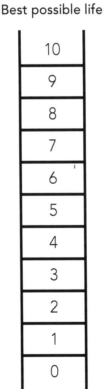

Best possible life

Worst possible life

Life Satisfaction Scale

For children and young people aged eight to eighteen. This is a questionnaire where the responses give an indication as to how satisfied a child or young person is with their life. There are no right or wrong answers. The questions are show below:

Mark how much you agree or disagree with the following statements	Strongly agree	Moderately disagree	Mildly agree	Moderately agree	Strongly agree
1	I have a good life					
2	I am happier than most young people					
3	I have what I want in life					
4	I am happy with my family					
5	I like where I live					
6	I enjoy the school/college I attend					
7	I have people who will help me if I have problems					

Chapter 7: Wellbeing and positive psychology

A new paradigm

As we saw in Chapter 1, the paradigm shift made by positive psychology was to challenge the historical emphasis of psychology on either alleviating or preventing mental distress in individuals, and to move the focus instead on to promoting personal emotional growth. While the prevention of mental distress and the promotion of emotional growth may at first glance appear similar, the reality is that they have some crucial differences.

Key Point

Positive psychology focuses on what makes life worth living for an individual, and how this can be achieved.

The prevention of mental health problems involves looking at the core skills needed by an individual to avoid such conditions as depression or anxiety. So Cognitive Behavioural Therapy (CBT), for example, aims to provide people with the skills to challenge negative thinking traps that can lead to or invite negative emotions. The promotion of personal emotional growth means looking at how to equip and enable people to flourish. Therefore, positive psychology focuses more on what makes life worth living for an individual, and how this can be achieved.

A good way to think of this in visual terms is to consider the scale below:

< Mental illness					Neutral				Wellbeing >	
-5	-4	-3	-2	-1	0	1	2	3	4	5

The primary aim of traditional psychology is to move people experiencing some form of mental distress from -5 to 0. Positive psychologists argued that this did not mean that they would be any happier; just that they would not have the symptoms of anxiety, depression or whatever their problem had been. For positive psychologists, the ultimate aim was not to move people in distress from -5 to 0 but to move people who were not in distress from 0 to +5. Achieving this would mean that they could actually be happier and more productive, not just problem-free.

Positive psychology focuses on the power of positive emotions. The energy of positive emotions drives people to try out new activities, face new challenges and engage with the world. By contrast, negative emotions lead us to shut down, withdraw inwards and avoid the world. The idea of positive emotions is also linked closely to the concept of happiness and wellbeing. This is a different concept from simple pleasure, which is about satisfying basic needs for survival; it is a more sophisticated form of enjoyment that come from intellectual involvement and creativity.

Wellbeing, then, is much more than just the absence of disease symptoms. A list of the major topics studied by positive psychologists serves to highlight the key issues that are of interest:

- Love and humanity
- Positive emotions
- Strengths and virtues
- Compassion
- Humour
- Courage

Antecedents of positive psychology

Needless to say, positive psychology did not emerge from thin air. There were already a number of key figures who were advocating a more positive approach for psychology – in a sense, these figures anticipated the need for a shift in thinking decades before it actually happened. In a lecture of 1974 the American community psychologist James G. Kelly (1929–2020) said:

> "The work of psychologists is moving from an emphasis upon the troubles, the anxieties, the sickness of people, to an interest in how we acquire positive qualities and how social influences contribute to perceptions of wellbeing, personal effectiveness and even joy." (Kelly, 1974)[31]

---

31   Kelly G & Lernihan U (1974). Kinship Care As A Route to Permanent Placement. In Iwaniec D (Ed.) (2006) *The Child's Journey Through Care: Placement Stability, Care Planning, And Achieving Permanency* (pp. 99–112). Hoboken, NJ: Wiley-Blackwell.

A particularly important example of these antecedents, and one who in fact dates from earlier still, is American humanistic psychologist Abraham Maslow (1908–1970). In 1943 Maslow first proposed his 'hierarchy of needs', which began with basic physiological needs (food, water, warmth, rest) and progressed through safety needs, belongingness and love needs, and esteem needs to culminate in 'self-actualisation' – when a person achieves self-fulfilment and becomes their ideal self.

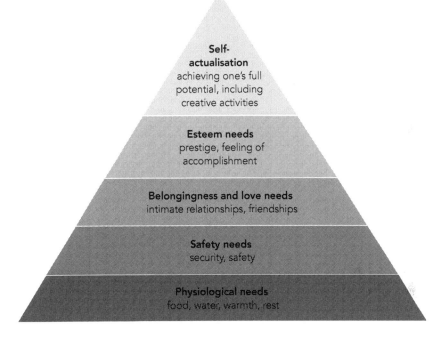

In his later years Maslow developed his theory still further by proposing 'transcendence', a sixth tier which he described as *"the very highest and most inclusive or holistic levels of human consciousness, behaving and relating, as ends rather than means, to oneself, to significant others, to human beings in general, to other species, to nature, and to the cosmos"* (Maslow, 1971).[32] While the detail of Maslow's hierarchy of needs has always been contested (and Maslow himself noted that there was little scientific basis for it), the general principle of human beings constantly striving to reach higher in a motivational and spiritual sense continues to have resonance across the fields of psychology, sociology, marketing and beyond.

---

32 Maslow A (1971) *The Farther Reaches Of Human Nature*. New York, NY: Viking Press.

The modern founders

Returning to the modern field of positive psychology, its two main founders are generally considered to be Martin Seligman and Mihaly Csikszentmihalyi. It is primarily the ideas of Martin Seligman that will concern us in this book, though it is important to note that the work of Csikszentmihalyi has had a significant influence on the field as a whole. Together, they defined positive psychology as:

> "The scientific study of optimal human functioning that aims to discover and promote the factors that allow individuals and communities to thrive." (Seligman & Csikszentmihalyi, 2000)[33]

A simpler and more direct definition was provided by Christopher Peterson (1950–2012), another positive psychologist with an important influence on the field:

> "Positive psychology is the scientific study of what makes life most worth living." (Peterson, 2008)[34]

Positive psychology has a very distinct view of human nature, and of how we as human beings create meaning and identity. Traditional psychology was concerned with explaining the way people are now by looking into past factors. So the way a person is could potentially be explained by their earlier history or the way their parents treated them as a child. Positive psychology is more concerned with where people are going than where they have been. So the focus is on how to adapt the present to create a better future, rather than on how to understand the present by interpreting the past.

In this book, our key interest is in how positive psychology can be applied to the wellbeing and resilience of children and young people. With the ongoing and rising concerns of the mental health of children and young people globally, it is not surprising that positive psychology – with its emphasis on wellbeing and happiness – should be considered of value and the model has been used and developed in many countries around the world. The above definitions, after all, can be reasonably summarised as aiming to develop a scientific study of happiness. So can positive psychology help support wellbeing, and help children and young people to live happy and meaningful lives?

---

33 Seligman MEP & Csikszentmihalyi M (2000) Positive Psychology: An Introduction. *Am Psychol* 55(1): 5–14.

34 Peterson, C (2008) What is positive psychology and what is it not? *Psychology Today,* May 16 2008

Chapter 8: How positive psychology can improve wellbeing

The PERMA model

In his 2011 book *Flourish*, Martin Seligman put forward a theoretical model of psychological wellbeing and happiness that he had developed by studying how people's lives were enhanced by their use of core personal strengths.[35] Seligman believed that some of these strengths were courage, persistence and wisdom. The new wellbeing theory replaced his previous focus on authentic happiness and allowed for a broader field of concepts, variables and outcomes to be included.

Expert View

"The topic of positive psychology is wellbeing, the gold standard for measuring wellbeing is flourishing, and the goal of positive psychology is to increase flourishing."

Martin Seligman

Seligman proposed that wellbeing involved five elements, collectively known as PERMA:

- **Positive emotion**. This includes key indicators of happiness.

- **Engagement**. This draws on Csikszentmihalyi's idea of flow (1990), which means being totally immersed in an activity that uses strengths and talents, resulting in an engaged life.[36]

- **Relationships**. Meaning a desire to be with an in meaningful relationships with others.

- **Meaning**. This refers to a sense of belonging to something that is bigger than oneself.

- **Accomplishments**. Pursuing achievements for their own sake and not for what they may bring.

---

35 Seligman M (2011) *Flourish: A New Understanding Of Happiness And Well-Being – And How To Achieve Them: A New Understanding Of Happiness And Wellbeing: The Practical... Psychology To Make You Happier And Healthier*. London: Nicholas Brealey Publishing.

36 Csikszentmihalyi M (1990) Flow: The Psychology Of Optimal Experience. New York, NY: Harper and Row.

The PERMA model is multidimensional, and it argues that wellbeing is much more than just having positive emotions; it equates more to a full way of life. For Seligman, each of the five PERMA components is independent of the others. Each is pursued for its own sake, not as a means to something else, and each contributes independently to an individual's wellbeing and happiness.

Let us consider in turn the five components of the model – positive emotion, engagement, relationships, meaning, and accomplishment.

Positive emotion

The first component of PERMA is positive emotion. Does feeling good equate to positive outcomes? Do people who are happy have better lives than people who experience more negative emotions? Certainly, positive emotions activate biochemical changes in the brain. They load our brains with dopamine, serotonin, and endorphins – neurotransmitters that stimulate the brain's reward system and are associated with positive moods, motivation, pleasurable sensations and enhanced cognitive abilities.

Expert View

"The positive emotions of joy, interest, contentment, pride, and love broaden people's momentary thought-action repertoires, widening the array of the thoughts and actions that come to mind."

Barbara Fredrickson

The *broaden and build* theory developed by the American social psychologist Barbara Fredrickson offers an explanation of these salutary effects. Fear and stress activate our primitive 'fight or flight' response for survival purposes, restricting our thoughts and actions. Therefore, when we experience negative emotions, we have a narrowed range of thought responses – we are in a quick and immediate mode of heightened stress. Conversely, positive emotions lead to broadened and more flexible responses, widening the array of thoughts and actions that are possible and over time building new skills and resources. When we experience positive emotions, we are more thoughtful, creative, and open to various intellectual, social, and physical resources (Fredrickson, 2001).[37]

Deliberately creating a positive mindset prior to a task or experience has been shown to produce positive results. In an experiment, it was found that adults who are primed for positive emotions have more creative

37 Fredrickson B (2001) The role of positive emotions in positive psychology. *Am Psychol* 56(3): 218–26.

and diverse ideas and solutions than those who are not (Fredrickson & Branigan, 2005).[38] Likewise, high school students who were told to think about the happiest day of their lives before taking a maths test were found to perform better than those who received no such instruction. The implications of this feed into the expanding field of Positive Education. Seligman himself has played an active role in this area, managing a whole-school project at Geelong Grammar School in Australia.

The *broaden and build* theory argues that positive emotions allow us to engage more with the world. When we feel good, we see more. So positive feelings do more than just help us feel good; they broaden such behaviours as curiosity, awareness and discovery. All these behaviours have a definite role to play in the classroom.

Fredrickson argues that there is a need for a high ratio of positives to negatives – she suggests that three positives are required for every negative. This is because the human brain is over-biased towards the negative for good evolutionary reasons. The negative is likely to be a warning of something threatening, whereas the positive generally means that things are okay. Threats to survival always take precedence in evolutionary terms, so the brain prioritises negatives.

How to help – promoting positive emotions

☞ The table below shows some key ideas for promoting positive emotions from Barbara Fredrickson's toolbox:

TOOL	DESCRIPTION
Create high-quality connections	When relating to others, be focused on the here and now. Use non-verbal communication skills to show that you're being fully attentive.
Cultivate kindness	Each day, find times when you can perform random acts of kindness.
Create high-quality connections	When relating to others, be focused on the here and now. Use non-verbal communication skills to show that you're being fully attentive.

---

38   Fredrickson B & Branigan C (2005) Positive emotions broaden the scope of attention and thought-action repertoires. *Cogn Emot* 19(3): 313–32.

TOOL	DESCRIPTION
Create high-quality connections	When relating to others, be focused on the here and now. Use non-verbal communication skills to show that you're being fully attentive.
Cultivate kindness	Each day, find times when you can perform random acts of kindness.
Develop distractions	Make a list of positive distractions that you enjoy, e.g. going for a walk or listening to music. Whenever negative thoughts or feelings threaten your wellbeing, do something nice that will bring you back to a positive state. This is especially important if we know we have negative distractions that only make matters worse – for example, over-eating.
Dispute negative thinking	Developed form Seligman's work, this involves writing negative thoughts on cards, choosing a card at random and reading it out loud, then disputing the negative thought (still talking out loud).
Ritualise gratitude	Make a point of appreciating family, friends, work colleagues and other people around you. Show them that you appreciate them. This will assist you in seeing the many good things that exist in your life.
Savour positivity	Think of a time when you were with someone special. Examine this memory from many different angles. What were you feeling? Where were you? Practise having those feelings again.

Engagement

The second component of the PERMA model is engagement. It is the work of Csikszentmihalyi that defines engagement. This is when one is completely immersed and absorbed in the moment. Time passes quickly when we're fully engaged with what we're doing. Sometimes we're doing something but our mind is elsewhere. When we're fully engaged in an activity, we can enable self-development, improve our skills and experience a sense of fulfilment and happiness.

Expert View

"The best moments in our lives usually occur if a person's body or mind is stretched to its limits in a voluntary effort to accomplish something difficult and worthwhile."

Mihaly Csikszentmihalyi[36]

Linked to engagement is the term 'flow', which refers to the psychological and behavioural state we experience when we are totally immersed in an activity. When we fully engage with a hobby, we can become totally immersed in the task at hand; we achieve a state of 'flow' in which our sense of time is distorted, our focus is heightened and our productivity is raised. Engagement and flow do not necessarily have to spring from an activity of supreme importance; it could be something as simple as cooking or working out in the gym. A common expression conveying a similar idea is being 'in the zone'. The point, as far as we are concerned in this book, is for children and young people to be aware of the feelings they have and the sensations they experience when they are fully engaged.

High engagement is associated with involvement, enjoyment, effort, mastery and interest. In contrast low engagement is associated with boredom, passivity, apathy and inattentiveness. A wide range of in-school activities can allow children and young people to engage with different possible selves. Through, art, music and sport, they can be given the opportunity to experiment with and refine their self-concept. In addition, researcher Rich Gilman (2001) found that the engagement of young people in extra-curricular activities was linked to a higher sense of life satisfaction.[39]

 How to help – Increasing engagement

☞ Here are five strategies for promoting higher levels of engagement (adapted from Stack, 2015)[40]:

- **Quieten down** – it's easiest to achieve flow in silence
- **Remove distractions** – e.g. switch phone to silent, turn off email alerts
- **Single task** – focus on one task that is achievable
- **Relax** – jangling nerves stifle inspiration
- **Be mindful** – treat the present moment as all there is

---

39   Gilman R (2001) The relationship between life satisfaction, social interest, and frequency of extracurricular activities in adolescent students. *J Youth Adolesc* 30: 749–67.

40   Stack S (2015) Learning outcomes in an online vs traditional course. *IJ-SoTL* 9(1): 1–18.

Relationships

The third component of the PERMA model is relationships. As a species we are wired to relate to others. From birth we form meaningful emotional relationships with significant others, and wellbeing is closely linked to having good secure relationships. As Christopher Peterson put it:

"Other people matter. Period."[36]

Our relationships with others produce feelings of connection, love and intimacy. We have a sense of empathy and a need to support others in times of stress. However, there are skills needed to form a relationship. Many children and young people learn through observing others and gradually testing out new skills. They will make lots of mistakes, or perhaps a better description would be 'virtuous errors'. The child who interrupts adults is not necessarily being rude – he or she might be keen to join in but lacking mastery of the skills that would enable it.

 ## How to help – Forming relationships

☞ Some of the key skills involved in forming relationships with children and young people are:

- **Spending time together**. Being with a young person for no other reason than being with them sends a powerful message that there is no ulterior motive. So making time to be together is important. It could be sharing in an activity that you both enjoy, cooking, drawing, watching TV or playing a game.

- **Active listening**. Adele Faber and Elaine Mazlish's popular 2012 book *How To Talk So Kids Will Listen And Listen So Kids Will Talk* is a must for many adults.[41] Often, we don't really listen when other people are talking; instead we rehearse in our minds what we'll say once they stop. So turn-taking is a very basic skill. Then there are micro-skills that we emit to tell someone we're listening. Skills like maintaining an appropriate degree of eye contact, nodding and saying 'Hmm...' show that we're actively engaged. When we're passive, the lights may be on but no one's home.

41 Faber A & Mazlish E (2012) *How To Talk So Kids Will Listen And Listen So Kids Will Talk.* London: Templar Publishing.

■ **Empathy**. Empathy is about not judging, blaming, giving advice or even trying to fix a problem. It's about showing someone else that you perceive and understand what they're feeling. Often, we need to check that we genuinely know how they're feeling. So we sometimes need to say: "I imagine that made you feel very angry; is that right?" This shows the other person that you're really trying to understand their world.

Being able to talk about feelings with children and young people shows them that how they feel is normal. Having a vocabulary is about being emotionally literate. As adults we need to model how we feel under different circumstances – frustrated, annoyed, sad or happy – and how we express these feelings. What we feel is never wrong; where problems occur is in how we express our feelings. So children and young people need to learn that feeling angry is okay, but hitting or hurting others is not.

Expert View

"People will forget what you said. People will forget what you did. People will never forget how you made them feel."

Maya Angelou

In many situations, the adult is the one who can make or break a relationship. In school it is not unusual for some young people to actively want a teacher not to like them. There may be many reasons for this, but if the adult is not careful then they can be drawn into a negative relationship. How often in schools it is the same learners who are in detention? It may be that some children and young people have learned that negative attention is better than no attention at all. There are many simple ways in which school staff can develop positive relationships, and catching a child doing something right can be the first step towards them valuing the support an adult is offering. To quote the title and central message of Paul Dix's 2017 book on school behaviour:

"When the adults change, everything changes."[42]

Meaning

The fourth component of the PERMA model is meaning. For Seligman, having meaning in life comes from using our unique strengths to achieve a goal that is bigger than who we are – something that transcends who

---

42   Dix P (2017) *When The Adults Change, Everything Changes*. Wales: Independent Thinking Press.

we are. Too often our goal is simply to better someone else and is not to maximise our own personal pleasure or satisfaction. This is the narrative we make to understand our lives.

The Austrian Holocaust survivor, psychiatrist and author Victor Frankl (1905-1997) believed that a search for meaning is the primary motivation in life. He founded 'logotherapy' based on this premise.[43] The American psychologist Michael Steger makes an important distinction between searching for the meaning *of* life and searching for meaning *in* life.[44] The latter is concerned with who we are and understanding our purpose in life – we each seek to feel that our life and experiences make sense and matter. For Steger, who directs the University of Michigan's Centre for Meaning and Purpose, meaning for young people is acquired through developmental stages.

Research into the nature of children and young people's search for meaning stresses the role that can be played by the many extra-curricular activities that schools make available. Having meaning in life appears to serve as a protective factor for young people during adolescence, and evidence also suggests that there is a positive relationship between meaning in life is a good predictor of health status – including subjective health and psychological wellbeing (Brassai, Piko & Steger, 2011).[45]

Accomplishments

The fifth and final component of the PERMA model is accomplishments. Having goals in life is important; they motivate us to push ourselves and drive us to achievements. Wellbeing ensues from being fully engaged in the pursuit of personal meaningful goals. We pursue goals not just to reduce a need within us, but also for more complex reasons; for a sense of competence and mastery, and for control in our world. Continuing with Steger's model, establishing and pursuing goals during adolescence is an important step in the search for meaning in life.[44]

Expert View

"People want to know what their lives are all about and how they fit into the grand scheme of things and the world around them."

Michael Steger[44]

---

43   Frankl V (2004) *Man's Search For Meaning*. London: Rider.

44   Steger M (2009) Meaning In Life. In Lopez SJ & Snyder CR (Eds.) *The Oxford Handbook Of Positive Psychology*. Oxford: Oxford University Press.

45   Brassai L, Piko BF & Steger MF (2011) Meaning in life: is it a protective factor for adolescents' psychological health? *Int J Behav Med* 18: 44–51.

Chapter 9: Signature strengths

What are signature strengths?

Positive psychology is not the only area of science and practice where the emphasis has moved in recent years from weaknesses to strengths, but it is especially relevant to children and young people in a school context. If we are to help children and young people achieve a sense of wellbeing, then knowing their existing strengths – especially as they relate to wellbeing, and to moderating psychological distress - is just as important, if not more so, as knowing their deficits and weaknesses.

Also known as character strengths, *signature strengths* are essentially natural traits that can be nurtured. Focusing on a young person's strengths is a proven way to enhance wellbeing. Children and young people are more likely to engage with and work on programmes that aim to strengthen their personal qualities and help them achieve their goals, rather than those that try to eliminate problem behaviour(s) that may concern adults more than themselves. Signature strengths are also believed to work as a form of psychological buffer against mental illness.

> ## *Key Point*
>
> *Signature strengths are essentially natural traits that can be nurtured. Focusing on a young person's strengths is a proven way to enhance wellbeing.*

Signature strengths are ways of thinking, feeling and behaving that are natural to an individual. When using these, a young person is functioning to the best of his or her ability. Using the top five signature strengths for a person is thought to be the best way to enhance wellbeing. Chris Peterson, working with Martin Seligman, developed the Values-in-Action (VIA) Signature Strengths Test, which can be taken for free at *www.authentichappiness.org* and *www.viacharacter.org*.

Strengths are different from talents and abilities, which are more genetically determined. Talents such as athleticism, musical ability and artistic creativity are more often associated with concrete outcomes and they may be wasted; a natural musician chooses not to develop it into a career. By contrast, signature strengths such as honesty, kindness and determination may not be used in an explicit way for personal or career development, but rarely are they wasted.

Characteristics of strengths:

- We each have a family of strengths.
- Some strengths are more changeable than others.
- Strengths are measurable.
- Strengths can be added to.

Strengths-based assessment is a:

> *"Measurement of the emotional and behavioural skills,*
> *competencies, and characteristics that foster a sense of personal*
> *accomplishment, contribute to supportive and satisfying*
> *relationships with family members, peers and adults, enhance one's*
> *ability to cope with challenges and stress, promote one's personal,*
> *social and academic development."* (Rashid et al, 2015)[46]

There are several factors that need to be considered if we are to identify, reinforce and develop signature strengths in children and young people:

- Understanding the individual's development stage. The positive strength of *being fair* means very different things to a seven-year-old and a twelve-year-old. The younger child is likely to see being fair as *treating everybody the same*; by the age of twelve most children understand that being treated equally is not always fair, and *equity* is more important. For example, being praised for sitting still is appropriate for the restless child who is always out of his seat; but praising children who are always in their seat would feel patronising.
- Context is also important. While *honesty* is a definite signature strength, when a five-year-old asks *"Do you like my picture?"* being completely truthful is not necessarily the kindest thing.
- The child or young person's socioeconomic background may be a factor. *Being prudent* might mean *managing money well* to one child, whereas for another it might mean *living a simple life using few resources.*

---

46 Rashid T, Anjum A, Lennox C & Quinlan D (2015) *Assessment Of Character Strengths In Children And Adolescents.* Available at: https://www.researchgate.net/publication/281765645_ Assessment_of_Character_Strengths_in_Children_and_Adolescents [last accessed 4 February 2021]

The language of signature strengths

If children and young people do not yet have a language to describe signature strengths, then it can be helpful to turn the strength into actions. For example, if Nelson Mandela is accepted as having been a *forgiving* person, ask: *"What did he do to make us think of him as forgiving?"* Focus on one specific strength and create different situations where that strength might be seen. For instance, ask: *"If someone was being kind to a homeless person, what do you think they would be doing?"*

In most schools, some common strengths are needed for a class to function adequately. These would typically include cooperation, self-control, sharing, honesty, curiosity, kindness, perseverance and listening. Staff can introduce these strengths into everyday conversations in a range of ways. For example, commenting on the way a group of children are working together, one could say: *"I like the way you're taking turns and sharing ideas with each other."*

Other approaches that can be helpful are focusing on strengths and problem-solving with strengths.

To focus on strengths, choose a strength and discuss with the group examples of behaviour that show it in action – for example: *"What is meant by kindness?"*. Take photos of the pupils helping each other, and set the whole class the task of showing kindness throughout the day.

When problem solving with strengths, use examples to discuss those signature strengths that would be helpful in tackling a particular problem. For instance:

- "If we are to solve pollution in the world, what strengths do we need and why?"
- "If we are to tackle road accidents, what strengths do we need and why?"
- "If we are to tackle bullying in school, what strengths do we need and why?"

The American school psychologist Michael Furlong and his colleagues (2014) coined the term *covitality* to refer to the co-occurrence of certain positive traits in young people, and defined it as: *"The synergistic effect of positive mental health resulting from the interplay among multiple positive-psychological building blocks."*[47]

When they exist together, these positive traits have a stronger impact on an individual's wellbeing than any one of them can manage on its own. They are more powerful collectively than individually – 'the whole is greater than the sum of the parts'. The overall result of covitality of signature strengths appears to be that children and young people feel accepted, respected, included and supported in the school context. In other words, they have a good sense of wellbeing.

Expert View

"The combination of positive psychological characteristics and their synergic effects is more important than any individual characteristic for positive youth development."

Michael Furlong

There are thought to be four core personal signature strengths:

- Gratitude – Being aware of and thankful for good things that happen.
- Optimism – Expecting good things to happen.
- Zest – An excitement and energy towards new experiences and projects.
- Persistence – The ongoing determination to complete started projects.

A study by Wilkins, Boman and Mergler (2015) predicted that children and young people who scored highly across these four signature strengths would also have a positive relationship with their schoolwork and school.[48] That is, the covitality of the four collective strengths would enhance their level of school engagement. Using a variety of measures, they were able to conclude that these four signature strengths were also effective in promoting health and wellbeing. Interestingly, they found that gender did not moderate the impact the covitality of the strengths.

---

47 Furlong M, Gilman R & Huebner E (2014) *Handbook Of Positive Psychology In Schools.* Abingdon: Routledge.

48 Wilkins B, Boman P & Mergler A (2015) *Positive Psychological Strengths And School Engagement In Primary School Children.* Available at: https://www.cogentoa.com/article/10.108 0/2331186X.2015.1095680 [last accessed 4 February 2021]

How to help – Signature strengths

☞ Signature strengths exercise 1: Who am I?

By completing the questionnaire below, children and young people can come to understand themselves better and identify key areas of individual strength and weakness.

INSTRUCTIONS:
Answer truthfully as many of these questions as you can. There are no right or wrong answers. Don't worry about your writing or spelling.

1	My favourite pastime is:	
2	The colour I like best is:	
3	My lucky number is:	
4	A favourite memory I have is:	
5	If I were a grown up I would:	
6	The funniest TV programme I ever saw was:	
7	The music group I like best is:	
8	I wish:	
9	The tastiest meal I could ever have would be:	
10	My favourite thing to wear is:	
11	If I were an animal I would to be a:	
12	If it were my birthday tomorrow, I would wish for:	
13	The country I would most like to visit is:	
14	My favourite sport is:	
15	The best film I ever saw was:	
16	The luckiest thing that ever happened to me was:	
17	The cleverest thing I ever did was:	
18	The thing I can be relied on to do well is:	
19	I feel good in school when I:	
20	The best thing about a friend is:	
21	My favourite game is:	
22	I'm at my best when I:	
23	I like people who:	
24	The book I enjoyed most is:	
25	I like it when my favourite teacher:	

☞ Signature strengths exercise 2: Identify your strengths

INSTRUCTIONS:

Circle FOUR strengths from the list that best describe you.

Wisdom	Artistic ability	Curiosity	Leadership
Empathy	Honesty	Open-mindedness	Persistence
Enthusiasm	Kindness	Love	Social awareness
Fairness	Bravery	Cooperation	Forgiveness
Modesty	Common sense	Self-control	Patience
Gratitude	Love of learning	Humour	Spirituality
Ambition	Creativity	Confidence	Intelligence
Athleticism	Discipline	Assertiveness	Logic
Optimism	Independence	Flexibility	Adventurousness

☞ Signature strengths exercise 3: Celebrate past successes

Think of a challenge you have faced successfully in the past. Describe what it was. What were the strengths you used to be successful?

The challenge was:	
The strengths I used were:	

☞ Signature strengths exercise 4: Keep a 'strengths' diary

Just like a muscle, the more you use your signature strengths the stronger they will become.

DATE	STRENGTH USED	HOW IT HELPED

☞ Signature strengths exercise 5: Positive endings

At the end of each day it's easy to think about what went wrong, or what didn't work as planned. Instead, a good habit is to make a point of finding three good things that happened.

Date:	
The *first* good thing that happened today was:	
What this good thing that happened means to me:	
The *second* good thing that happened today was:	
What this good thing that happened means to me:	
The *third* good thing that happened today was:	
What this good thing that happened means to me:	

Signature strengths exercise 6: Watch a movie!

Children and young people like to watch movies, right?! Well, there are many films that can play a part in helping young people of various ages to see various signature strengths in action and develop their own. Examples include *Inside Out, Brave, Ferdinand, Forrest Gump, Life Is Beautiful* and *My Left Foot*.

Part 3: Wellbeing and development

Chapter 10: Child and adolescent development

"If we are to improve the lives of children... we must face the reality that the human infant and young child is incapable of autonomous self-protective behaviour... the human species gives birth to offspring that experience years of physical, emotional and mental development almost entirely controlled and influenced by significant adults responsible for nurturing and care. While maturational processes are built into the developing organism, each of these processes requires a nutritious diet, physical care, social stimulation and consistent parenting." George W Albee (1997)[49]

Before we embark on ways to develop wellbeing in children and young people we need to consider the nature of child and adolescent development. There will be practical implications if we are trying to strengthen a child of seven compared with an adolescent of thirteen. In the past, the main concern regarding children was their physical health. Advances in sanitation and vaccines have greatly improved their health.

There are many theories of children and young people's development. Many see development in terms of stages, roughly corresponding to certain ages, where children and young people gradually develop skills and competencies from the simple to the more complex. Two influential theorists to be considered briefly are Vygotsky and Bronfenbrenner. These are especially important as they stress the contexts in which children and young people are developing. This view is especially important as we come to explore how wellbeing can be developed.

Vygotsky developed a sociocultural approach to cognitive development. Learning is how children and young people acquire cultural knowledge and skills. It is through social interaction with 'knowledgeable others' that children and young people learn how to think and what to think about. Thought is an internalised language, therefore children and young people from different cultures will learn different ways of thinking. The knowledge a child needs to learn is first experienced at a social level before it is internalised and becomes part of the child's own psychology.

---

49   Albee GW, Bond LA & Cook Monsey TV (1992) *Improving Children's Lives: Global Perspectives On Prevention.* Thousand Oaks, CA: Sage.

For Vygotsky, the environment a child or young person grows up in will influence how they think and what they think about. The language that a child or young person learns sets how they will think and perceive their world. So, for example, the Inuit have many words to describe snow, whereas we have very few. Contrast this with the number of words we have to describe different types of cars.

The second theorist is Bronfenbrenner. For Bronfenbrenner, a child or young person is influenced by multiple environments. Some may be directly experienced and others are not, but each will have an impact on a child or young person's development. An example of how a distant environment can influence us is world economics of the time. If there is a downturn in the Chinese economy, fewer cars are purchased from the West, which may result in people being made redundant in the UK car industry. As an indirect consequence a family may become poorer through redundancy and the parents or carers become more distressed. This in turn may affect their ability to parent as well as they would under more benign circumstances. So a child's early experiences are being negatively influenced by forces well beyond their immediate world.

Expert View

"There is no more critical indicator of the future of a society than the character, competence, and integrity of its youth."

Urie Bronfenbrenner

Children and young people do not exist in a vacuum, they live in a society where the values and customs are socialised into them. We all suffer from a form of social egocentricity in that we believe the way we do things is the right and normal way. It is only when we study or visit other societies that we realise our way is just one of many possible ways.

Bronfenbrenner's *Ecological Systems Theory* (1979) showed that different contexts affect how a child or young person grows and develops.18 His model can be viewed as a set of Russian dolls, each being separate but in a relationship with the others.

He identified four systems, which are briefly:

■ The **microsystem** – How the immediate family and other care providers interact with a child's inherited temperament.

■ The **mesosystem** – How the family's interaction with school and other local support services influences a child's development.

- The **ecosystem** – This is one that the child may not directly experience, such as their parents/carers' workplace. Whether a parent is made unemployed or promoted will have a definite impact on any child.
- The **macrosystem** – This is the one most distant form the child's experience, but one that none the less impacts their development. This is the law made by the government, the state of the economy and cultural/religious values.

Bronfenbrenner's work played an important role in the development of the US's Head Start Program, which aimed to support the development of disadvantaged pre-kindergarten children.

So what of the children and young people of today? What is life like for them?

Every country is concerned with the wellbeing of its children and young people; we cannot expect them to thrive if they are unhappy and stressed during their formative years. The social world at any time has always been in a state of change, so children and young people today are faced with a technologically complex world. They are often referred to as the 'guinea pig' generation, in that they are the first to face such an array of different communication systems, while being parented by adults who are well-intentioned but technologically ignorant.

Of increasing concern in many modern Western societies is the growing number of children and young people facing social, emotional and mental health issues during their early years. Many are distressed and unhappy, displaying such worrying symptoms as eating disorders, anxiety, depression, self-harm and suicide. This has put wellbeing and resilience to the forefront for all who care and support children and young people.

Key Point

Children and young people today are the first to face an array of different communication systems, while being parented by adults who are technologically ignorant.

At one level we can understand the increase in mental health problems as a result of the increased pressures that children and young people face in today's world – i.e. the pressure from school, peer pressure and family expectations. However, for many there is no specific reason as to why they feel so stressed, it is something that is 'just there'. As an actress in the TV series Fleabag says: *"I want someone to tell me how to live, because so far I think I've been getting it wrong."* This seems to suggest that life has become too complex, with too many decisions; in fact, too many choices can be just as stressful as having too few (Toffler, 1984).[50] The stress and anxiety that many children and young people experience is now a fact of life.

There are four key areas that are involved with a child or young person's wellbeing.

A good place to start is to think of how we would like children and young people to be. That is why we need to have the end in sight before we can ask: what are the outcomes we are hoping to achieve for children and young people? One answer could be *"[engaging] in productive activities deemed significant by one's cultural community, fulfilling social relationships, and the ability to transcend moderate psychosocial and environmental problems"* (Pollard & Rosenberg, 2012).[51]

It is worth stressing here that, although good wellbeing will enable children and young people to manage and cope with moderate problems, it should not be seen as an antidote to mental illness. It is possible to have good wellbeing but still have a mental health problems. For example, a child or young person could have a serious phobia towards spiders, but a good sense of wellbeing. Wellbeing is a necessary condition for mental good health but is not sufficient to prevent mental ill health.

While each of the areas will overlap and interrelate, having the basic physical necessities for existence must be the first and most important need for any child or young person. Only then can a child or young person develop a sense of emotional wellbeing through the care they experience.

50   Toffler A (1984) *Future Shock*. New York, NY: Random House.

51   Pollard L & Rosenberg M (2012) The Strengths-Based Approach To Child Well-Being. In Bornstein M, Davidson L, Keyes C & Moore K (Eds.) *Well-Being: Positive Development Across The Life Course* (p. 14). Mahwah, NJ: Lawrence Erlbaum Associates.

Chapter 11: Wellbeing and physical development

Exercise and wellbeing

The human body was designed for activity. In our past, whether we were hunters or gatherers, we relied on our physical ability to survive. In today's world exercise, for many, has taken a back seat. With the growth of technology and labour-saving devices we have become more and more

> ## Key Point
>
> *Being physically active is now known to be a factor in mental health and wellbeing.*

sedentary. Children and young people walk far less than their parents or grandparents did. In many countries, efforts are being made to increase the physical wellbeing of children and young people. More than just an improvement in general fitness, physical activity allows children to socialise, which will improve their self-esteem and academic achievement.

What is physical activity?

"Physical activity or functioning is defined as the ability to be physically *active, to play, and to participate in activities or sports without limitation or restriction."* (Connor, 2012)[52]

It has long been known that exercise plays an important role in health. However, until recently there was a clear distinction between mental health and physical health. Being physically active is now known to be a factor in mental health and wellbeing.

Exercise serves two purposes:

- It reduces the secretion of stress hormones.
- It releases feel-good chemicals such as endorphins into the brain.

---

52 Connor JM (2012) Physical Activity And Well-Being. In Bornstein M, Davidson L, Keyes C & Moore C (Eds.) *Well-Being: Positive Development Across The Life Course.* New York: Psychology Press.

There is also evidence that exercise:

- Reduces the risk of heart disease.
- Reduces the risk of diabetes.
- Reduces the risk of colon cancer.
- Reduces the risk of Alzheimer's.

Factors that increase physical activity

In the UK boys seem more likely than girls to take part in some form of vigorous exercise. Children and young people from more affluent families are no more likely to take part in exercise than those from poorer ones. A study in 2013 found that only 18% of children aged five to fifteen achieved the recommended level of physical activity (Payne, 2013).[53]

There is a recognised lack of information on the biological role the sex of a child or young person has on the level of activity engaged in. There are physiological differences – for example, women have smaller conducting airways than men (Sheel, 2016)[54] and blood pressure in hypertension is regulated differently (Briant, 2016)[55] – but these do not explain the discrepancy between the sexes in exercise. Boys engage more frequently in physical exercise than girls. The reasons for the differences are many, including body image, social norms, fewer opportunities after leaving school and work pressures.

Body image is understandably a highly sensitive issue for many children and young people. In any class there are likely to be students who are more vulnerable and fall into one or more of these categories:

- is or has been bullied about their weight or appearance
- has or is at risk of developing an eating disorder
- exercises excessively
- knows or is related to someone with some of these issues
- is facing issues over their sexual orientation or gender identity that affect body image.

53 Payne S (2013) The physical activity profile of active children in England. *Int J Behav Nutr* 10: 136.

54 Sheel A (2016) Sex differences in the physiology of exercise: an integrative perspective. *Exp Psychol* 101(2): 211–12.

55 Briant LJB, Charkoudian N & Hart EC (2016) Sympathetic regulation of blood pressure in normotension and hypertension: when sex matters. *Exp Physiol* 101: 219–29.

It is fair to assume that to some degree many children and young people have issues around the way they look. It is, as they say, part of the zeitgeist. Today children and young people report feeling *"besieged by sexualised and unrealistic images of beauty"* (Teacher Guidance: Key Standards In Teaching About Body Image). When discussing such issues with groups of children and young people, the best advice is to assume that they are all vulnerable. The PSHE Association provides information and guidelines for teaching issues linked to body image.[56]

At home parents and carers are natural role models for children and young people. It is less about what adults say and more what they do that matters most – therefore, seeing their family value and engage in exercise has more influence than telling children and young people the value of exercise.

In school the amount of exercise children and young people engage in today is alarmingly small. In the US only twenty-five per cent of children aged six to seventeen take part in an hour of physical activity every day. The benefits of exercise are well enough known for this to concern all involved with the wellbeing of children and young people.[57]

The challenge is to marry initiatives that will promote exercise with the competing curriculum demands. When the emphasis is on academic progress, combined with these results being published in league tables, it is hardly surprising that physical exercise is a poor relative.

---

56 PSHE *Teacher guidance: key standards in teaching about body image.* (pshe-association.org. uk/curriculum-and-resources/resources/key-standards-teaching-about-body-image)

57 CDC Healthy Schools Physical Activity Facts. (cdc.gov/healthyschools/physicalactivity/facts. htm)

How to help – exercise and wellbeing

☞ Exercise is a protective factor for wellbeing because it:

- strengthens bones
- helps concentration
- improves posture and balance
- leads to improved academic results
- strengthens self-esteem

☞ Guidelines for healthy exercise are to keep it fun, avoid over-competitiveness and build up little by little. The table below shows exercise activities that are suitable for children and young people at a range of ages.

Children not yet walking

- Floor play – reaching and rolling
- Making sounds – e.g. with saucepans
- Water games
- Singing

Early walkers:

- Ball games, throwing and catching
- Trampolining
- Walking to the shops
- Playing in the park

Ages 5-16 – moderate:

(heartbeat raised but still able to talk)

- Martial arts
- Cycling
- Walking
- Frisbee

Ages 5-16 – vigorous:

(heartbeat/breathing faster; talking difficult)

- Running
- Swimming
- Football
- Rugby

References and resources

- gosh.nhs.uk
- www.nhs.uk
- activekids.com
- verywellfamily.com

Nutrition and wellbeing

Nutrition naturally links closely to physical wellbeing as it concerns what we eat to fuel the body. A balanced diet is essential, both excess and dearth will have marked effects. In the early years, when children are developing, good nutrition is essential for healthy development. Poor nutrition at this stage can result in general developmental delay and, specifically, impaired cognitive processing (Briefel et al, 1999).[58] With all the evidence the one area that remains difficult is how can healthy nutrition be provided for children? The challenge is that, if children have poor nutritional habits, how can their behaviour be changed?

Why are junk foods so addictive?

Two factors work together to explain why junk foods are so addictive to children and young people: neurological and social. As parents and carers, we often feel the need to give our children a treat or a gift. It may be for achieving something in school, learning a new skill or perhaps being helpful. We want to give something that is special, not something they have often. In this way food can become a reward. It is given in recognition for something achieved, *because you have practised the piano/completed your homework*. It may also be given as conditional reward, i.e. *when you..., I will give you...* . So, here we are using food as a kind of incentive, perhaps a way of motivating a child to do something they would rather not do, e.g. *if you tidy up your room, I will let you choose your favourite pizza.*

Sometimes parents and carers feel the reward is essentially being used as a bribe, and that they should not use rewards for this. A bribe, strictly defined, is when you aim for the person or child to do something that is either illegal or immoral. Trying to incentivise a child to tidy up their room does not fit that definition.

The food treats we give also have special addictive features. First, they are very well-packaged and look attractive, but more importantly they contain excessive sugars and unsaturated fats. Unsaturated fats have been found to increase the risk of coronary artery disease. When we eat them they cause an increase in the release of dopamine in the nucleus accumbens. This area in the brain has become known as the brain's pleasure centre. The neural pathways to the pleasure centre in the brain become hardwired and, as the saying goes, neurones that fire together

---

58   Briefel R (1999) *Universal-Free School Breakfast Program Evaluation Design Project: Review Of Literature On Breakfast And Learning.* Princeton, MJ: Mathematica Policy Research.

wire together. As a result, a neural pathway is formed, and eating these foods is reinforced because of the pleasant feeling they cause.

In addition, the brains of children are not fully developed. The area of the brain where children learn impulse control is the prefrontal cortex. As this is still developing, children are likely to find impulse control more difficult. The pleasure-seeking centres of the brain, which are developed, win the desire for pleasure. Early exposure to junk food may make addiction to other stimulants later in life more probable. So, as parents and carers, we may unwittingly encourage children to become addicted to junk foods. It is unintentional, though, so we should not be too hard on ourselves.

Although much is known about the need for nutrition in a child's daily intake, achieving behavioural changes in parents and carers is proving more challenging. The task is how to prevent this addiction or how to break it. There are three main areas in which good nutrition can be promoted – in the home, care settings and schools.

How to promote healthy eating

If the answer to this issue was straightforward, the problem would be resolved and there would be no need to include it. The fact that so much is written on *children's bad eating habits* should make us realise how difficult an issue this is. Below are some well-established ideas. If you are already using these, well done. If not, it is worth considering or adapting some to your family's circumstances.

- Use low fat dairy products
- Lean cuts of meat
- Use fruit and vegetables with meals

It is not unusual for children to go through a 'picky eater' phase. Why does it happen? It is feasible that it is down to our biology. We are hardwired to be cautious around food, in the same way that we are more likely to develop a phobia about snakes or spiders than about car journeys or sharp knives. So being choosy about what we eat is a natural survival trait that our ancestors needed. The problem today is that there are too many different choices; when there was a limited range of food it was rare to see children being picky. Now we have many healthy foods but children are also exposed to junk foods, which are particularly addictive.

Why children either are or aren't picky eaters is probably due to a cocktail of factors. Parents and carers are so keen to see children eat healthy foods that mealtimes often turn into a highly charged emotional experience. Look at some of the feelings that are often present at meal times:

- Anger: "I am the adult! I know what is best for you, so eat!"
- Anxiety: "You will fall behind in growth, or become ill."
- Guilt: "What kind of parent am I that I can't feed you properly?"
- Shame: "What will my friends think of me?"

Children will often be aware of these. You do not need language to feel strong emotions, so any mealtime can develop into a battle zone: "*Yes, you will!*" "*No, I won't!*" For some children, especially if they already have a strong-willed disposition, being forced will actually strengthen their resolve to not comply. Then when a small morsel of the right food is eaten, the positive encouragement is overwhelming, which just reinforces how important this issue is.

☞ How to help – nutrition and wellbeing

☞ Healthy eating

The world outside the home is designed to encourage children to overeat, and to overeat the wrong foods. The best place to develop good healthy eating habits is at home. So let's accept that children being picky over their food is not unusual, and is a universal part of human development.

☞ Teach good eating habits

DOs

- Eat together
- Prepare food together
- Grow herbs to add to meals
- Be persistent, keep offering

DON'Ts

- Give rewards and praise
- Insist on a clear plate

☞ Special treats

We often give food as a special treat, perhaps when something has been achieved. This is where junk food hits its mark; being brightly packed – it looks special. Develop, with your children, a range of possible treats for such special occasions, including some of their treats but also activities and healthy options.

☞ Examples of good practice

- nutrition.org.uk
- fit.webmd.com

Chapter 12: Wellbeing and emotional development

Emotions are central to what it is to be human; they are essential for our survival. Emotions are something innate – that is, we are born with them. Ekman (2004) believes there are six basic emotions that are found in all societies.[59] Each of these are thought to have unique neural networks that trigger specific thoughts, behaviours and subjective experience.

- Anger
- Fear
- Happiness
- Surprise
- Disgust
- Sadness

Expert View

"Emotions change how we see the world and how we interpret the actions of others."

Paul Elkman

These emotions have become hardwired in us as a means of survival. In contrast to this, it is popularly held that, although emotions have a biological base, they are more flexible and are influenced by the person, context and social circumstance. As is so often with complex issues, both these approaches probably contain an element of truth.

What concerns us more is the role of emotions in children and young people's development and their role in wellbeing. Emotions such as fear, anger and disgust have played a key role in protecting us from threats in our past. The preprogrammed *fight* or *flight* response is a clear example of how the brain quickly responds to a threat – a flight response and we run, an anger one and we fight. This was appropriate when we were faced with dinosaurs and the like. Today they can be triggered by exams, or even bank statements. The problem is that the lower part of the brain that controls these emotional responses is the first part of our brain to develop and is outside of direct conscious control. Having to think of a response in a life-threatening situation makes no sense, so instead we react first and think later.

Therefore, we have inherited a biological system that is still programmed for us to survive in the jungle, just like animals, rather than in a technological, communication-based environment. Through necessity our emotions have

59 Ekman P (2004) Emotions Revealed: *Understanding Faces And Feelings*. St Ives, UK: Phoenix Paper Ball.

evolved and adapted to a more complex social world, so we have developed many more than our ancestors had, and have added new social ones such as guilt and shame. So emotions have been the driving force that enabled our survival but also the subjective experience of emotions means that we have positives and negatives. This means that we tend to engage more with activities that give us pleasurable emotions and avoid those that give us negative ones. Not only do they aid our survival but they also help us evaluate the interactions we have with our world.

Emotions and wellbeing

The studies below suggest that positive emotions are good for our wellbeing:

- When children visualise situations that make them feel good, the positive mood increases their performance on creative problem-solving and mathematical tasks (Bryan & Bryan, 1991).[60]

- Positive mood states have been found to have good effects on patients with AIDS and cancer (Salovey et al, 2000).[61]

- A positive emotional state decreases the susceptibility to illness, suggesting the immune system is better able to resist illness (Cohen et al, 1995).[62]

While there is a link between positive emotions and wellbeing, it would be naive to say this is always the case. Negative emotions are not always followed by poor outcomes – for example, being angry when one's moral code has been broken is justified.

Emotional development in children and young people is believed to follow a number of stages, each of which contributes to the success of the next. For example, Colley and Cooper (2017) wrote of five core competencies that each need to be successfully mastered.[63]

- **Emotional self-awareness** – A child can recognise and understand their own feelings and name their emotions and how they impact on their behaviour.

---

60 Bryan T & Bryan J (1991) Positive mood and math performance. *J Learn Disabil* 24(8): 490–94.

61 Salovey P, Rothman AJ, Detweiler JB & Steward WT (2000) Emotional states and physical health. *Am Psychol* 55: 110–21.

62 Cohen S, Doyle WJ, Skomere DP, Fireman P, Gwaltney JM & Newsom JT (1995). State and trait negative affect as predictors of objective and subjective symptoms of respiratory viral infections. *J Pers Soc Psychol* 68(1): 159–69.

63 Colley D & Cooper P (2017) *Attachment and Emotional Development in the Classroom: Theory and Practice.* London: Jessica Kingsley Publishing.

- **Emotional self-regulation** – Emotional impulses can be controlled and responses are sensitive to the context.
- **Social awareness (empathy)** – The ability to feel how others are feeling, and respect for others.
- **Relationship management** – Can manage differences constructively.
- **Responsibility and decision-making** – Able to weigh up advantages/ disadvantages of different options.

Children and young people's fears and anxieties

There are many emotional fears and anxieties associated with normal development at different ages and some are common to most children and young people. It is of course the emotional stage of development that is the key factor and not the age of a child. A child may be seven years old but, for various reasons, still responds more like a four-year-old to new situations.

The following provides a general framework.

Childhood fears and anxieties

Age	Source of fear	Anxiety disorder
Early infancy 0 – 6 months	loss of support loud noises	normal response
Late infancy 6 – 12 months	stranger separation	normal response
Toddler 2 – 4 years	imaginary fears	separation anxiety
Early childhood 5 – 7 years	natural disasters floods	animal phobia
Middle childhood 8 – 11 years	esteem school performance	school phobia
Adolescence 12 – 18	peer rejection	social phobias

(Carr, 2014)[64]

---

64 Carr A (1999) *Handbook Of Child And Adolescent Clinical Psychology: A Contextual Approach*. London: Routledge.

Nature and the role of early attachment

There are many aspects of children and young people's emotional development that are important for wellbeing. This section will explore the nature and role of early attachment and the processes involved. Second, it will look at how children and young people develop internal emotional self-regulation. This is especially important for any child and young person's successful inclusion in both school and their wider social network.

Supporting children and young people at these different stages can take many forms. We will consider the work of Clarke and Dawson (1998a) and their Cycles of Development.[65] In their account, there are various stages of human development and each stage has set tasks for the individual to achieve as part of the attachment process before they can successfully move on. If they are not managed successfully then difficulties will occur in later development. Their approach is valuable as they provide practical ideas as to what a parent or carer can do to facilitate each stage. A brief overview of their model is shown below.

  How to help – developmental stages

☞ **Stage 1: Being (birth to six months)**

Tasks of the child
- Call for help
- Signal needs
- Accept nurture
- Bond with carers
- Trust caring adults

Affirmations:
- I'm glad you are here
- You belong here
- What you need is important to us
- We are glad you are you
- You can grow at your own pace
- You can feel all of your feelings
- We want you to be here and we want to care for you

---

65   Clarke J (1998a) *Growing Up Again: Helping Ourselves, Helping Our Children*. Seattle, WA: Parenting Press.

How to help:

- Affirm the child in doing the developmental tasks for this stage
- Provide consistent care as needed
- Think for the child when required, while monitoring development through the stage
- Use touch, holding, talking, singing, and intuition

☞ Stage 2: Doing (six to eighteen months)

Task of the child:	How to encourage:
■ To explore their environment	■ Affirmations
■ To signal needs	■ You can explore and experiment and we will support and protect you
■ To trust others and self	
■ To continue to form secure attachments	■ You can do things as many times as you need to
■ To get help in times of distress	■ You can use all of your senses when you explore
■ To start to learn that there are options	■ You can know what you know
■ That not all problems are easily solved	■ You can be interested in everything
	■ We like you when you are active and when you are quiet
	■ We like to watch you grow and learn

How to help:

- Affirm the child in doing the developmental tasks for this stage
- Provide a safe environment and protection from harm
- Provide nurturing touch and encouragement
- Say 'yes' more than 'no'
- Offer a variety of sensory experiences
- Listen to the child, especially if he/she is struggling to express something
- Feedback observations of behaviour and model new language
- Respond when your child initiates activity

Stage 3: Thinking (eighteen months to three years)

Task of the child:

- To establish ability to think for themselves
- To test reality; to push against boundaries and other people
- To learn to think and solve problems with cause-and-effect thinking
- To start to follow simple safety commands – stop, come here, stay here, go there
- To express anger and other feelings
- To separate from adults without losing security
- To start to give up beliefs about being the centre of the universe
- To continue earlier tasks

How to encourage:

- Affirmations
- I'm glad you are starting to think for yourself
- You can say 'no' and push the limits as much as you need to
- It's OK for you to be angry, and we won't let you hurt yourself or others
- You can learn to think for yourself, and others can too
- You can think and feel at the same time
- You can know what you need and ask for help
- You can be yourself and we will still care for you

How to help:

- Affirm the child in doing the developmental tasks for this stage
- Help transition from one activity to another
- Give simple clear directions, including basic safety commands
- Be consistent in setting limits and ensuring they are kept
- Accept all of the child's feelings without getting into win–lose battles.
- Give reasons, and provide information to move child on in his/her thinking
- Expect the child to think about their own and others feelings
- Give time for new thinking to develop, e.g. cause-and-effect

Stage 4: Identity and Power (three to six years)

Task of the child:

- To assert an identity separate from others
- To acquire information about the world, self, body and gender role
- To discover effect on others and place in groups
- To learn to exert power to affect relationships
- To practise socially appropriate behaviour
- To separate fantasy from reality
- To learn extent of personal power
- To continue earlier tasks

How to encourage:

- Affirmations
- You can explore who you are and find out about others
- You can try out different ways of being powerful
- All of your feelings are okay here
- You can learn the results of your behaviour
- You can be powerful and ask for help at the same time
- You can learn what is pretend and what is real

How to help:

- Affirm the child in doing the developmental tasks for this stage
- Expect the child to express feelings and to connect feeling and thinking
- Teach clearly that it is okay to be who you are, and that both sexes and all cultures are okay
- Answer questions accurately, provide information and correct misinformation
- Be clear about who is responsible for what in the classroom and playground
- Encourage fantasy while being clear about what is fantasy and what is reality
- Acknowledge and respond to appropriate behaviour

☞ Stage 5: Structure (six to twelve years)

Tasks of the child:

- To learn skills, learn from mistakes and decide to be 'good enough'
- To learn to listen in order to collect information and think
- To practise thinking and doing
- To reason about wants and needs
- To check out family/school rules and structures
- To learn the relevance of rules
- To experience the consequences of breaking rules
- To disagree with others and still be wanted
- To test ideas and values
- To develop internal control
- To learn what is one's own and others' responsibilities
- To learn when to flee, to flow and when to stand firm
- To develop the capacity to cooperate
- To test abilities against others
- To identify with one's own sex

How to encourage:

- Affirmations
- You can think before you say 'yes' or 'no'
- You can learn from your mistakes
- You can trust your intuition to help decide what you want to do
- You can find ways of doing things that work for you
- You can learn the rules that help you live with others
- You can learn how and when to disagree
- You can think for yourself and get help instead of staying in distress
- We still want to be with you when we differ and we can learn together

How to help:

- Affirm the child in doing the developmental tasks for this stage
- Teach conflict resolution and problem-solving skills
- Give lots of strokes for learning, thinking and finding own way to do things
- Encourage skills development
- Be encouraging, enthusiastic, reliable and consistent

- Respect the child's opinions and beliefs and allow discussion
- Be clear that mistakes are part of learning
- Challenge negative behaviour and confront discounting
- Encourage participation in rule-making, and be clear about negotiable and non-negotiable rules

☞ Stage 6: Integration (twelve to nineteen years)

Task of the adolescent:

- To take steps towards independence
- To achieve a clearer emotional separation from family
- To emerge as a separate independent person with own identity and values
- To be competent and responsible for own needs, feelings and behaviours
- To integrate sexually into the earlier developmental tasks

How to encourage:

- Affirmations
- You can know who you are and learn and practise skills for independence
- You can develop your own interests, relationships and causes
- You can grow in your femaleness or maleness and still need help at times
- You can learn to use old skills in new ways
- We look forward to knowing you as an adult
- We trust you to ask for support when you need it

How to help:

- Affirm for doing developmental tasks
- Continue to offer appropriate support
- Accept adolescent's feelings
- Confront unacceptable behaviour
- Be clear about school's position on drugs, etc
- Encourage growing independence
- Expect thinking, problem-solving and self-determination
- Confront destructive or self-defeating behaviour
- Celebrate emerging adulthood, personal identity, etc
- Negotiate rules and responsibilities

Managing developmental challenges

A useful metaphor that helps us appreciate the importance of children and young people successfully managing the challenges at each of the different stages is the 'Stack of Pennies' story, developed by Eric Berne.[66]

Picture a stack of pennies. Each penny represents a developmental task, starting with Stage 1 on the bottom and adding additional pennies for each of the tasks and stages in turn. When all the pennies are flush and even, the foundation of the stack is firm. You can add any number of pennies and they won't topple over. If, however, one or more of the pennies that form the base of the stack is slightly bent, curved or irregular, then the stack becomes skewed or starts to zigzag. All the pennies stacked on top of the uneven ones are less secure, regardless of how true or even they are. The uneven pennies change the direction and balance of the stack. Recycling (deliberately repeating the stage later in life) offers opportunities to make the bent pennies true and to redirect and rebalance our developmental stacks.

Expert View

"The pennies of childhood, the quarters of adolescence, and the silver dollars of maturity. One bent penny might eventually cause thousands of silver dollars to tumble in chaos."

Eric Berne

Internal emotional self-regulation

It is worth clarifying some of the terms that are used when considering children's emotional development. Emotions are considered a physiological arousal within the nervous system, triggered by an external event. A feeling is the cognitive interpretation of that arousal. For example, two people are climbing a rock face, both are emotionally aroused; one is feeling terrified and worried about falling because they have not climbed before, while the other is a regular climber and feels excited at the challenge ahead.

A key developmental milestone for children and young people is their increasing ability to control feelings – or 'self-regulation', as it is known. We can clearly see a lack of self-regulation in the typical two-year-old; they will frequently have a tantrum when they cannot have a treat or similar. This is a normal response. However, when that same child is seen at the age of four, they now seem able to wait and enjoy the treat later on when it is explained to them by the adult. What has happened? Through brain maturation and interaction with parenting, the child has acquired the

66 Frances P (2013) *Coin Metaphor* (E Berne). Available at: http://understandingta.blogspot.com/2013/06/transactional-analysis-in-psychotherapy_15.html [last accessed 4 February 2021]

ability to not be controlled by impulsive feelings. They can contain and self-regulate these feelings. This is also described as delayed gratification.

The growth of self-control is best seen in the 'marshmallow' experiment carried out by Mischel (1970), which has become one of psychology's classic experiments.[67] Pre-school children were offered a less-preferred immediate reward or a better one if they could wait, i.e. delayed gratification. Follow-up studies have found a correlation between pre-school children who could delay gratification with competency and academic scores. Later research suggests that those who could delay gratification had more activity in their prefrontal cortex.

Self-regulation is how we refer to a child or young person who can control their feelings. There are two types of regulation: internal and external. An internally self-regulated child is one that has learnt that cheating or stealing is wrong, so they will not steal or cheat even when the opportunity exists. An externally regulated child will refrain from stealing or cheating because of adult supervision and fear of the consequences, but will deviate if the opportunity arises when left on their own. Both are regulated, but only the first one can be described as being in control of their feelings, i.e. self-regulated.

How is emotional self-regulation developed?

A major influence for regulating emotions is the family. When children and young people have such feelings as sadness, anxiety, fear and anger it is their cognitive ability that allows them to manage or contain these emotions. Researchers have studied how relationships within the family help or hinder this process. At first children and young people depend on adults to

> ## *Key Point*
> *If adults are emotionally positive and sensitive to a child or young person's emotions, they will indirectly support developing self-control.*

soothe and de-stress them through their caring and soothing responses; gradually adults will influence how a child self-manages their emotions. This is achieved both directly and indirectly. If adults are emotionally positive and sensitive to a child or young person's emotions, they will indirectly support developing self-control. This enables them to regulate their own distress as they move from infancy to toddlerhood (Raver, 1996).[68] As adults talk through their own emotions, they can coach

---

67 Mischel W (2015) *The Marshmallow Test: Understanding Self-Control And How To Master It.* Ealing, London: Corgi Imprint.

68 Raver C (1996) The relations between social contingency in mother-child interactions and 24-month-olds' social competence. *Deve Psychol* 32: 850–59.

children to use problem-solving skills to calm themselves down – from such basic ones as counting to ten through to breathing techniques.

For some children and young people who are exposed to high levels of adult anger, sadness and withdrawal, neuroscience suggests that they will have their emotional regulation skills compromised. For example, children exposed to chronic adult anger become hypervigilant and oversensitive to emotionally negative stimuli (Hagenaars, Satins & Roelofs, 2011).[69] This shows that children and young people will adapt to the prevailing conditions they find themselves in. While this pattern is adaptive in the stressful setting where it was learned, it becomes a problem elsewhere. In such a situation, the child can see and react to threats where none exists.

How to help – developing emotional literacy

☞ Supporting children and young people in their emotional development is no easy task. The best method is to break the process down into subskills. Each skill can then be focused on and developed.

The skills are:

- **Emotional awareness** – Being able to identify different emotions, rate their intensity and express them.
- **Understanding** – What triggers emotions; physical changes associated with different ones and how to hide them.
- **Empathy** – Recognising emotions in others, sharing and caring.
- **Prevention** – Lifestyle, how it helps and hinders emotions.
- **Mastery** – Being good at it.
- **Expression** – Self-expression; to share or not.
- **Cognitive** – Thoughts and feelings.
- **Specify emotion skills** – Managing anger, sadness and anxiety.

(Southam-Gerow, 2016)[70]

---

69   Hagenaars M, Stins J & Roelofs K (2011) Aversive life events enhance human freezing responses. *J Exp Psychol* 141(1): 98–105.

70   Southam-Gerow MA (2016) *Emotion Regulation In Children and Adolescents*. New York: The Guilford Press.

Chapter 13: Wellbeing and cognitive development

The ideas of Vygotsky (Karpov, 2014) are especially relevant here.[71] Vygotsky was a Russian psychologist who developed his theories at the same time as Piaget (1920s and 1930s), and whose work has become known as Social Developmental Theory. When we compare the development of human babies to most other animals, it is clear that the human infant takes a long time to become capable of functioning as a mature adult, whereas most animals are pretty much independent quickly after birth. Their key survival behaviours are hardwired into them, they do not need to learn them. For the human baby, some reflexes are hardwired; for example, if you stroke the cheek of a baby they will turn their head in search of food – the rooting reflex. Most other behaviours are learned, and the key one for Vygotsky is the acquisition of language.

Expert View

"Language is the main vehicle of interaction, and it is a determining factor in development of the mind."

Lev Vygotsky

Vygotsky's approach to child development

Cognitive development is the result of social interaction. When adults play with babies/infants they use simple language. Language is used to describe the actions they are doing: *"Let's change this nappy for you."* The baby is learning how to describe actions through language. They will soon mimic what the adults say: *"Me put toys away"* or *"Me good girl/boy."* So the child is beginning to see the world through the language of their parents and carers. This is how the culture of their community is passed to them. The fact that they are described as a 'boy or girl' is providing them with ways of thinking about themselves and others in gendered terms.

Importantly for Vygotsky, thought and language are two separate systems. We can think without language, e.g. knowing where the light is in a room when it is dark is intuitive knowledge. We can have language without thought, such as the verbal babbling of a baby. Cognitive development depends on the internalisation of language. It is via interaction with others, referred to as a 'more knowledgeable other', that a child is helped to learn more and more complex higher mental

---

71 Karpov Y (2014) *Vygotsky For Educators*. New York, NY: Cambridge University Press.

functions. Schaffer (1996) gives the example of a child doing their first jigsaw; they struggle, then an adult sits with them and gives them different strategies: *"Find the corner pieces first and then the edges."*[72] For Vygotsky, this reflects social interaction involving cooperation through using language to promote cognitive development.

This is very different from Piaget. For Piaget, children and young people go through stages of cognitive development. Each stage involves developing new and more complex schemas – these are internal mental representations of the external world. Piaget's influence was very significant; it changed how children and young people were seen. They were not miniature adults, but needed to grow through set stages. The role of experience was stressed as children and young people gradually became able to think with abstract concepts.

Stages do not figure in Vygotsky's account. Instead, social factors are more important. Children are born with the basic tools for cognitive development, but it is social interaction that enables them to develop. For Vygotsky there is a key role for the more knowledgeable other. This is the adult who can enable a child to move onto higher mental functioning. The child has a 'zone of proximal development', which is what they can do on their own, but then with a knowledgeable other they can move on.

A key feature of a child's cognitive wellbeing is to be able to control themselves and not be dominated by their emotions. A two-year-old will be prone to tantrums when a goal they wish for is blocked. So in the supermarket we can expect them to have a tantrum when they are refused a treat. When we revisit that same child at age four, we see a difference. Now the four-year-old is told and accepts that they can have the treat when the shopping is completed. What is it that enables the four-year-old to stay in control, to override their emotional drive for the treat?

Piaget could explain they now have new schemas, whereas for Vygotsky it shows that the child's zone of development has been increased through the active support of an informed adult.

---

72   Schaffer R (1996) *Social Development*. Oxford: Blackwell.

Sociodramatic play, self-regulation and school readiness

Sociodramatic play is when children joint role-play a plot that reflects aspects of social relationships – for example, playing shop or nursing a baby. Children want to be adults, and play is the means through which they explore adult roles and relationships. Adults help children move from using objects to acting out social roles – for example, by using a spoon to feed a doll to playing the role of a caring mother/father who is nursing the child.

Parents and carers should actively encourage sociodramatic play. Through play a child learns to self-regulate – when they act out a role, the child must act in accordance with that role; they cannot just do as they wish. There are rules as to how they should behave. This is an obvious key skill of school readiness. Children need symbolic thought to imagine how to act out a role. Thinking through language is an essential school skill.

Adults should actively engage with children in sociodramatic play to promote self-regulation and school readiness skills.

  How to help – sociodramatic play

☞ Adults should actively engage with children in sociodramatic play to promote self-regulation and school readiness skills. An example is shown below.

Emma is playing with bricks. The adult models how to play 'shopkeeper' with the bricks.

Adult: Hello, Mr Shopkeeper, I would like to buy some shoes. (Points to the bricks.)

Emma: Which ones?

Adult: I think I would like these blue ones. (Picks up two bricks.)

Emma: Would you like to try them on?

Adult: These seem to be a bit tight. Do you have any in a size bigger?

Studying the brain

Our understanding of the human brain has increased dramatically on account of new techniques of research and investigation, and this has developed into the contemporary scientific field of cognitive neuropsychology. It was an understanding of how neurons transmitted messages and the energy needed for such activity that led to scientific breakthroughs in how the brain could be studied. These techniques were mainly driven by medical needs for better treatments of pathological conditions.

The brain's prefrontal cortex has long been thought of as where cognitive processes took place. This is where impulse control, planning and goal directed behaviour is controlled. Through current brain research, we can explore how children and young people come to be able to control their actions through cognitive processes. The aspect we will focus on is known as executive functioning skills (EFS.) These are fundamental to children having self-control and are essential for wellbeing. Studies have shown that without such skills they experience problems in controlling their behaviour (Batmanghelidjh, 2007;[73] Nadeau & Nolin, 2013;[74] Barkley & Murphy, 2006[75].

A brief account of the procedures that have been developed to study the human brain will show how the link between the brain and behavioural self-regulatory skills are studied today.

At first the brain was understood anatomically through autopsies. However, once researchers found that neurons were electrically charged, they were able to develop the electroencephalograph (EEG). This involved recording electrical activity through the scalp, which was of particular value for medical practitioners studying epilepsy.

The fact that neurons are electrically charged means that magnetic fields would be produced through activity. In the 1960s a new research tool, the magnetoencephalograph (MEG), was developed to research into perceptual and cognitive brain processes.

---

73 Batmanghelidjh C (2007) *Shattered Lives: Children Who Live With Courage And Dignity.* London: Jessica Kingsley Publishers.

74 Nadeau M, Nolin P, Chartrand C (2013) Behavioral and emotional profiles of neglected children. *J Child Adolesc Trauma* 6: 11–24.

75 Barkley RA & Murphy KR (2006) *Attention-Deficit Hyperactivity Disorder: A Clinical Workbook (3rd ed.).* New York: Guilford Press.

A little earlier, in the late 1950s, positron emission tomography-computed tomography (PET-CT) was developed, again to aid medical diagnoses, and this has advanced oncological research and treatments.

Today, the dominant technique that has contributed to research in neuropsychology is functional magnetic resonance imaging (fMRI). This measures brain activity indirectly through detecting changes in blood flow. An increase in blood flow is indicative of neuronal activity. This technique has enabled europsychologists to localise brain activity to within millimetres.

While fMRI shows biological changes occurring in localised areas of the brain, it does not enable us to see thinking and learning. This gap in our understanding is bridged by psychological models that relate to cognitive processes. Cognitive neuropsychology explores the link between the biology of the brain and the cognitive processes of the mind (Howard-Jones, 2014).[76]

With fMRI, neuropsychologists are able to study the brain while it carries out different processes. This has enabled specific areas of the brain to be located for different functions. Using fMRI, Fassbender et al (2004) found that the control of behaviour could be separated into distinct functions which were performed by discrete cortical regions.[77]

Cognitive neuropsychology and executive functioning skills (EFS)

Most human functioning is managed by a set of processes known as executive functioning skills (EFS), that can be separated into distinct psychological functions.

"A great deal of an individual's everyday functioning is monitored by an overriding 'executive' or 'managerial' process, a process that controls what, and how much, behaviour is displayed."
(McAtee, 1999)[78]

---

76 Howard-Jones P (2014) Neuroscience and education: myths and messages. *Nat Rev Neurosci* 15: 817–24.

77 Fassbender C, Murphy K, Foxe J & Wylie J (2004) A topography of executive functions and their interactions revealed by functional Magnetic Resonance Imaging. *Brain Res Cogn Brain Res* 20(2): 132–43.

78 McAtee EC (1999) *Investigation Of Deficits In Higher Level Executive Functioning As A Prerequisite For Adult Basic Education Intervention, Final Report, Fiscal Year 1998–1999.* Edinboro, PA: Northwest Tri County Intermediate Unit.

Typically cognitive theorists consider EFS to be an umbrella concept that includes such processes as:

- Maintenance of a problem-solving set for future goals (Pennington, Bennetto, McAleer & Roberts, 1996).[79]
- Organising behaviour over time (Denckla, 1996).[80]
- Self-monitoring and self-regulation (Borkowski & Burke, 1996).[81]
- Conforming to rules of social behavior (Price, Daffner, Stowe & Mesulam,1990).[82]
- Skillful use of strategies (Graham & Harris, 1996).[83]
- Using rewards and punishments to enhance learning (Giedd et al, 1996).[84]

Executive functioning skills are essentially the functions that the brain carries out to control our attention and behaviour (Morraine, 2012); they allow goals to be set and achieved.[85]

Executive functioning skills and maturation

We are not born with EFS but the potential is there, just as the potential for language and other complex processes is. These are innately *hardwired* potentials; their development will be the result of the interaction between a child's genetic inheritance, biological and environmental factors. When language has developed children can *stop, think and choose*, and having this skill enables them not to be distracted by external stimuli.

---

79   Pennington BF, Bennetto L, McAleer O & Roberts RJ (1996) Executive Functions And Working Memory: Theoretical And Measurement Issues. In Lyon GR & Krasnegor NA (Eds.) *Attention, Memory and Executive Function* (pp. 327–48). Baltimore, MD: Paul H. Brookes Publishing Co.

80   Denckla MB (1996) A Theory And Model Of Executive Function: A Neuropsychological Perspective. In Lyon GR & Krasnegor NA (Eds.) *Attention, Memory and Executive Function* (pp. 263–78). Baltimore, MD: Paul H. Brookes Publishing Co.

81   Borkowski JG & Burke JE (1996) Theories, Models And Measurements Of Executive Functioning: An Information Processing Perspective. In Lyon GR & Krasnegor NA (Eds.) *Attention, Memory and Executive Function* (pp. 235–62). Baltimore, MD: Paul H. Brookes Publishing Co.

82   Price BH, Daffner KR, Stowe RM & Mesulam MM (1990) The compartmental learning disabilities of early frontal lobe damage. *Brain* 113: 1,383–93.

83   Graham S & Harris KR (1996) Addressing Problems In Attention, Memory And Executive Functioning: An Example From Self-Regulated Strategy Development. In Lyon GR & Krasnegor A (Eds.) *Attention, Memory And Executive Function* (pp. 263–79). Baltimore, MD: Brookes.

84   Giedd JA, Snell JW, Lange N, Rajapakse JC, Casey BJ, Kozuch PL (1996) Quantitative magnetic resonance imaging of human brain development: Ages 4–18. *Cereb Cortex* 6(4): 551–60 .

85   Morraine P (2012) *Everyday Executive Functions*. London: Jessica Kingsley Publishers.

Executive functioning skills begin to emerge in the developing brain at a very early stage. A baby's brain develops sequentially from the *bottom up*. The older parts of the human brain developed first; these contain behavioural patterns linked to survival and are hardwired into the brain. At birth babies have neurons wired together for such essential behaviours as breathing, eating, sleeping and crying. New behaviours are the result of experiences that create new neural pathways. Complex processes emerge through the interaction between brain and the environment. Learning thinking skills depends on experience – for example, the brain has the innate propensity to develop a language, but which language will be acquired depends on exposure to a particular language.

Maturation, which is the development of the prefrontal cortex, is central to an understanding of child development.

> *"It has long been believed that the development of the frontal cortex allows the child to move away from being bound by external stimuli. The development of frontal control mechanisms allows children to demonstrate voluntary control of actions and to delay gratification. The child's ability to resist control from current input gives rise to our feeling that toddlers, unlike infants, have a mind of their own."*
> (Posner & Rothbart, 2007)[86]

It is maturation of the brain's neural pathways, in conjunction with environmental experiences, that allow the emergence of EFS. From as young as three to six months, babies show signs of emerging EFS. Research has found that a baby's eyes will follow a moving object but, also, will sometimes start to focus slightly ahead of the moving object. This suggests that the baby is anticipating where the object is going (Eliot, 1999).[87] The neural growth in the frontal cortex is enabling the baby to choose where to look. Just as we don't need to teach our stomachs to digest food, we don't need to teach the brain to think. It does so naturally; it is what it was designed for.

To summarise, then, EFS are essential to be able to:

■ Control feelings

■ Persist with set goals

■ Have flexibility

■ Control impulses

---

86   Posner MI & Rothbart MK (2007) Research on attention networks as a model for the integration of psychological science. *Annu Rev Psychol* 58:1–23.

87   Eliot L (1999) *What's Going On In There?: How The Brain And Mind Develop In The First Five Years Of Life*. New York, NY: Bantam Books.

- Plan and prioritise
- Start work on set tasks

For most children and young people, these skills are fully acquired by the time they are ten or eleven years old.

It is fair to say that many children and young people who face social, emotional and behavioural challenges often struggle with:

- Control of feelings
- Sustained attention
- Response inhibition
- Task initiation
- Goal-directed persistence

Executive functioning skills depend on the development of specific areas of the brain. Children and young people with a range of different medical conditions, such as Attention Deficit Hyperactivity Disorder (ADHD), autism, attachment disorders, Asperger syndrome and Conduct Disorder, all share one thing in common. They have underdeveloped EFS; however, this does not mean that environmental factors play no role.

Today we appreciate much more how early socialisation experiences can affect neural growth (De Bellis, 2001).[88] The wide differences in EFS between children and young people suggests that this is the case. The development of EFS in children and young people from low-income households differs significantly to those from better-off homes. Some of the reasons for these differences will be considered later; for now, suffice it to say that low income is a proxy for several stressors that probably act cumulatively or interactively to affect the course of children's executive control development (Clark et al, 2014).[89]

---

88   De Bellis M, Hooper S, Spratt E, Woolley D (2001) Neuropsychological findings in childhood neglect and their relationships to pediatric PTSD. *J Int Neuropsychol Soc* 15(6): 868–78.

89   Clark AC, Martinez MM, Mize-Nelson J, Wiebe SA & Espy K (2014) Children's Self-Regulation And Executive Control: Critical for Later Years. In Landry SH & Cooper CL (Eds.) *Wellbeing: A Complete Reference Guide, Volume 1: Wellbeing in Children and Families.* Hoboken, NJ: Wiley-Blackwell

Executive functioning skills and wellbeing

Clearly a child or young person's ability to control what they think, feel and do will have a major impact on their wellbeing. The lack of EFS is a predictor of poor developmental outcomes in both personal and educational settings. The child or young person with good EFS will cope with failures and disappointments in a healthy way, whereas the child or young person who lacks EFS is more likely to have an emotional tantrum that will not be considered appropriate for their age. When children and young people are seen behaving with a lack of self-control, it is reasonable to assume that their normal development has been disrupted in some way.

How to help – executive functioning skills

☞ **The 'Turtle Technique'**

The National Center for Pyramid Model Innovations in the USA has a range of reproducible resources designed to improve the social, emotional, and behavioral outcomes of young children with, and at risk for, developmental disabilities or delays. Its scripted story 'Tucker Turtle Takes Time to Tuck and Think' is designed to assist with teaching children the 'Turtle Technique' – learning to stop, calm down, think and then choose, rather than acting impulsively.[90]

90   Lentini R, Giroux L & Hemmeter ML (2019) *Tucker Turtle Takes Time to Tuck and Think.* National Center for Pyramid Model Innovations (https://challengingbehavior.cbcs.usf.edu/docs/TuckerTurtle_Story.pdf)

Chapter 14: Wellbeing and social development

Our focus in this chapter will be on adolescent peer relationships. Is having friends a luxury or a necessity? After the family, it is peers that can have a significant influence on the pathway teenagers take to adulthood. When young people mix with their peers they are mixing with equals; this is in contrast to when they mix with adults. Adults will often have more knowledge and power over the young people than peers. It is their peers that young people will grow with, and have mature relationships with.

Sadly, the word 'teenager' is associated with negativity and words such as:

- selfish
- materialistic
- monosyllabic
- untidy

Many myths have developed around adolescents, mostly that they are worse today than they ever were! Yet we can easily find quotes from long ago:

> *"The children now love luxury; they have bad manners, contempt for authority; they show disrespect for elders and love chatter in place of exercise. Children are now tyrants, not the servants of their households. They no longer rise when elders enter the room. They contradict their parents, chatter before company, gobble up dainties at the table, cross their legs, and tyrannise their teachers."*
> (Socrates, quoted in Patty & Johnson, 1953)[91]

Today we understand much more of the changes and challenges that young people face during the adolescent years. The idea that it was

---

91 Patty WL & Johnson LS (1953) *Personality And Adjustment* (p. 277). New York, NY: McGraw-Hill.

a time of *storm and stress* is in part explained by the fact that young people who were struggling were usually referred to psychiatrists. As a result, psychiatrists developed a biased view of adolescence, often over-generalising from the few that they saw to the many that they didn't.

There are major changes occurring for all young people at this time that can result in difficulties, especially at home. Young people want increasing independence and personal autonomy, especially with regard to family rules. Sexual maturation means that mixing with peers of both sexes begins to take on a new meaning and time spent with peers becomes more attractive than spending time with adults. We also know from research that different regions in the brain develop at different rates. Importantly, the brain's reward system develops before the control centres in the prefrontal cortex, and this can result in young people being prone to risk-taking and pleasure-seeking. They are more aware of the thrill an experience will give than of the possible dangers involved.

Key Point

The brain's reward system develops before its control centres, and this can result in young people being prone to risk-taking and pleasure-seeking.

Brain research can help us understand what is taking place. The limbic system, which is responsible for social–emotional learning, becomes more active at puberty, increasing adolescents' attention to rewards, emotional arousal and short-term gratification. As a result, there is little regard to social norms. The control system, which is situated in the pre-frontal cortex, and is responsible for impulse control, planning, self-regulation and resistance to social pressures does not fully mature until the late teens. The result is that the limbic system is left relatively unchecked until the later development of the control system. These changes can explain why the teenage brain requires extra sleep, in order to organise and manage the many changes that are occurring.

This brief account shows that risk-taking behaviours combined with conformity to adolescent sub-cultures are a normal part of adolescent development. However, a cautionary note is needed here. This is not always true as there are variations between adolescents (Blakemore, 2018).[92] So when we speak of teenagers as though they were one group sharing very similar characteristics, we are making a mistake. The majority of young people are not alienated from their families. They do not have major psychiatric illnesses, do not experience a total breakdown of

---

92 Blakemore SJ (2018) *Inventing Ourselves: The Secret Life of the Teenage Brain.* London: Doubleday.

communication with their parents, and do not experience this period as a time of storm and stress (Coleman & Hendry, 1999).[93]

Tasks of adolescence

In today's fast-changing postmodern societies, the challenges facing our young people are all the more demanding. In more traditional societies, young people knew what kind of work they were going to do – for example, if their father was a fisherman, then they knew that they were also likely to become a fisherman. Today the jobs that young people will eventually fulfil often do not yet exist. With the ever-increasing role of Artificial Intelligence (AI), many contemporary jobs are fast disappearing.

Common tasks and goals of modern young people include:

- Increased pressure for educational success.
- Developing sexual identity and relationship.
- Maintaining peer relationships.
- Acquiring a set of values and an ethical system.
- Becoming socially responsible.
- Achieving independence from parents and carers.
- Preparing for one's own family.

(Dogra, Parkin, Warner-Gale & Frake, 2018)[94]

So, what are the key influences that shape young people?

It seems that, although nature provides the building blocks, it is nurture that designs the outcome. It is not the parents and carers that have the greatest influence on a young person's beliefs and values but the other young people they mix with who share similar values to themselves.

It is interesting to note that theories of adolescent development stress the importance of friends as being necessary for mentally healthy individuals. However, the majority of research focuses on the negative effects of peer relationships, such as criminality, drug abuse, school failure and mental health problems – not the benefits.

---

93 Coleman J & Hendry L (1999) *The Nature Of Adolescence*. London: Routledge.
94 Dogra C, Warner-Gale F & Parkin A (2018) *A Multidisciplinary Handbook Of Child And Adolescent Mental Health*. London: Jessica Kingsley Publishers.

So how are peer relationships good for wellbeing? Mixing with peers enables young people to explore their emerging thinking skills; at this stage they begin to be able to think and reason abstractly. For Piaget they are now at the formal–logical stage of thinking. This means that, as Vygotsky put it, "*a whole world with its past and future, nature, history, and human life opens before the adolescent*" (Karpov, 2014). This can be a time of challenges at home, and for this reason wellbeing can become an issue.

Some of the reasons for family stress may be summarised as:

- Young people can be seen as being overly self-centred, paying little attention to the needs of others.

- With new thinking skills, young people are faced with the ability to imagine their future, i.e. what kind of person they hope to become. They define themselves less in terms of the skills they have or have not mastered and more in terms of personality traits. *I am something of an introvert.*

- Their newly developed reasoning skills can lead to confrontations in the family. Young people are less happy now to simply accept the views of their parents and carers. Instead, they will expect reasons and justifications for any view presented. They also observe what the adults in their lives say and what they do.

A large number of teenagers experience fluctuating self-esteem, meaning that they could feel self-confident one day, but spend the next feeling self-critical and depressed. Some will even vary significantly within the same day. For the most part there is a relatively stable self-concept, i.e. how young people generally believe themselves to be. This allows them to have a predictable aspect of who they are. There is also a malleable aspect to their emerging personality, which is flexible and can change depending on situational factors (Rosenberg, 2001).[95] So young people can behave differently when the situation demands, without changing their core beliefs as to who they are – for example, being shy and withdrawn with new people does not alter their core belief that they are extrovert.

As we have already noted, it is adults in the family that have a significant influence in shaping how young people see the world. So it follows that the parenting style used in the family can be of particular relevance. Studies have conceptualised two basic styles that are of relevance here:

---

95   Rosenberg M (2001) *Extending Self-Esteem*. Cambridge: Cambridge University Press

Authoritarian – characteristics of children parented in this style are:

- Over-constrained by authority.
- Lack of self-respect.
- Compliant when parent present.
- Inhibited, unable to express feelings.

Authoritative – characteristics of children parented in this style are:

- Self-aware.
- Compliant when parent absent.
- Generally well-adjusted.
- Polite, obedient.

When an authoritarian style is used, the adults use force and coercion to parent. They tend not to reason with their children as to why certain rules need to be followed. For example, a young person asks: *"Why must I be in by 9pm?"*. Adult: *"Because I am your father and I say so."* This contrasts with the authoritative parenting style, which would be more likely to reason that *"you have school tomorrow and need your sleep!"* It might not always impress the young person but they become used to reasons for the adults' decisions. They learn to see that the world is not black and white and that there are many different ways of looking at and understanding the same event.

It is the authoritarian parenting style that is more likely to increase tensions and confrontations in the family. The adult will be dismissive of their young person's views, insisting that the young person is wrong and they are right. Some of the differences can be characterised as follows:

- The authoritarian style will see the young person as rebellious. The authoritative will see the young person as growing in independence.
- The authoritarian style will see the young person as being rude when they interrupt adults. The authoritative will see the young person as learning social skills.
- The authoritarian style will see the young person as being excessively self-centred. The authoritative style will see the young person as developing their own identity.

During this transformative period of development, young people are more at risk of developing mental health issues. For example, one in six young people aged sixteen to twenty-four have some symptoms of common mental disorders, such as depression or anxiety (Young Minds, 2016).[8] Fifty per cent of seventeen-to-nineteen-year-olds with a diagnosable mental health disorder have self-harmed or attempted suicide.

The deviant behaviour that is observed in some young people, such as violence, drug-taking and criminal activity, is more often associated with gang membership. It is not the norm for the majority of young people during this time of their lives. Although the causes will be many and complex, one factor is ineffective parenting practices. When the norms and values of the family have either not been internalised by a young person, or there is abuse and criminality within the family, then there is an increased likelihood of the young person joining a gang as a substitute family. They will then follow the norms and values of the gang as a way of finding order and security at a time of change within themselves.

To summarise, it is normal for young peoplpe to mix more with their peers as they move towards adulthood. Usually they will mix with peers who come from similar backgrounds to themselves. Young people will practise new thinking skills both at home and with their peers. Some parenting styles can be more protective of young people's wellbeing at this stage than others. Understanding the emotional, cognitive and social changes young people are experiencing can enable parents and carers to be more tolerant and less critical of the behaviours at this time. Young people will need time to integrate the many changes they are experiencing for them to develop an integrated personality.

How to help – social development in adolescence

☞ Adolescent challenges

It can seem a 'health paradox' that when teenagers are moving towards their peak physical health, they are at most likely to engage in 'risky' activities such as experimentation with alcohol/drugs, unsafe sex, poor diet, etc (Blakemore, 2018).[92]

If adolescents can become involved in organised activities, they can satisfy the need for challenges in controlled ways. It will also mean that they are socialising with peers with similar interests.

☞ Ideas to explore

Outdoor activity
NCS Summer No We Can

https://www.action4youth.org/event/ncs-summer-2020-wave-three-programme/

Sports
Sport England

https://www.sportengland.org/our-work/children-and-young-people/

Creativity
Access Art

https://www.accessart.org.uk/be-a-creative-producer/

Safe thrills
Boundless

https://www.boundless.co.uk/be-inspired/travel-tips/unusual-uk-days-out

Part 4:
Wellbeing at home and in school

Chapter 15: Wellbeing and the family

The first influence in a child or young person's life is the family; whether they are with their biological parents or adoptive/caring ones, the family is their most important role model. It is in the family that they will begin to develop their unique personality. In the preschool years, children begin their unique journey to adulthood. The uniqueness of their personality is shaped in their family as to how they relate to others through:

Key Point

A child will be influenced by the way they are parented from the earliest moments

- Cooperation and coordination – give and take.

- Engaging in and sharing fun.

- Understanding and responding to feelings.

- Regulating everyday tensions.

As well as:

- Managing frustrations.

- Accepting delays and disappointments.

- Operating in their environment autonomously.

(Sroufe, 1990)[96]

A child will be influenced by the way they are parented from the earliest moments. For example, how an adult changes a baby's nappy can be a positive or negative experience, and one that begins to shape how the individual feels about themselves and the world they find themselves in. A nappy can be changed in a loving and fun way, or in a hostile and negative way. Understanding about relationships will begin to develop as the baby interacts with significant others, which will form the basis for future social relationships. We are each a *presenting past*; we create our present interactions based on past experiences.

96 Sroufe L(1990) An Organisational Perspective On The Self. In Cicchetti D & Beeghly M (Eds.) Transitions From Infancy To Childhood: The Self (pp. 281–307). Chicago: University of Chicago Press.

Attachment in the family

A child is born programmed to attach to their caregiver. The Bowlby/ Ainsworth theory of attachment believed that there was a basic need for all children to form a strong bond or attachment to another person, usually the primary care giver. For Bowlby (1998) attachment forms a lasting psychological connectedness between human beings.[97]

Becoming attached is essentially how a baby will survive. They will need protection as well as food, shelter and warmth. Just as the young of animals imprint on the adult, so human infants imprint on their carer. At birth it is the lower part of the brain that is fully connected and functioning. A child's growing brain needs comfort, affection and nurture. A baby will typically experience many signs of being positively cared for, through touch, sight, smell and sound. The baby is soothed with gentle words, fed when hungry, and cuddled when distressed. All of these signals bathe the lower brain in feelings of trust and security. It is experiencing the world as a safe and caring place. As it looks at its mother, it sees itself (we use the term 'mother' here to refer to the main carer, irrespective of gender.) Having no language, the baby does not experience itself as being separate from her. The gentle, caring and responsive behaviour of a mother is the first building block of an internal working model of the world. This can be contrasted to a baby that experiences harshness and neglect, who hears unkind words towards them, who is handled roughly and is left crying when distressed (Krumwiede, 2014).[98]

Expert View

"We do as we have been done by."

John Bowlby

If the baby is under stress then the normal wiring up of the brain is compromised. Stress interferes with the normal development of the prefrontal cortex. As covered earlier, this is the part of the brain that controls more complex thinking processes. Referred to as the 'executive centre' of the brain, it is here that a child learns gratification, to plan, to reason and to control their impulses. The neurons are ready to make connections, but due to stress the focus is more on lower brain functions such as *fight or flight* responses. The name of the game is survival, so energy needed for the development of higher processes is delayed because the immediate threats that are being experienced take priority.

---

97 Bowlby J (1998) *Separation: Anxiety And Anger: Attachment And Loss (Volume 2)*. New York, NY: Pimlico.

98 Krumwiede A (2014) *Attachment Theory According To John Bowlby And Mary Ainsworth*. Norderstedt, Germany: Open Publishing.

So internal working models form from the relationship a child is experiencing. They can be modified, confirmed or disconfirmed through experiences of new and influential attachment relationships – although to teach a child trust and love after initial abuse and neglect will take time, skill and patience.

A user-friendly way to think of this process is that a baby learns to 'dance the steps of its mother'. These steps are usually repeated when they enter into new relationships. So when they are left at a nursery or their first day at infant school, the adult carers they meet are usually 'dancing' similar steps to those the child learned at home. So all is well. The difficulty is when the child has had to learn very different steps, through being in an abusive relationship. Because things that happen frequently to a child become the norm, they will expect other adults to *dance* in a similar way. This sadly can be the experience of those children who have attachment disorders. So early attachment defines, essentially, how a child will relate to the various people in their lives.

A child's early wellbeing, then, is very dependent on the positive attachment experiences they have in their family. When children are securely attached they do better on cognitive tests, measures of intelligence and language development than those who are insecurely attached (van Ijzendoorn, Dijkstra & Bus, 1995).[99] Secure attachment in the early years has been found to predict good positive peer interactions (Fagot, 1997).[100]

In the family, secure attachment is achieved when an adult with a child:

■ Celebrates a child's achievements.

■ Shows affection.

■ Shows how a child is progressing.

■ Highlights developmental milestones.

■ Spends special time with a child.

■ Shares a mutually enjoyable activity.

99   van Ijzendoorn MH, Dijkstra J & Bus AG (1995) Attachment, intelligence and language: A meta-analysis. *Soc Dev* 4: 115–28.

100 Fagot BI (1997) Attachment, parenting, and peer interactions off toddler children. *Dev Psychol* 33(3): 489–99.

∬2ℎ How to help –
How to Help strengthening attachment

☞ **Here are some ideas to strengthen attachment:**

■ You take part in a fun activity together and laugh a lot.

■ You both talk enthusiastically about a planned future event.

■ You give the child in your care a spontaneous high-five/hug.

■ You ask the child to give you a quick high-five/hug.

■ At the end of the day you go through all the enjoyable events shared during that day.

■ You spot something that the child is doing well and let them know.

■ You spot that the child is a little unhappy and you sit down together and chat about this.

■ The child spontaneously shows affection to you and you respond warmly.

■ You enjoy a funny story together.

■ You accidentally do or say something silly and you and the child sit down and have a good laugh about it, or both retell the story to others.

Parenting methods

So, given the abundance of evidence for the importance of secure attachment, what is known about parenting methods? We have already considered the advantages of using a more authoritative parenting style rather than an authoritarian one. But, in fact, we can explore much further and give a deeper understanding of what is an incredibly subtle and complex process.

Let's say that early researchers into parenting were viewing the process from some distance. The models they suggested were very general, like large brush strokes. It is not that they were wrong, but when parenting is examined close up the finer detail reveals a much more varied and complex picture.

The view that parents should follow one style over another simplifies matters. Later researchers have brought in more variables that need to be included if a more informed understanding is to be achieved.

Previous parenting models made the assumption that all children in a family would react in the same way to the parenting style used. We now know that this assumption is wrong. As we are concerned with the wellbeing of children, it is only right that we try to understand how the family affects the development of a child from their perspective. Children are not passive receivers of their parents' and carers' parenting, they are actively engaged in making sense of what is happening. Two children in the same family will experience the same parenting technique differently. One may accept guidance as fair while another may reject it. This involves us understanding the meaning children give to their parent's actions. When a parent asks *"But I treated them both the same, why are they so different?"*, it does not allow for the child's perception of what was happening to them.

Parenting – the child's perspective

Temperament

As we are concerned here with wellbeing in children, it seems only right to understand how the family can help or hinder wellbeing from a child's perspective.

When researchers in the past were studying parenting styles they looked at the relationship between what a parent or carer did and how it affected a child's behaviour. So, for example, if a reward was given for a child helping in the home, did it increase helpful behaviour? What was not included were variables known as 'moderators', which affect the strength of a relationship between a cause and effect. A parent or carer might use strict parenting to ensure compliance, so the moderator in this situation might be the temperament of the child. So a child with a difficult temperament might view the parent's behaviour as being rejecting, whereas another with a easy temperament might see the same behaviour as a sign of care.

So the temperament, which is biologically based and is a relatively stable factor, can easily result in children viewing their parents' care in different ways.

Expert View

"All children test the boundaries, and in a loving nurturing environment they come to understand that they cannot always get what they want."

Kate Cairns[101]

---

101 Cairns K (2001) The Effects Of Trauma On Childhood Learning. In Jackson S (Ed.) *Nobody Ever Told Us School Mattered: Raising The Attainments Of Children In Public Care*. London: British Association for Adoption and Fostering (BAAF).

Research in this area has focused on the use of discipline to control children. How does parental discipline effect children's behaviour? Kochanska (1997) found that children who had inherited a fearful temperament, became over-anxious when disciplined strictly.[102] Other studies have shown:

- That children with an irritable temperament behaved worse with hostile parenting (Morris et al, 2002).[103]

- That very young boys with a difficult temperament responded well to positive parenting (Belsky & Pluess, 2009).[104]

- That parents who were inconsistent in their discipline of temperamentally fearless preschoolers were less empathetic (Frick & Connell, 2007).[105]

- That children who were temperamentally prone to negative emotion had fewer problems when their mothers were low in rejecting disciplinary methods (Lengua, 2008).[106]

So, while the picture is complex, one thing that emerges is that the effectiveness of any parenting style needs to be considered with respect to the individual child's temperamental disposition. The temperament of a child can moderate or alter the impact of different kinds of parenting (Bates & Pettit, 2007).[107]

Children's perceptions

How do children interpret the actions of their parents and carers? To answer this, we must question whether children differ in how they make sense of the actions of parents and carers, and if they differ in how they see events depending on where the events occur.

---

102 Kochanska G (1997) Multipole pathways to conscience for children with different temperaments: From toddlerhood to age 5. *Dev Psychol* 33: 228–40.

103 Morris I (2015) *Teaching Happiness And Well-Being in Schools: Learning To Ride Elephants.* London: Continuum.

104 Belsky J & Pluess M (2009) The nature (and nurture) of human plasticity in early development. *Perspect Psychol Sci* 4(4): 345–41.

105 Frick P & Cornell AH (2007) The moderating effects of parenting styles in the association between behavioral inhibition and parent-reported guilt and empathy in preschool children. *J Clin Child Adolesc Psychol* 36(3): 305–18.

106 Lengua L (2008) *Anxiousness, Frustration, And Effortful Control As Moderators Of The Relation Between Parenting And Adjustment In Middle-Childhood.* Available at: https://onlinelibrary.wiley.com/doi/abs/10.1111/j.1467-9507.2007.00438.x [last accessed 4 February 2021]

107 Bates J, Pettit G, Keiley M, Laird R & Dodge K (2007) Predicting the developmental course of mother-reported monitoring across childhood and adolescence from early proactive parenting, child temperament, and parents' worries. *J Fam Psychol* 21(2): 206–17.

An understanding by parents and carers of how their children perceive them can be a critically important insight that helps to explain family confrontations and suggest ways forward.

Grusec, Saritas and Daniel (2014) suggest three components involved in adults understanding how a child is perceiving any situation.[108]

- Knowledge of the individual child helps predict the best parenting technique. This means that when a parent understands their child, their developmental level and their temperament, they are better placed to find the best parenting technique. When a child refuses to cooperate, a knowledgeable parent or carer will choose a different technique to achieve compliance, for example humour, incentives or consequences.

- How knowledge affects adult behaviour. When a parent or carer has knowledge of their child, this can then affect the way they will parent that child. This won't always produce the best results. If a child has an anxious temperament, the knowledgeable parent can over-protect the child, which can be less than helpful. Alternatively, knowing how a child will respond to various forms of discipline can be useful information for managing a strong-willed child.

- How adults become knowledgeable about their children. The key source of information is through the adult listening.

The factors that help children and young people to disclose information to their parents are:

- Being available.

- Disclosing information about themselves.

- Being in a good mood themselves.

- Recognising a child or young person's mood state.

(Tokic & Pecnik, 2010)[109]

What can parents and carers do that will strengthen the skills and attributes that underpin wellbeing?

---

108 Grusec, J, Saritas D & Daniel E (2014) The Nature of Effective Parenting: Some Current Perspectives. In Landry SH & Cooper CL (Eds.) *Wellbeing In Children And Families* (Vol 1, pp. 157–77). Hoboken, NJ: Wiley-Blackwell.

109 okic A & Pecnik N (2010) Parental behaviours related to adolescents' self-disclosure: Adolescents' views. *J Soc Pers Relat* 28: 201–22.

We have already considered attachment and its importance for developing neural networks, as well as the emotional health of the baby. Without this secure attachment, we now know that children can have serious relationship difficulties throughout their lives, including:

- Ongoing distrust in relationships.
- Greater risk of psychosocial disorders.
- Problematic school relationships with staff and peers.

Communication in the family

Many difficulties in family relationships can be the product of poor or unintended communication. Here are some examples of the difference between what is said by the adult and what is heard by the child.

- Adult says: *"I want you to be happy and involved in things you enjoy."*
  Child or young person hears: *"I should always be happy and comfortable. When I feel sad, upset, frustrated, or disappointed, someone should make me feel better."*

- Adult says: *"I want you to be stimulated and enriched."*
  Child or young person hears: *"I should never be bored. I should only be asked to do things that are stimulating and enriching, not things that are tedious and boring. In fact, if it's not interesting, I won't do it."*

- Adult says: *"I want you to make your own choices."*
  Child or young person hears: *"No one should tell me what to do; I should be allowed to make up my own mind."*

- Adult says: *"I want you to be included in family decisions."*
  Child or young person hears: *"Adults should not make any decisions without consulting me first. I should be part of the management team."*

- Adult says: *"I want you to be treated equally and fairly."*
  Child or young person hears: *"I should be treated the same as adults. If other people can do it, I should be able to do it too."*

How to help – active listening

☞ A parent or carer can find opportunities to have short, meaningful exchanges with their children. Look out for good times to listen – for example at bedtime, at mealtimes, or during a car journey (it can help to have less eye contact).

When you do:

- Step 1 – Decide to listen, switch off your own feelings.
- Step 2 – Listen for the feelings: "What are they feeling?"
- Step 3 – Put into your own words what you hear: "Are you feeling depressed because of the low marks you got in that test?" Check out your understanding: "Have I got this right? You feel [upset at your friend] because [they left you out of the game]?"

When a child or young person has strong feelings, active listening can help. It is less appropriate when their behaviour is disrespectful.

Self-esteem for adolescents

Given the complex nature of adolescence, how can parents and carers support young people and help to build their self-esteem? Steps taken by adults are often rejected by adolescents; however, this does not mean that they were the wrong steps and it is important to understand and accept this. The general consensus of researchers is that the following parental traits will be of value in strengthening the self-esteem of children and young people:

- Approval
- Encouragement
- Support
- Warmth

How will these be experienced?

Actions speak louder than words in this area. The young person's perception of parental behaviours matters a lot. So, spending time with them, doing things together, complimenting them and playing with them all matter. The fact that a teenager is likely to resist, reject and rebel against such behaviours is to be expected. What will strengthen and support the young person's self-esteem is knowing that they matter to their parents and carers, they are important to them and they care about what happens to them.

Following on from what has already been said, it is the authoritative parenting style that is considered best for young people. In this style parents and carers will use reasons and explanations to justify their decisions and actions. They will monitor, supervise and restrict young people's behaviours, but with justifications.

Peer relationships

Peer approval is all-important. This can mean that physical appearance and social acceptance by peers are valued more highly than academic competence. Being with peers contributes and stimulates a range of necessary skills in young people: these include reasoning skills, same- and opposite-sex relationships and cooperation skills. It is important to remember that when a young person is with their peers they are with their equals; there is not the difference in power and status that exists when they are with adults (Bornstein, 2013).[110]

Can the family/adults influence peer relationships?

The answer is yes, but before not after. There are core skills that good peer relationships will nurture and develop. How well any individual will link to their peers is established before they even meet. How any individual will link with and relate to their peers is a reflection of the skills they have already acquired from their family. We are, as it were, a product of our past. How the young person negotiated with their parents and carers for increased personal autonomy will shape how they will negotiate with their peers on contentious areas. How it was achieved will have become part of a young person's skill repertoire.

Enabling young people to meet and work with adults outside the family, for example on community-based projects, can help them to connect with adults in meaningful ways, and come to see themselves as autonomous individuals making valuable contributions to the community that they belong to.

---

110 Bornstein MH, Jager J & Steinberg LD (2013) Adolescents, Parents, Friends/Peers: A Relationships Model. In Weiner I, Lerner RM, Easterbrooks MA & Mistry J (Eds.) *Handbook Of Psychology, Vol 6: Developmental Psychology* (2nd ed., pp. 393–434). New York, NY: Wiley.

In the pre-teen stage, there will probably be areas of interest that the individual is developing. These may range from sporting activities to particular hobbies such as dancing or martial arts. Opportunities to join interest groups of this kind will serve three main benefits:

■ The young person will experience independence from the family.

■ They will strengthen a sense of their own unique personality.

■ As they grow in skill competency, their own self-esteem will be enhanced.

If encouraged at this stage to join clubs where such skills can be developed, it can be the beginning of an interest that lasts for many years.

To summarise, the better the relationship the parent or carer has in the pre-teen years, the better the relationship during the teenage years.

Wellbeing for parents and carers

"If Mama ain't happy, nobody ain't happy"
('Mama Ain't Happy' by Tracy Byrd)

It is a fact of life that if anyone in a family is unhappy, then there will be a knock-on effect to everyone else. Even if no one will talk about the unhappiness it will still have an effect. Sometimes it can be like the 'elephant in the room' - everyone can see plainly that there is an elephant in the room, but everyone also knows the unwritten rule that no-one talks about it.

It is important to conclude this chapter with some thoughts on the wellbeing of the parents and carers. When the adults in a family have mental health problems, such as anxiety and depression, then there is an increased likelihood of the children having emotional and/or behavioural problems (McLaughlin et al, 2012).[111] The adults in a family model behaviours to their children; they transmit core values. Parents and carers need to be as concerned with what they do in front of their children, as well as what they say. The emotional strength of parents and carers is especially relevant. To this end, here are some key ideas and strategies to support. They are presented in a daily toolbox format, with the recommendation that you use either something from each compartment, or something that fits just as well, every day.

---

111 McLaughlin K, Greif Green J, Gruber M, Sampson N, Zaslavsky A, Kessler R (2012) Childhood adversities and first onset of psychiatric disorders in a national sample of US adolescents. *Arch Gen Psychiatry* 69(11): 1,151–60.

H2h How to help – parent and carer wellbeing

☞ **Wellbeing for your body**

As a parent or carer, the list of tasks to complete each day can seem endless, and may often mean doing several of them at the same time. There are many different roles to fulfil each day – teacher, comforter, adviser, mediator, nurse and more. The need to be physically fit is essential. Below are some general ideas – if they help, use them; if not, leave them. But taking care of yourself is a 'must', not an option. If you don't, who will? And if you don't do it now, when will you?

- Sleep – Aim for a good night's sleep. Sleep allows the body to rest and the mind to refresh. Seven to eight hours per night is good. What will help? Reduce light in the bedroom, and if possible reduce noise. Leave iPads and the like outside.

- Exercise – Resistance training is weight exercises that strengthen and develop muscle tone. Use lighter weights than needed to build muscle bulk. See the NHS Strength and Flex exercise plan, *How To Improve Your Strength And Flexibility* (https://www.nhs.uk/live-well/exercise/strength-and-flex-exercise-plan/). Aerobic exercise increases the heart rate to seventy-five per cent of maximum capacity, whether it is a brisk walk or a swim.

☞ **Wellbeing for your heart**

At the end of each day a good habit is to reflect on what has happened and find one or two things that made you feel good. Perhaps record them. The act of reviewing your day from a positive perspective will challenge that innate tendency we all have, which is to remember the bad parts over the good ones.

- Head – Having a sense of *being in control* is good for anyone's sense of wellbeing. It could involve planning your day to include time when you do something purely for yourself – no matter how short a time, be it two minutes or thirty. The fact that you think it important is part of the solution. Perhaps read a book or do a puzzle. Make time to engage your thinking.

■ Social life – When we consider who we are, it is usually defined in terms of a relationship with someone. A parent has children, a spouse has a partner, a teacher has students. So clearly our identity is strongly defined by social relationships. Whether you have a role as a friend, a neighbour, a volunteer, a member of a church or a grandparent, such roles are to be valued and nurtured.

☞ Wellbeing for your soul

Feeling good about the life you are leading is to be able to see the meaning it has. Being a parent or carer has meaning over and above the everyday acts that make up your day. Perhaps some photographs of the milestones that you have enabled your children to make can act as a daily reminder.

Chapter 16: Wellbeing in school

In many modern countries there are campaigns against the current emphasis on exam success. School leaders, teachers and parents are all challenging the existing educational system. Statistics show that:

- Ninety per cent of school leaders claim to have seen an increase in anxiety, stress, low mood and depression over the past five years.
- Seventy-three per cent of parents would choose a school where their child is happy over a school with better exam results.
- Eighty-three per cent of teachers think that the focus on exams has become disproportionate to overall wellbeing.

So, while all parents and carers want their children and young people to succeed academically, they place a higher value on their children being *happy* and *confident*. In other words, they value the wellbeing of their children.

Similarly, schools are naturally concerned with producing positive outcomes for their learners. Wellbeing is more and more becoming an integral part to any school's general education policy. The importance of wellbeing has increased significantly over the past few years. One of the driving reasons for this lies in the alarming numbers of children and young people diagnosed with some form of mental health problem. The figures have already been presented, but are worth restating – some fifty per cent of all mental disorders emerge before the age of fourteen years. This means that any initiative to strengthen the wellbeing and mental health of children and young people needs to have the support of all involved.

Expert View

"What a difference it makes to our youth when our schools and communities are places of welcome that prepare them for a future full of options."

Michael Resnick[112]

There are two key questions that are relevant to wellbeing in school. First, how can a sense of wellbeing be measured? And second, what are the key indicators of a school ethos that promotes wellbeing?

112 Resnick M (2005). Healthy youth development: Getting our priorities right. *Medical Journal of Australia*, 183(8), 398–400.

How to help – measuring wellbeing in schools

 There are many issues that need to be fully considered before any measure of wellbeing in school is attempted - for example, how will the questions that are used to evaluate wellbeing be phrased? Questions such as *"Do you feel cared for and supported in school?"* and *"Are you happy with your life in school?"* are incredibly sensitive and potentially upsetting for children and young people who are coping with difficult circumstances. It is important that the questions are all concerned with a child or young person's life in school. They are not intended to probe aspects of their life outside school.

 When asking questions the following should be borne in mind:

- Where? – Children or young people should not be expected to sit in rows as if they were taking an exam. It is not intended to be seen in that way.

- When? – Timing will make a difference. After the summer holidays may produce different results to the end of the Christmas term.

- Why? – A full and clear explanation needs to be given as to the purpose of the questions. How will the results be used? Who will have access to them?

- What? – Some children and young people may need assistance with reading the questions.

- Who? – How can those children and young people who are in care settings be supported as they answer questions about a life that we know to be less than satisfactory?

 An excellent compendium of measures of wellbeing is one produced by Public Health England, called *Measuring And Monitoring Children And Young People's Mental Wellbeing: A Toolkit For Schools And Colleges*.[113] This provides information on some thirty different scales, with detailed information on each.

---

113 Public Health England (2016) *Measuring and Monitoring Children and Young People's Mental Wellbeing*. (Available at: basw.co.uk/resources/measuring-and-monitoring-children-and-young-people's-mental-wellbeing-toolkit-schools-and).

Can school ethos and wellbeing be measured?

Positive psychology is playing a growing role in promoting wellbeing in education. Most schools have a policy in place to manage student behaviour; however, the majority rely on some form of reward and sanction system. Over recent years, increasing awareness that many young people have social, emotional and mental health (SEMH) needs has led to such approaches being questioned. Consequently, more and more schools are moving from trying to change the behaviour to trying to understand the reasons behind the behaviour.

Coupled with this change in the way behaviour is being conceptualised is the growing belief that schools can play an important role in preventing some of the SEMH issues through preventative strategies. There have already been many initiatives, SEAL (social and emotional aspects of learning) being one. Positive psychology provides a framework that is focused on strengthening the necessary skills in children and young people to cope with an ever more complex world.

Much of what SEAL includes can readily be subsumed under positive psychology. What positive psychology offers is a more coherent and sound base for a new approach. Instead of schools trying to prevent problem behaviours, positive psychology turns the argument on its head and argues that an increase in those behaviours that can protect children and young people from SEMH issues. The fact that positive psychology is more concerned with where children and young people are going than where they have come from, is ideal for schools. Schools are in the business of increasing a child or young person's behavioural repertoire, rather than reducing it. So positive psychology is about building on, developing and teaching new skills that will contribute to the wellbeing of children and young people. This is the bread and butter of schools – to improve the health of learners, rather than to treat them for a range of pathological conditions.

Peer relationships and wellbeing

Several studies have found that peer-to-peer relationships play a significant part in the wellbeing of children and young people in schools. Friendship is an umbrella term and includes a wide range of features, so to use it to promote wellbeing some form of model is needed. Are there different types of relationships that can help us use friendships more effectively to promote wellbeing?

The relationships that children and young people form with their peers have the potential to influence how they think, feel and behave (Ladd, 2005).[114] Children and young people's relationships are of course very complex and change with development. Some general trends do however exist, which allow for a framework to be developed to assist in how we think about this important aspect of development. Ladd et al (2014) suggest that there are four distinguishable features of relationships:[115]

- **Friendships** – Typically friendships are voluntary and involve a positive emotional tie. They depend on mutual consent and last only as long as those involved choose. Children who engage successfully in friendship relationships are usually considered to be socially skilled, have such prosocial skills as complementary and reciprocal play, communication clarity, information exchange, ability to find and share common activities, and conflict resolution. Being part of a friendship group contributes significantly to a child or young person's positive adaptation to school.

- **Acceptance vs rejection** – This concerns a child or young person's status within a group, or the degree to which they are liked/disliked. A predisposing feature for rejection is if a child or young person lacks prosocial skills and shows aggressive or withdrawn behaviours. These seem to discourage peers from forming relationships. This is likely to have a negative impact on their school performance through limiting possible interpersonal resources and benefits such as peer approval and mutual problem-solving. Rejected children are also less likely to be chosen to join in learning activities, study groups or play activities.

- **Peer victimisation** – This is where one or more of a peer group behave aggressively, physically or psychologically against a specific child who cannot stop the harassment. It seems that such behaviour occurs at all levels of schooling, including kindergarten. Research suggests two behavioural sub-types. First are those children who are more solitary, sensitive and with submissive behaviours. The second type are more activeaggressive, tend to overreact and have irritable traits. These are classified as 'passive' and 'proactive' victims (Kumpulainen et al, 1998).[116] Olweus (1978), a major researcher into bullying, classifies these as *passive* and *provocative victims*.[117]

114 Ladd G (2005) *Children's Peer Relations And Social Competence: A Century Of Progress.* New Haven, CT: Yale University Press.

115 Ladd G, Kochenderfer-Ladd B & Sechler C (2014) Classroom Peer Relations As A Context For Social And Scholastic Development. In Landry S & Cooper CL (Eds.) *Wellbeing In Children And Families* (pp. 243–70). Oxford: John Wiley & Sons, Ltd.

116 Kumpulainen K, Rasanen E, Henttonen I & Almqvist F (1998) Bullying and psychiatric symptoms among elementary school aged children. *Child Abuse Negl* 22: 705-17.

117 Olweus D (1978) *Aggression In The Schools. Bullies And Whipping Boys.* Washington, DC: Hemisphere, Wiley.

■ **Work partnerships** – Teachers frequently assign children or young people to work with set partners. As they work together, they will build reputations as to the kind of partner they are – for example, good/desirable to be with as opposed to bad/undesirable and to be avoided if possible. The core skills that seem to be valued are being focused, cooperative and supportive (Ladd et al, 2012).[118] This finding has valuable implications for the use of Cooperative Group Work as a means of promoting wellbeing.

In-school belonging

Feeling that you are part of your school, that you are accepted and valued, enhances a child or young person's sense of meaning and value. The need to feel that we belong is a universal one that is driven by our very nature as social animals. While we can override this, as children and young peple the value to belong is a motivator that has many positive outcomes. For some, the term *connectedness* is preferred to *belonging*. Whichever is used, the implications are the same.

Expert View

"Students' sense of belonging is the extent to which they feel personally accepted, respected, included, and supported by others in the school social environment."

Carol Goodenow and Kathleen Grady [115]

The fact that a sense of belonging has such positive consequences for children and young people has raised the profile of this issue. International research has found that as many as one in four children report feeling that they *don't belong* to their school. Studies indicate that, although the majority do have a sense of belonging to school, it is disadvantaged and first-generation immigrant children who are more likely to feel that they don't belong. In addition, there appears to be a link between school belonging and children and young people presenting with either internalising or externalising behaviours (Wilkinson-Lee et al, 2011)[119]

---

118 Ladd G, Kochendefer-Ladd B, Visconti K & Ettekal I (2012) *Children's Classroom Peer Relationships And Social Competence As Resources For Learning And Achievement At School.* Charlotte, NC: Information Age Publishing.

119 Wilkinson-Lee AM, Zhang Q, Nuno VL & Wilhelm MS (2011) Adolescent emotional distress: The role of family obligations and school connectedness. *J Youth Adolesc* 40(2): 221–30.

120 Goodenow C & Grady KE (1993) The relationship of school belonging and friends' values to academic motivation among urban adolescent students. *J Exp Educ* 62(1): 60–71.

Schools need to be concerned about these findings, as there are proven benefits for a child or young person with a *sense of belonging*. Personal benefits to the child or young person include:

- Lower anxiety
- Fewer behavioural problems
- Stronger self-control

There are also academic benefits:

- Higher expectation of success
- Greater engagement with tasks
- Improved effort

(Mace, 2019)[121]

The cost to schools are also significant, as children and young people who lack a sense of belonging are more likely to have problems with:

- Substance abuse
- Absenteeism
- Early sexual initiation
- Violence

In the US, belonging was studied as a factor in bullying. It was found that belonging is a predictive factor that correlates to bullying; an increase in belonging leads to a decrease in bullying (Slaten, 2019).[122]

In general, a sense of in-school belonging seems to improve children and young people's wellbeing. A lack of belonging is associated with a range of negative outcomes, including:

- Poor behaviour
- Loneliness

---

121 Mace R (2019) *All Together Now: Why Schools Should Foster A Sense Of Belonging.* Available at: https://www.tes.com/magazine/article/why-schools-should-foster-sense-belonging [last accessed 4 February 2021]

122 Slaten C (2019) *Students With A Greater Sense Of Family And School Belonging Are Less Likely To Become Bullies.* Available at: https://education.missouri.edu/2019/07/students-with-a-greater-sense-of-family-and-school-belonging-are-less-likely-to-become-bullies/ [last accessed 4 February 2021]

■ Psychological distress

■ Psychosocial disturbances and mental illness

(Allen & Bowles, 2012)[123]

A study in 2014 found that children and young people who scored highly on social and emotional indices succeeded academically and were more fully engaged in school life. The study suggested that the level of wellbeing a child or young person has is a better indicator of academic success than other demographic characteristics, namely gender, social class, and Special Educational Needs (SEN) status (Department for Education, 2014).[124] It also found that children and young people who scored highly on emotional wellbeing made better progress in primary school and on transfer engaged more fully in secondary school.

It is worth exploring what belonging means to children and young people, and especially to those who are more vulnerable as they have special educational needs. A study of children and young people with additional needs found that there were several themes to a sense of belonging:

■ Teaching and learning – Working as a team and receiving support.

■ Environment – Being familiar with the physical layout.

■ Extra-curricular activities – Sport and club activities.

■ Relationships – With peers and school staff.

(Midgen et al, 2019)[125]

A mediating factor in belongingness is age. As we have already considered, during adolescence it is the peer group that becomes more influential. This was the finding in a study by Gowing (2019), who found that for young people it was their peer group relationships that gave them the most value in attending school.[126] The link was even stronger for those who reported low-connectedness to school.

123 Allen KA & Bowles T (2012) Belonging as a guiding principle in the education of adolescents. *Aust J Educ Dev Psychol* 12: 108–19.

124 Department for Education (2014) *The Impact Of Pupil Behaviour And Wellbeing On Educational Outcomes*. Available at: https://www.gov.uk/government/publications/the-impact-of-pupil-behaviour-and-wellbeing-on-educational-outcomes [last accessed 15 February 2021]

125 Midgen T, Theodoratou T, Newbury K & Leonard M (2019) 'School for Everyone': An exploration of children and young people's perceptions of belonging. *Educ Child Psychol* 36(2).

126 Gowing A (2019) Peer-peer relationships: A key factor in enhancing school connectedness and belonging. *Educ Child Psychol* 36(2): 64–77.

Having a sense of connection to their school also seems to act as a preventative factor against risky behaviours. Using the Social and Emotional Health Survey, with questions such as:

- I am lucky to go to my school (Gratitude)
- I expect good things to happen at my school (Optimism)
- I get excited when I learn something new at school (Zest)
- I keep working until I get my school work right (Persistence)

Furlong et al (2014) found that those children and young people who had a sense of engagement seemed to have some form of protection from:[49]

- Substance abuse
- Absenteeism
- Sexual involvement
- Violence

How to help – measuring school belonging

Sceptics often argue that woolly concepts such as belongingness cannot be usefully measured; they are too vague to be useful. However, there are several measures that challenge this:

☞ **School Belonging Scale**

This measure looks at three aspects of feeling involved: a sense of belonging, a feeling of being supported, and an acceptance of school rules as being fair. It is a brief measure, having twelve items, but it has support for being both reliable and a valid measurement in this hypothetical construct.

Example questions are:

- Can I get good support from my school?
- Do I feel good about being in my school?
- Can I accept the rules and procedures set by my school?

(Parada, 2019)[127]

---

127 Parada R (2019) Assessing perceived school support, rule acceptance and attachment: evaluation of the psychometric properties of the School Belonging Scale (SBS). *Educ Child Psychol* 36(2): 106–16.

School Belongingness Scale

This is a ten-item self-report questionnaire. It has two sub-scales, with one measuring Social Exclusion:

- I feel I don't belong in school
- I feel myself excluded in this school
- In this school I feel ignored

And the other measuring Social Inclusion:

- I can really be myself in school
- I see myself as part of this school
- I have close /sincere relationships with my teachers and friends

(Arslan & Duru, 2017)[128]

 Psychological Sense of School Membership

This is an eighteen-item self-report scale, using a three-point scale: never, sometimes, always (Goodenow, 1993).[129]

Example questions are:

- I feel like a real part of [name of school]
- Most teachers at [name of school] are interested in me
- People here know I can do good work

---

128 Arslan G & Duru E (2017) Initial development and validation of the school belongingness scale. *Child Ind Res* 10(4): 1,043–58.

129 Goodenow C (1993) The psychological sense of school membership among adolescents: Scalke development and educational correlates. *Psychol Sch* 30: 79–90.

Chapter 17: Wellbeing in the classroom

Whether a child or young person makes good progress is less dependent on the school than on the class they are in. A student may be in a good school but for various reasons not relate well to their key teachers. Similarly, in a poor school a student make good progress because the relationship with key teachers is extremely good. This chapter will link research and practice to explore how a classroom can promote the wellbeing and resilience of children. Masten and Coatsworth (1998) offer the following functional definition:

> *"Resilience is how children overcome adversity to achieve good developmental outcomes."*[130]

The diagram below shows the different relationships any student will have. Each is important to their wellbeing.

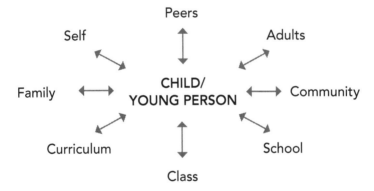

Improving any of these relationships will make a significant contribution to the student's wellbeing. There are a number of areas that ideally need to be addressed to achieve this aim. Today, after some fifty years of classroom research (Doll & Lyon, 1998), we are in a good position to itemise the variables that enable children and young people to feel good and succeed.[131] These are the in-class factors that have been found to protect all children and young people, especially vulnerable ones:

---

130 Masten AS & Coatsworth JD (1998) The development of competence in favourable and unfavourable environments: Lessons from research on successful children. *Am Psychol* 56: 227–38.
131 Doll B & Lyon M (1998) Risk and resilience: implications for the practice of school psychology. *Sch Psychol Rev* 27(3): 348–63.

- Teacher-to-learner relationships
- In-class peer relationships
- Learner self-determination
- Learner self-control
- Expectations for success

(Doll, 2014)[132]

A further factor that will not be considered here, but is of equal importance, is the connection between home and school.

The challenge is to operationalise each of these factors. This can help us design a tool to highlight how well a class is doing, with suggestions for improvement. It is worth noting that it is not theories that apply in the real world, but the practical implications based on them. It should also be noted that while assessment tools for wellbeing exist, off the shelf solutions do not always fit. No two schools are alike.

132 Doll B (2014) Enhancing Resilience In The Classroom. In Goldstein S & Brooks RB (Eds.) *Handbook Of Resilience In Children*. London: Springer.

133 Creasey G, Jarvis P & Knapcik E (2009) A measure to assess student–instructor relationships. IJ-SoTL 3(2): 14.

How to help – classroom wellbeing MOT

While recognising the limitations that exist when seeking to assess wellbeing in schools, the following framework may serve as a helpful tool in specific contexts. Part 1 is to be completed by the child or young person, and explores how they see the classroom. Do they feel safe and valued, and that they belong? Part 2 is to be completed by the teacher (or support staff). The framework is derived from the work of Gary Creasey, Pat Jarvis and Elyse Knapcik.[133]

☞ Wellbeing MOT Part 1– the learner.

The following statements concern how you feel about your class.
There are no right or wrong answers.
Your name is not required on the form.

Indicate how much you agree with the statements by circling a number between 1 and 7.

1 means you do not feel the statement applies,
7 means you think it does.

Adult–learner relationship

1. I feel very safe with this teacher.

1	2	3	4	5	6	7

2. I find it easy to ask this teacher for help.

1	2	3	4	5	6	7

3. I think this teacher has favourites.

1	2	3	4	5	6	7

4. I know this teacher would help if I had a problem.

1	2	3	4	5	6	7

5. I feel this teacher really cares about everyone in the class.

1	2	3	4	5	6	7

Peer relationships

1. I get along with most of the class.

1	2	3	4	5	6	7

2. There is very little teasing in this class.

1	2	3	4	5	6	7

3. I am always happy to lend equipment to classmates.

1	2	3	4	5	6	7

4. If I am stuck I can rely on help from classmates.

1	2	3	4	5	6	7

5. This is one of the friendliest classes I have been in.

1	2	3	4	5	6	7

Learner self-determination

1. I always feel I have some control over what I do in this class.

1	2	3	4	5	6	7

2. I have a strong feeling of success at the end of a project I have chosen.

1	2	3	4	5	6	7

3. I feel our teacher likes us to make choices over the work we do.

1	2	3	4	5	6	7

4. I know that our class representatives are listened to.

1	2	3	4	5	6	7

5. I enjoy discussing the class rules at the beginning of each term.

1	2	3	4	5	6	7

Self-control

1. When I have a problem, I have learned to persevere.

1	2	3	4	5	6	7

2. When problems happen at playtimes, I rarely lose my cool.

1	2	3	4	5	6	7

3. I understand the different feelings I have.

1	2	3	4	5	6	7

4. I get nervous when we have tests but can stay in control.

1	2	3	4	5	6	7

5. I have ideas to help me solve problems.

1	2	3	4	5	6	7

Expectations for success

1. I feel my teacher expects me to do well.

1	2	3	4	5	6	7

2. When I make mistakes my teacher helps me learn from them.

1	2	3	4	5	6	7

3. I have made good progress through my teacher supporting me.

1	2	3	4	5	6	7

4. I have learnt to be more confident since working with my teacher.

1	2	3	4	5	6	7

5. I know I can make progress through effort and determination.

1	2	3	4	5	6	7

Now, take the average score for each area (add the scores for the 5 questions in a given category together, divide them by 5 and round to the nearest whole number), and mark them on the Radar Graph below. The nearer to the centre the number, the greater the need for development in that area.

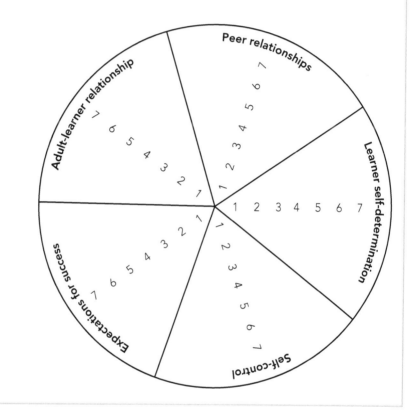

☞ Wellbeing MOT Part 2 – the teacher

The following statements concern how you feel about your class.
There are no right or wrong answers.
Your name is not required on the form.

Indicate how much you agree with the statement by
circling a number between 1 and 7.

1 means you do not feel the statement applies,
7 means you think it does.

Relationships

1. I often try to imagine what it must be like for a student in my class.

1	2	3	4	5	6	7

2. I look for opportunities to spend one-to-one time with my students

1	2	3	4	5	6	7

3. I am sensitive to the mood changes of individual students.

1	2	3	4	5	6	7

4. I often highlight relationship issues through the curriculum.

1	2	3	4	5	6	7

5. Individual knowledge of my students increases my ability to be flexible.

1	2	3	4	5	6	7

Self-esteem

1. I ensure students have the opportunities to support each other.

1	2	3	4	5	6	7

2. Students record their personal competencies and successes, and update them.

1	2	3	4	5	6	7

3. Students are taught positive self-statements.

1	2	3	4	5	6	7

4. Students experience responsibility through a range of roles.

1	2	3	4	5	6	7

5. Students' unique strengths are utilised in lessons.

1	2	3	4	5	6	7

Emotional climate

1. My lessons always aim to promote self-control and choice.

1	2	3	4	5	6	7

2. Students are sensitively supported by adults and peers.

1	2	3	4	5	6	7

3. Students learn that their views are valued.

1	2	3	4	5	6	7

4. Respect is a core value that is modelled and recognised.

1	2	3	4	5	6	7

5. All students actively participate in the day-to-day running of the class.

1	2	3	4	5	6	7

Physical

1. I ensure that the room temperature/ventilation is comfortable for students and myself.

1	2	3	4	5	6	7

2. In my class, graffiti and damage are removed/repaired immediately.

1	2	3	4	5	6	7

3. In my class, desks are arranged to suit the learning process taking place.

1	2	3	4	5	6	7

4. My display boards are colourful and changed/updated regularly.

1	2	3	4	5	6	7

5. I can see all students wherever they are in the class.

1	2	3	4	5	6	7

Troubled learners

1. I assess all students to identify learning difficulties.

1	2	3	4	5	6	7

2. Students with behavioural challenges record their progress towards agreed targets.

1	2	3	4	5	6	7

3. I frequently convey my high expectations to all students.

1	2	3	4	5	6	7

4. I see a misbehaviour as an indication of needs.

1	2	3	4	5	6	7

5. I do not give up when their progress is slow.

1	2	3	4	5	6	7

Now, as with Part 1, take the average score for each area (add the scores for the 5 questions in a given category together, divide them by 5 and round to the nearest whole number), and mark them on the Radar Graph below. The nearer to the centre the number, the greater the need for development in that area.

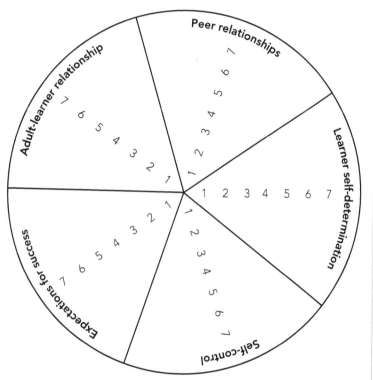

For both the learner and the teacher, the Radar Graph can be used to formulate an action plan to develop/strengthen those areas of weakness. The statements themselves give ideas as to the possible strategies that could be used to improve matters.

Chapter 18: Behaviour and school policies

In a book on wellbeing and resilience, it is only right that we include information on how to understand and promote these qualities in those children and young people who have faced adverse experiences. These children and young people often have a range of behavioural difficulties. It is wrong and unlawful to apply a one-size-fits-all behaviour policy.

> *"Published behaviour policies need to be consistent with the legal requirement that treating all pupils the same may be unlawful where a disability affects behaviour. It may be unlawful to apply a behaviour policy that treats all pupils the same if a pupil's disability makes it harder for them to comply with the policy than other pupils who are not disabled."* (Department for Education, 2018)[134]

It is worth considering this issue in more detail.

Challenging behaviour policies – misunderstandings, inappropriateness and unfairness

Many schools are questioning their reliance on traditional reward and sanction type behaviour policies (BPs). These policies aim to promote orderly learning environments through rewarding good behaviour and sanctioning misbehaviours. Such approaches follow government guidelines, stressing that headteachers should draw up policies that effectively promote good behaviour by using rewards to reinforce and praise good behaviours, as well as setting out the disciplinary sanctions to be used if pupils misbehave (Department for Education, 2016).[135]

---

134 Department for Education (2018) *Mental Health And Behaviour In Schools*. Available at: https://assets.publishing.service.gov.uk/government/uploads/system/uploads/attachment_data/file/755135/Mental_health_and_behaviour_in_schools__.pdf [last accessed 4 February 2021]

135 Department for Education (2016) *Behaviour And Discipline In Schools: Advice For Headteachers And School Staff*. Available at https://assets.publishing.service.gov.uk/government/uploads/system/uploads/attachment_data/file/488034/Behaviour_and_Discipline_in_Schools_-_A_guide_for_headteachers_and_School_Staff.pdf [last accessed 4 February 2021]

There are three serious weaknesses with this approach:

- They reflect a poor understanding of rewards and sanctions, and the unforeseen consequences associated with them.

- They are an inappropriate method for teaching repeat offenders how to behave appropriately.

- They are unfair, when applied as a one-size-fits-all measure, and result in children and young people with social, emotional and mental health disabilities having a higher chance of being excluded.

Misunderstandings

Much has been written on the problems of reward and sanction systems (Kohn, 1999).[136] For many the focus of their behaviour policy is to reduce behaviours. More time and energy is spent on correcting and managing inappropriate behaviours than promoting appropriate ones. As educationalists our aim should be to increase students' behavioural repertoire, not reduce it. Children and young people are often trying to solve a problem, not be one, but because of their immaturity they have limited skills at their disposal. Their goals might be, for example, to avoid work or obtain teacher attention. An over-reliance on correction techniques can mean that staff are unwittingly meeting a student's needs.

Key Point

Children and young people are often trying to solve a problem, not be one, but because of their immaturity they have limited skills at their disposal.

B. F. Skinner was the arch proponent of using consequences to influence behaviour. He wrote of how positive and negative reinforcement could shape behaviour and less about rewards and sanctions. In fact something could only be either a positive or negative reinforcer after its effect on the behaviour was observed. It is worth noting that, strictly speaking, it is the behaviour that is being reinforced not the student. The effectiveness is judged by observing whether the behaviour changes. So, while a student might not like being put into detention, the observed fact that they continue to have detentions shows that detention is not a negative reinforcer for the behaviour (Woolard, 2010).[137]

---

136 Kohn A (1999) *Punished By Rewards*. New York, NY: Houghton Mifflin Company.
137 Woolard J (2010) *Psychology For The Classroom: Behaviourism*. Oxon: Routledge.

Furthermore, whenever an adult reacts to a child or young person's behaviour, it is the child or young person who is in control. Their behaviour causes a response from the adult. If we accept that behaviour is rarely random and is usually motivated to obtain something or avoid something, then it would seem that the child or young person is in control. It is not difficult to see that if the focus is on correction techniques then school staff are more likely to experience failure and frustration as they unwittingly help meet a child or young person's – for example, the student who does not like a lesson misbehaves and is sent out. Are they being sanctioned or rewarded? From a behaviourist's point of view, the behaviour is being positively reinforced, i.e. rewarded.

We know from the Elton Report (1989) that those schools spending time encouraging appropriate behaviours had fewer problem behaviours than those schools trying to eliminate poor behaviours.[138]

The appeal of rewards and sanctions

In the 1980s there was a growing concern about behaviour in schools. A survey by the Professional Association of Teachers found that members believed indiscipline was on the increase, and roughly one in three reported having been attacked by a pupil at some point in their career (Elton,1989).[139] Of the many psychological theories of child and adolescent development, behaviourism seemed the most appropriate for schools to endorse. This approach was the most compatible with the existing methods schools were applying to control behaviour. As one teacher put it: "*I was smacked at home and caned in school; there was harmony.*" So sanctions were well established. While there were other educational theories on child development (Vygotsky, 1986;[139] Bruner, 1996[140]), it was the work of Skinner (1974) that was the most user-friendly – advocating that behaviour was functional, predictable and changeable.[141] This approach has given us Applied Behaviour Analysis (ABA), which is a rigorous way of analysing and changing behaviour that is still of significant value today.

Expert View

"The trick is to restrict the time we spend in the negative energy zones to necessity and aim to get ourselves in the positive energy zones as much as possible."

Ian Morris[102]

138 Elton Report (1989) *Discipline In Schools: Committee Of Enquiry Report*. London: Her Majesty's Stationery Office.

139 Vygotsky L (1986) *Thought And Language*. Cambridge, MA: Massachusetts Institute of Technology Press.

140 Bruner J (1996) *The Culture Of Education*. Cambridge, MA: Harvard University Press.

141 Skinner BF (1974) *About Behaviourism*. New York: Knopf Doubleday Publishing.

Rewards

Schools will typically use such rewards such as:

- Positive feedback
- Points for prizes
- Sticker awards
- Certificates, letters of commendation
- Prize draws
- Special responsibilities

The potential problems with rewards are as follows:

- They devalue learning. When a student is told, *"Do X and I will give you Y"*, then whatever X may be it is devalued, i.e. it becomes a means to an end (Kohn, 1999).[136]

- Intrinsic motivation is weakened. If a student is motivated to do a task for extrinsic reasons, later when they can freely choose to do the same task, they are less likely to do it. The task has become a means to an end (Greene, Nisbett & Lepper, 1973).[142]

- Rewards do not teach personal responsibility. Behaviour is under the control of external factors, so the individual is not responsible for it (deCharms, 1968).[143]

- Performance on a task can be increased through the use of rewards, but a learner's attitude to learning task is weakened (Dweck & Leggett, 1988).[144]

- Learners are treated as a means to an end, namely a score – the learners' interests and other basic needs are ignored.

Sanctions

While schools vary in the type of sanctions they give, typically they will involve some of the following:

- Verbal warning
- Detention

---

142 Greene D, Lepper MR & Nisbett RE (1973) Undermining children's intrinsic interest with extrinsic reward: A test of the "overjustification" hypothesis. *J Pers Soc Psychol* 28(1), 129–37.

143 DeCharms R (1968) *Personal Causation: The Internal Affective Determinants Of Behavior.* New York: Academic Press.

144 Dweck CS & Leggett EL (1988) A social-cognitive approach to motivation and personality. *Psychol Rev* 95(2): 256–73.

- Time-out with senior staff
- Task to make amends (under supervision)
- Fixed-term or permanent exclusion

The potential problems with sanctions are as follows:

- Misbehaviour may be motivated to obtain attention. To administer a sanction will usually involve adult attention, this attention given in conjunction with the sanction may actually be rewarding and thereby maintaining the misbehaviour.

- If a sanction is frequently given by the same adult, then any negative emotional arousal linked to the sanction is likely to generalise to the person responsible and a conditioned fear may be acquired. This may result in a negative relationship which can prevent the adult being supportive or helpful in the future. It is not unusual for one member of staff to be seen in such a negative light through their association with sanctions.

- When the threat of a sanction is present children and young people may control their behaviour, but when the threat is removed the misbehaviour returns. It is not uncommon for children and young people to misbehave when taught by supply teachers, or during free time, but not in class time.

- Often the time gap between the misbehaviour and the sanction is so long that there is no association for the children and young people to learn a link. For any reinforcer to be effective there needs to be a closeness in time for the association to be made and learned.

- For a minority of children and young people, behaving badly is their way of obtaining attention. They have habituated to the negative aspect and find the unforeseen side effects positive.

- Sanctions make the assumption that the children and young people could have behaved differently. The assumption is that they had a choice. As will be explored later, some students may be punished for not using a skill they do not possess (punishment problems and negative side effects).

Inappropriateness

So why are behaviour policies inappropriate? In an everyday school there will be a significant number of children and young people who already possess the skills required for the classroom. These will be such skills as the ability to:

- Say 'please' and 'thank you'
- Take turns
- Share
- Cooperate with others
- Listen

These children are school-ready.

Many children will have acquired these skills at home, as their parents and carers will have modelled and taught them through repeated practice. A school behaviour policy is almost not needed for these young people. In fact, they are so often well-behaved that to praise and reward them for their behaviour can be condescending. They are nearly always well-behaved. In fact, it is often these children that school staff feel are overlooked. As a result, some schools have introduced *golden time*, or similar, so that these children and young people can feel that they are recognised for behaving well.

Key Point

Having a behaviour policy is directing energy towards a problem that for many children and young people just doesn't exist – a hammer to break a non-existent nut.

So you could argue that having a behviour policy is directing energy towards a problem that for many children and young people just doesn't exist – a hammer to break a non-existent nut. If the aim of any behaviour policy is to enable children and young people to engage more fully in their learning, then perhaps the school policy could be more appropriately focused on motivation and engagement for learning.

Learning Power (Claxton, 2018)[145]

Realistically, every day teachers are involved in encouraging children and young people to stop doing things they enjoy and instead do things they probably won't enjoy. So there is every likelihood of conflict. To this can be added the fact that during the teenage years there is a desire by adolescents to be treated like an adult, despite often acting like a child. We now appreciate that the brain of a teenager is not fully wired up until sometime in their twenties. This process is known as reconfiguration, which is when old and unused neural connections are pruned and new ones made (Blakemore, 2018).[91]

---

145 Claxton G (2018) *The Learning Power Approach.* Carmarthen: Crown House Publishing.

So school staff can realistically expect to face some degree of misbehaviour in even the most emotionally secure and neurotypical children and young people. In such circumstances of low-level disruptive behaviours, good classroom management techniques would be all that are needed. Research suggests that if teachers focus their energy on children and young people behaving appropriately then the frequency of low-level disruptions decreases (Ford, 2018).[146]

Such evidence supports those who have long argued for positive techniques to increase appropriate behaviour, rather than those who advocate a zero tolerance strategy to manage misbehaviours.

Unfairness

"Behaviour Policies work for those who don't need them, and are unfair for those who do." (Long, 2020)[147]

While all schools are aware of the Equality Act (2010), it is worth considering some key points that will strengthen the argument against a one-size-fits-all behaviour policy. It is unfair to children and young people with Special Educational Needs and Disabilities (SEND), and/or other risk factors, for behaviour policies to be applied indiscriminately.

Discrimination has different implications when applied to disability issues. Under the Equality Act (2010) disability includes a mental impairment that has a substantial and long-term negative effect. This implies that many children and young people who display persistent misbehaviours may well have an underlying mental health problem.[148]

The government's recent green paper on mental health provision provides the alarming data that there are 850,000 children and young people with a diagnosable mental health disorder in the UK. It also highlights the vulnerability of the following groups to having mental health problems:

■ Looked-after children
■ Lesbian, gay, bisexual and transgender children

146 Ford G (2006) *The New Contented Little Baby Book*. London: Vermilion.
147 Long R (2020) *Behaviour Policies: SEBDA Newsletter.* Available at: https://www.sebda.org last accessed 15 February 2021]
148 UK Government (2010) *Equality Act 2010. Available at: https://www.legislation.gov.uk/ ukpga/2010/15/contents* [last accessed 4 February 2021]

- Young people involved in gangs
- Young people not in education, employment or training (NEETs)

Schools are permitted to treat disabled pupils more favourably than non-disabled pupils. This implies that holding rigidly to a consistency policy on behaviour may discriminate against children and young people with SEND or other disabilities. Furthermore, a school must not do anything that applies to all pupils that is more likely to have an adverse effect on disabled pupils. This implies that giving rewards or sanctions for children and young people who do or do not display readiness to learn skills will adversely affect SEND children and young people, who may not have the necessary skills or may have them in a weaker form than their peers.

In many schools there are often a small number of children and young people responsible for a disproportionately high number of misbehaviours (the proportion can be as low as three per cent). Most students who have been misbehaving will have been initially dealt with through the schools behaviour policy. Exclusion will be the final step, with all previous sanctions and/or rewards having failed.

Exclusion figures

- The rate of permanent exclusions across all primary, secondary and special schools increased slightly from 0.07% (2014–15) to 0.08% (2015–16).

- The number of fixed period exclusions across primary, secondary and special schools increased from 302,975 (2014–15) to 339,360 (2015–16). That is approximately 1,590 per day (2014–15) increasing to 1,790 (2015–16).

- The rate of fixed period exclusions across all primary, secondary and special schools also increased from 3.88% (2014–15) to 4.29% (2015–16) for pupil enrolments. [149]

We can reasonably assume that a high number of those who are excluded, either for a fixed period or permanently, will have been through a school's behaviour policy for managing persistent misbehaviours. The question that follows is: are there any indications that make some children and young people more likely to be excluded than others? Data suggests the answer is yes.

---

149 Department for Education (2017) *Permanent And Fixed Period Exclusions In England: 2015 To 2016.* Available at: https://assets.publishing.service.gov.uk/government/uploads/system/uploads/attachment_data/file/645075/SFR35_2017_text.pdf [last accessed 4 February 2021]

Four categories emerge from the data; some children and young people may be included in more than one category, and therefore counted several times.

■ **Free school meals** – Children and young people eligible for and claiming free school meals are four times more likely to receive a permanent or fixed period exclusion.

■ **Children in care** – The rate of permanent exclusions for looked after children and young people is higher than the rate for all children and young people. Looked after children and young people are more than five times more likely to have a fixed period exclusion. The statistics show that 11.44% of looked-after children and young people had at least one fixed period exclusion in 2016, compared with 2.11% of all children and young people. Looked-after children and young people are five times more likely to be temporarily excluded than children and young people overall.

■ **Ethnic group** – Children or young people of Gypsy/Roma heritage and travellers of Irish heritage have the highest rates of both permanent and fixed period exclusions. Afro-Caribbean children and young people are over three times more likely to be permanently excluded than the school population as a whole.

■ **Special Educational Needs (SEN) or Education, Health and Care (EHC)** plan – Nearly half of all permanent and fixed exclusions were identified as having Special Educational Needs and those receiving support were almost seven times more likely than those without SEN.

Questions posed with respect to these figures are:

■ Why is there such a strong correlation between exclusion rates and Special Educational Needs?

■ What can schools, parents and local authorities do to avoid the unnecessary exclusion of pupils with Special Educational Needs?

(Moorewood, 2017)[150]

Why are so many pupils with Special Educational Needs excluded from school? Because we are failing them. Children and young people with

---

150 Morewood G (2017) *For Pupils With SEND, Exclusion Is The Road To Nowhere.* Available at: https://blog.optimus-education.com/pupils-send-exclusion-road-nowhere [last accessed 4 February 2021]

special needs are grossly overrepresented in exclusion figures – we need a system that meets their needs (O'Brien, 2016).[151]

Typically the reasons for children and young people being excluded include:

- Persistent disruptive behaviour
- Physical assault against an adult
- Physical assault against a pupil
- Verbal abuse or threatening behaviour against an adult
- Verbal abuse of threatening behaviour against a pupil
- Damage
- Bullying

However, a more detailed analysis reveals much more, and the reasons now fall into the following categories:

- Mental health issues
- Social deprivation
- Ethnicity
- Special Educational Needs and Disability (SEND)

Jarlath O'Brien, drawing on the findings of a study by Strand and Fletcher (2015),[152] said that while he *"knew about the gross of representation of children with Special Educational Needs and Disabilities, [he] was horrified to find a similar bias when ethnicity was considered"*. For O'Brien the explanation for these findings is that there is a systemic bias at work. This bias may be partly the result of the belief that a school's behaviour policy should be applied equally to all.

The children and young people who are being excluded can fall into different categories, but they will all have certain characteristics that make their success in school difficult. So, while the causes of their problems may be different, the negative effects are similar.

151 O'Brien J (2016) *Why Are So Many SEN Pupils Excluded From School? The Guardian*, 27 October 2016. Available at: https://www.theguardian.com/teacher-network/2016/oct/27/why-are-so-many-sen-pupils-excluded-from-school-because-we-are-failing-them [last accessed 4 February 2021]

152 Strand S & Fletcher J (2014) *A Quantitative Longitudinal Analysis Of Exclusions From English Secondary Schools*. Oxford: University of Oxford.

As we saw in Chapter 13, executive functioning skills (EFS) are typically learned by young children via interaction with adults and neurological growth in the brain's prefrontal lobe. Executive functioning skills related to behaviour are:

- Inhibition – Control impulses; stop behaviour.
- Shift – Move freely from one activity/situation to another; problem-solve flexibly.
- Emotional Control – Modulate emotional responses appropriately.

Clearly difficulties in any of these will contribute to problems with behaviour.

The causes of some children and young people not developing such self-control in a neurotypical way are many, including ADHD, autism, poor parenting, Asperger's syndrome and attachment disorders. As Cooper-Kahn and Dietzel (2008) explain:[153]

> "Like a rash, executive dysfunction is a symptom that sometimes appears alone and sometimes is part of a larger problem. The broader diagnosis might be a learning disability (LD), autism spectrum disorder (ASD) or other condition, such as a range of neuro-developmental, psychiatric, and medical disorders."

So it would be fair to say that most children and young people who are excluded have some of the following difficulties:

- Low self-esteem
- Negative learning mindset
- Emotionally illiterate
- Poor self-regulation skills
- Poor problem-solving skills
- Poor group interaction skills
- Negative attitude towards authority

If a one-size-fits-all behaviour policy is applied to children and young people with these difficulties, then it seems highly likely that they will progress towards the ultimate sanction of exclusion. Imagine if a child

---

153 Cooper-Kahn J & Dietzel L (2008) *Late, Lost And Unprepared*. Bethesda, USA: Woodbine House Incs.

or young person is assessed and diagnosed as having dyslexia. The intervention to address this is to carry on teaching that individual in the same way as everyone else. Children and young people with social, emotional and mental health difficulties need support that addresses their specific issues. It is unfair to apply a behaviour policy that assumes that they have the skills to behave when in fact, like any child or young person with learning difficulties, there is a need for focused support.

So it seems reasonable to say that:

- A significant number of children and young people excluded have a range of Special Educational Needs and Disability issues.
- Certain ethnic groups are more vulnerable to exclusion.

Behaviour Policy Plus

So, if the typical school has a behaviour policy more relevant for the majority of learners, what would one designed to support those who are vulnerable to being excluded look like?

The following are actual statements made by schools, and are collected here as exemplars of progressive policies related to behaviour and inclusion.

"As a school we believe that all of our children and young people are whole and perfect. Our families send us their best children and young people. However, due to a range of circumstances, there are some children and young people who have developed patterns of behaviour that are potential barriers to them being successful learners or socially included."

"Initially when children and young people make behavioural mistakes, they will work through our structured Restorative Practice Programme. For children and young people who repeatedly make mistakes we will assess to determine how best to support and teach them."

"All of our children and young people have the right to learn and be safe. Children and young people who have, or are at risk of, SEND receive focused support."

"Data is collected to understand the conditions that can result in poor behaviour, as well as a consideration of the possible functions the behaviour serves."

"If we can predict problem behaviour, we should aim to prevent it.

"Our in-school behaviour specialist sets up a small action team to allow all involved with the children and young people to develop a programme that seeks to develop and strengthen the necessary skills needed to be a valued school member."

"Our school policy plus is guided by the following principles:

- *We believe in fighting fire with water. Through redirecting inappropriate behaviour in a non-confrontational manner.*
- *When faced with problem behaviour, we analyse we don't personalise.*
- *If we can predict problem behaviour, we work to prevent it.*
- *We do not have problem children, we sometimes have children with problems.*
- *Children are usually trying to solve problems, not be problems. But they may have inappropriate problem-solving techniques.*
- *Behavioural mistakes are learning opportunities.*
- *Our aim is to increase a child's behavioural repertoire."*

"Our curriculum to address a child or young person's SEMH difficulties covers the following key areas. There are resources and evidence based programmes available in each of these areas:

- *Executive functioning skills.*
- *Emotional literacy programme.*
- *Self-esteem development.*
- *Consequential learning.*
- *Cooperative group skills.*
- *Problem-solving skills."*

The way forward

When seeking to move beyond one-size-fits-all behaviour policies and instead design new approaches built around positive techniques to increase appropriate behaviour, it is important to bear in mind the following facts:

- Behaviour policies may work for the many but are unfair to those who have difficulties of various kinds.
- Behaviour policies over-rely on rewards and sanctions.

- Rewards weaken intrinsic motivation.
- Sanctions do not teach new skills.
- Misbehaviour is more often the symptom not the problem.
- Behaviour policies discriminate against the vulnerable.

Given all of this, how can any school claim with integrity that wellbeing matters if it continues to work with a one-size-fits-all behaviour policy? As Elizabeth Truss said:

"At the moment too many young people are unfairly labelled as trouble-makers when in fact they have unmet mental health problems."[154]

---

154 Truss E (2016) Cited in Nagel P (Ed.) *Mental Health Matters* (p.8). London: Bloomsbury.

How to help – evaluating school wellbeing approaches

☞ When seeking to assess your school as a learning environment that fosters wellbeing for all, a useful approach is to rate your current approaches across each of the following dimensions.

Are children and young people known by name and reasons for absences checked?								
1	2	3	4	5	6	7	8	9

Involved in activities/clubs								
1	2	3	4	5	6	7	8	9

Cooperative learning								
1	2	3	4	5	6	7	8	9

High expectations								
1	2	3	4	5	6	7	8	9

Mentoring systems								
1	2	3	4	5	6	7	8	9

Success and praise								
1	2	3	4	5	6	7	8	9

Chapter 19: School transitions and wellbeing

Children and young people move through many transitions on their journey to adulthood. Life is full of changes. Even as a baby there are many transitions. A baby moves from a cot to bed, they are weaned and they move from nappies to toilet. They learn to crawl and then walk. All of these are small but significant changes. Then there are the educational changes, from nursery to primary school and then from primary to secondary. All of these are very likely to be taking place while family changes are also occurring, such as bereavements, moving home and other disturbances.

Key Point

Transition is especially of concern to some vulnerable groups of children and young people.

In more traditional societies to transition from child to adult is marked by very specific rituals. Also when a child or young person becomes sexually mature and able to procreate, they are considered an adult. In Western societies the extended time children and young people spend in school has blurred the significance of biological maturity. The fact that the wellbeing of many is put at risk at this time makes it appropriate to consider.

Transition is especially of concern to some vulnerable groups of children and young people. These include *"girls, children with disabilities, ethnic minorities and those living in rural areas"* (UNICEF, 2012).[155]

The impact transition has on children and young people's wellbeing is clearly seen in a report commissioned by the Department for Education. It found that two out of every five pupils failed to make expected progress in the year following transition (Galton, Gray & Ruddock, 1999).[156]

Linked to transition is the idea of school-readiness. While this appears to be an easily definable term, appearances can be deceptive and it is open to misunderstandings through different interpretations. Kay (2019) found

---

155 UNICEF (2012) School Readiness: A Conceptual Framework. Available at: https://www.unicef.org/earlychildhood/files/Child2Child_ConceptualFramework_FINAL(1).pdf [last accessed 4 February 2021]
156 Galton M, Gray J & Ruddock J (1999) *The Impact Of School Transitions And Transfers On Pupil Progress And Attainment*. Research Report RR131. Nottingham: DfEE.

that school-readiness for children about to transfer into reception class concerns the children being toilet-trained and able to put their coats on.[157] When they are due to transfer into Year 1, it is about children being able to write and having basic mathematical skills. The more concerning finding from her research is that data for a lack of school-readiness seems to highlight certain groups of children:

- Those on free school meals.
- Those who have English as a second language.
- Those with Special Educational Needs and Disability (SEND)..
- Summer-born children.
- Gypsy and Roma children.

So it would seem that there are children who have more challenges than others and are more likely to suffer a poor sense of wellbeing on account of them not being school-ready.

They are consequently likely to be marginalised rather than understood and supported. Governments have an expectation of school-readiness but the fact that many can be expected to fall beneath this level should be seen as a social issue rather than an educational one. Schools are expected to address the shortcomings made by society and not by schools themselves (Kay, 2019).[157]

Another factor relevant to a child or young person's wellbeing is birthdate. Although countries may vary in where the school year begins, there will always be children who are younger than others on account of their birthdate. In the UK the school year begins on September 1, so the children most disadvantaged are those born during the summer months. In essence these children experience a year less than their peers before starting school. The effect of this can be seen in many areas, including:

- Significant differences in exam results between summer- and autumn-born children, the latter doing better.
- Disproportionate numbers referred for having additional special educational needs. The reasons are complex, but seem to involve summer-born children receiving less schooling and teachers failing to take the immaturity of summer-born children into account.

---

157 Kay L (2019) *School Readiness, Governance And Early Years Ability Grouping*. Available at: https://journals.sagepub.com/doi/abs/10.1177/1463949119863128 [last accessed 4 February 2021]

- Developmentally summer-born children are naturally more immature. (Sykes, Bell & Rodeiro 2016)[158]

A concerning finding in an American study was that there was a higher chance of suicide among those children who were the youngest in their school year (Thompson, Barnsley & Dyck, 1999).[159] It was suggested that poor academic performance may lead to lower confidence and self-esteem. These are typically found to be precursors to suicidal thoughts.

> **Key Point**
>
> With respect to wellbeing, transition at any stage clearly has the potential to negatively affect children and young people.

With respect to wellbeing, transition at any stage clearly has the potential to negatively affect children and young people.

The transition to be considered here is from primary to secondary school. In terms of psychological changes there are several key changes thought to occur at this age. Because this is a time of change for children and young people, it can cause stress and possibly impact negatively on their school career. A brief account of the challenges researchers believe children and young people experience at this time will help us consider how school transition can be most effectively managed.

For Piaget, it was the time when most young people move from concrete operational structures, where they need to see and manipulate objects, to their final stage of formal thinking. The formal operational stage begins at approximately age twelve and lasts into adulthood. As adolescents enter this stage, they gain the ability to think in an abstract manner and manipulate ideas in their head, without any dependence on concrete manipulation (Inhelder & Piaget, 1958).[160]

Secondary education curriculum demands are very different from primary. Children and young people are expected to think abstractly in subjects such as Mathematics and Science. The time of transition is rigidly fixed by age, but the actual stage of thinking for an individual child or young person may vary considerably.

---

158 Sykes E, Bell J & Vidal Rodeiro C (2016) *Birthdate Effects: A Review Of The Literature From 1990 On.* Available at: https://www.cambridgeassessment.org.uk/images/109784-birthdate-effects-a-review-of-the-literature-from-1990-on.pdf [last accessed 4 February 2021]

159 Thompson AH, Barnsley RH & Dyck RJ (1999) A new factor in youth suicide: The relative age effect. *Can J Psychiatry* 44(1): 82–85.

160 Inhelder B & Piaget J (1958) *The Growth Of Logical Thinking: From Childhood To Adolescence.* New York, NY: Basic Books.

We know, with evidence, that:

■ Cognitive development varies considerable in any school group selected by age.

■ The curriculum requirements of many secondary subjects are beyond the ability of many students.

■ Academic success correlates with cognitive ability not chronological age.

Research by Shayer and Adey (1981) found that the cognitive demands of the Science syllabus in the UK were beyond the cognitive developmental ability of secondary school students.[161] So using an age-determined criterion means that there will be many students who are not ready to meet the demands of their new curricula. As Casey (1994) put it:[162]

> "Early adolescents are in a transitional intellectual state between child-like (concrete) thinking and adult-like (formal) thinking... Because individual growth rates are variable, we cannot predict exactly when a child actually begins developing formal thinking processes."

The solutions suggested of by Shayer and Adey were: [161]

■ 'Reduce, reorganise or reschedule' the cognitive demands of the curriculum.

■ Or assess students for their cognitive readiness to cope with the curriculum demands.

The alternative solution was to design a programme to maximise the development of formal thinking structures. The programme, *Thinking Science*, which was developed from this work, was found to significantly improve success at secondary school.

So it would seem that for many children and young people there is a mismatch between exisiting thinking skills and the demands they face at transition. This is an obvious additional stress and a serious threat to any child or young person's sense of wellbeing (Shayer & Adey, 1981).[161]

---

161 Shayer M & Adey P (1981) *Towards A Science Of Science Teaching*. London: Helnemann.
162 Casey B (1994) In Howe A & Richards V (Eds.) (2011) *Bridging The Transition From Primary To Secondary School*. Oxford: Routledge.

James Marcia, a developmental psychologist, built on Erikson's theory of psychosocial development.[163] For Marcia, adolescence is when physiological, sexual and cognitive changes are occurring. In addition to identity achievement, where adolescents make a commitment to who they are, there also are three different states: identity diffusion, identity foreclosure, and identity moratorium.

Expert View

"Adolescence is marked by the central question of who we are in terms of an individual identity, place and role in life. Puberty forces all of us to ask and answer this question."

David Matsumoto[164]

An adolescent's identity is determined by the adoption of:

- Sexual orientation
- A set of values and ideals
- Vocational direction

Signs of transition distress

This brief look at adolescent development highlights why school transition needs to be carefully and sensitively managed. There are additional factors associated with those children who are at risk of not transferring successfully. These are when they have a low self-esteem, poor physical and/or mental health and poor peer relationships (Coleman & Hagell, 2007).[164]

Children and young people are likely to display clear signs of distress when they are not coping with the transition. Some of the negative consequences are outlined below.

Short-term effects:

- Outbursts of anger
- Crying and tearfulness
- Clinginess/need for affection
- Withdrawal

---

163 Marcia J (1966) *Identity Development Theory.* Available at: https://courses.lumenlearning.com/adolescent/chapter/identity-development-theory/ [last accessed 4 February 2021]

164 Coleman J & Hagell A (2007) *Adolescent Risk And Resilience: Against The Odds.* Chichester, West Sussex: John Wiley & Sons, Ltd.

- Tantrums in younger children
- Regression, bed-wetting, etc.
- Sleep problems
- Loss of appetite/eating more
- Loss of motivation
- Lack of concentration

Long-term effects:

- Self-harming
- Withdrawal
- Avoiding social contact
- Lack of concentration
- Not learning/developing
- Low self-esteem
- Strained relationships

How to help – transitions

 Transition has the potential to adversely impact children and young people in a variety of ways, especially those who are already vulnerable. It helps if adults:

- Explain what is going on
- Discuss what is happening and what will happen
- Provide distraction activities
- Have routines so the child or young person knows what to expect
- Organise family visits

 In addition, successful transitions are built on:

- Enabling children and young people to transfer with friends and facilitating the making of new friends. Older pupils/students befriending new ones especially helps with this.
- Good communication between the schools and home that addresses anxieties and provides opportunities to visit and meet key people.
- Matching new subject areas to the ability level of the individual; nothing breeds success like success. Having curriculum continuity in subjects across the phases.
- Knowledge and ability to practise the new routines, such as knowing where facilities such as toilets are.

 Good practice involves pre- and post-transfer actions:

- Presentations on how different secondary schools manage transition.
- Information that reiterates the same messages.
- Open-door policy to address questions and anxieties.

Pre-transition:

- A Year 6 curriculum that addresses social and emotional issues.
- Visits from secondary staff.
- Visits to secondary school.

Post-transition:

- Year 7 pupils attend school with no other students – familiarisation.
- Peer-mentoring programmes.
- Tutor group team building.
- Vulnerable individuals identified and given additional support.

Schools today are more aware of the factors during transition that can affect children and young people. They more readily understand Maslow's basic needs, including that children and young people have to:

- Feel safe
- Feel that they belong
- Feel they are valued

This is fully reflected when a child or young person receives a letter from their new school:

"Aside from welcoming the new students, we want to model an important aspect of our culture from the outset. I am making an authentic contact – as one human to another. I tell them about me... I invite them to write back... I receive many replies."
(Lee & James, 2010)[165]

---

165 Lee and James (2010) In Howe A & Richards V (Eds.) (2011) *Bridging The Transition From Primary To Secondary School*. Oxford: Routledge.

Part 5: Resilience and mental health

Chapter 20: Wellbeing for troubled children

The growing number of children and young people with mental health issues makes this chapter one of central importance. The moral standard of any society should be judged by the manner in which it cares for its most damaged and vulnerable individuals. Surely children and young people in this group must be included in any resource on wellbeing? A special focus will be on resilience, as this has been most studied in respect to children and young people who face adversity. It can also provide us with ideas to increase their wellbeing.

Troubled children and young people are typically the victims of events outside of their control. Just as we cannot control the weather, so children and young people can't control the negative events that befall them. Today we have arrived at a very different understanding of why many children and young people display behaviours that are inappropriate for the context they are in or

Key Point

The moral standard of any society should be judged by the manner in which it cares for its most damaged and vulnerable individuals.

their developmental stage. In the past the concern was to remove the problematic behaviour; today it is more to understand it. As a result, the behaviour is more often seen to be a form of communication for children and young people who have a limited repertoire of skills. A baby will cry when it needs feeding; similarly, a child or young person who needs more attention will find a way to achieve it. Be it negative or positive attention, they both meet the child or young person's need.

If we are to support troubled children and young people in their wellbeing, we need to have an understanding of:

- The reasons for problematic behaviour.
- Its effects on their development.
- How resilience can be a pathway to their wellbeing.

Reasons for problematic behaviour

Any disorder observed in children and young people is more often than not the result of a number of interacting factors. There are biological factors, such as the inherited temperament of a child or young person, and these will combine with environmental factors. We understand better today how these two interact to determine either adaptive or maladaptive outcomes. As Rutter (2001) put it:[166]

> *"It is appropriate that we consider what we have learned from psychosocial risk research and what are the challenges ahead. The dismissal of environmental influences by genetic evangelists is not justified. The rise during the past 50 years in rates of many disorders in young people makes it clear that environmental factors of some kind must be influential."*

A study that has highlighted the impact of adverse experiences on children and young people is the Adverse Childhood Experiences (ACE) study which we looked at briefly in Chapter 3. This was a US study that involved the childhood experiences, current health status and behaviours of some 17,000 individuals, and it was designed to investigate how early negative experiences such as abuse and neglect might be risk factors for problems in later development.

The results of this study show that as the number of risk factors in a child's life increases so also does the likelihood of problem behaviours and illnesses, such as:

- Risky behaviours, alcohol and substance abuse.
- Chronic health conditions, cancer and diabetes.
- Unplanned pregnancy.
- HIV/STDs.
- Depression/anxiety/suicide.
- Early death.

Having an increased number of ACEs does not mean that a child or young person will inevitably have poor outcomes, but there is an increased risk because of them. If a child has protective factors within

---

166 Rutter M (2001). Psychosocial adversity and child psychopathology. In Green J & Yule W [Eds] *Research and Innovation on the Road to Modern Child Psychiatry Volume 1*. Gaskell.

their lives, these will protect against the many possible negative health and life outcomes and the negative influence will be greatly reduced.

An ACE questionnaire was produced (https://acestoohigh.com/got-your-ace-score/). The higher a person's score the greater their risk. It was found that when child or young person had a score above four the risk was significantly increased.

As social disadvantage and the number of stressful life events accumulate for children, more protective factors are needed to act as a counterbalance. Risk factors are cumulative – for example, children exposed to multiple risks such as social disadvantage, family adversity and cognitive or attention problems are much more likely to develop behavioural problems (Brown, Khan & Parsonage, 2012).[167]

Key Point

As social disadvantage and the number of stressful life events accumulate for children, more protective factors are needed to act as a counterbalance.

Adverse conditions are factors that disturb the successful development of children and young people and, more specifically, a risk factor is a measurable and observable factor that predicts a negative outcome for the individual's development. This reinforces the definition of resilience as the ability of a child or young person to cope or recover from risk factors that would result in a child or young person having some form of social, emotional or mental health difficulties as a result.

So, what are the adverse conditions children or young people are likely to face? Some specific examples of Adverse Childhood Experiences (ACEs) are:

- Violence at home
- Abandonment through separation or divorce
- Abuse – physical, sexual and/or emotional
- Neglect – physical or emotional
- Parent or carer being in prison
- Alcohol or drug problems in the home

Other factors that can have a negative impact are:

---

167 Brown E, Khan L & Parsonage M (2012) *A Chance To Change: Delivering Effective Parenting Programmes To Transform Lives.* London: Centre for Mental Health.

- Poverty
- Bullying
- Peer rejection
- Racism
- Being in care
- Unsafe communities

Children and young people who observe adult violence and conflict find this affects their emotional regulation. They develop patterns of self-regulation that are biased in favour of being hypervigilant for threats (Hagenaars, Stins & Roelofs, 2011).[68] Such patterns are likely to be adaptive within the environments they are in but are maladaptive in new social situations (Pearce, 2016).[168]

Effects on development

The traits that an individual has, which can be observed, are the result of their genes, i.e. DNA. This is the genotype and it interacts with the environment and the individual's experiences to create what is then is called the phenotype.

Two individuals with identical genetics (i.e. the same genotype) can have different looks and behaviours to each other, which is their phenotype. As babies, identical twins are identical but as they grow up they become dissimilar through what they experience and environmental differences. Epigenetics in psychology studies how the expression of genes is influenced by the environment and individual experiences; the observed characteristics in behaviour, thought, personality and mental health is the result of these two factors interacting.

A possible analogy is to think of the design plan for a car. The actual design (the genotype) will be modified according to where the car is to be driven (the phenotype). In snowy areas the tyres will be fitted to cope with icy roads, but if the car was built to be driven in the outback of Australia the car would be a convertible or at least have air conditioning. So it is with children and young people – their genotype interacts with the environment to produce their phenotype.

Unless there are medical conditions, and providing they are well-cared-for, all babies develop at the same rate in the womb. Until the age of

---

168 Pearce C (2016) *A Short Introduction To Attachment And Attachment Disorder.* London: Jessica Kingsley Publications.

two all children achieve the same developmental milestones. It is when there are adverse conditions that neurotypical children begin to vary in their development. In the early stages it is the physical and emotional wellbeing of the mother that will impact most on a child's development.

How does this relate to troubled children and young people? It is clear that adverse conditions have long term consequences, as they *"increase the risk of later development of poor mental health, adverse behavioural responses, and a range of physical illnesses"* (van Woerden, 2018).[169] While some sixty-seven per cent of the population will have experienced at least one ACE, it is the combined and accumulative effect of several that seems to heighten the risk for problems.

Children and young people with four or more ACEs are:

- Fourteen more times likely to attempt suicide.
- Eleven times more likely to use intravenous drugs.
- Four-and-a-half times more likely to develop depression.

And figures show that some twelve per cent of the population have at least four ACEs.

Children and young people who have faced some of the above ACEs are more likely to:

- Laugh when disciplined
- Argue with adults when they see unfairness
- Tackle problems negatively and aggressively
- Have a poor procedural memory
- Not respect authority

This could be part of the explanation for the increase in children and young people with social, emotional and mental health problems. Without going into excessive statistical details, in 2017 a study found that one in nine children and young people had a mental health disorder – either emotional, behavioural, hyperactive, or other. The link between a child or young person being resilient or not depends on many variables interacting. A baby will be protected from many risk factors

169 van Woerden H (2018) *The Annual Report Of The Director Of Public Health*. Available at: https://www.nhshighland.scot.nhs.uk/Publications/Documents/DPH-Annual-Report-2018_(web-version).pdf

that a teenager is not, but a baby will be more vulnerable to attachment difficulties through abandonment. At different times of their development there will be different risk factors.

Children and young people are biologically programmed to live, and to survive, in whatever context they find themselves. The DNA of a child born into a chronically stressful environment is likely to be influenced to produce a personality that is better able to cope with stress – perhaps a hypervigilant personality. They are also likely to have an over-aroused nervous system that is over-sensitive to any possible threat, so evolution has equipped us with the ability to make subtle changes depending on the environment around us.

In normal contexts the attachment process that a baby develops with their prime carer will help programme the development of neural patterns in their nervous system. At this early bonding stage, the brain stem is learning how to react to safety and stress. The brain is organising neural pathways and these take time to develop. The more often a pathway fires, the stronger the association and likelihood of it firing again in the future becomes. As the saying goes, *neurons that fire together, wire together.* The baby that is being loved and cared for will develop a secure trusting bond with their carer.

> ## Key Point
>
> *Children and young people are biologically programmed to live, and to survive, in whatever context they find themselves.*

However, a baby's coping strategies to stress can be adaptive in the short term but maladaptive when applied in different contexts. If the baby is experiencing stress, then the neural pathways that will fire together are those that will enable the baby to develop stress resilience. Experiments with animals have shown that there is an association between rats that are maternally licked and groomed during the first week of life, and their ability later to cope with stress (Caldji et al, 1998).[170]

Children and young people that live in stressful and dysfunctional families are frequently distressed; dysfunctional families and distressed children go hand in hand. This is irrespective of the socioeconomic background of the family.

The causes of the issues and disorders that lead children and young people to become troubled are, then, many and complex. The key factors are:

---

170 Caldji C, Tannenbaum B, Sharma S, Francis D, Plotsky P & Meaney M (1998) Maternal care during infancy regulates the development of neural systems mediating the expression of fearfulness in the rat. *Proc Natl Acad Sci USA* 95(9): 5,335–40.

- Biological
- Psychological
- Environmental

Today a commonly used technique for understanding this is a bio-psychosocial model, which allows for the many contributory factors to be included and integrated.

In the following chapters we will look at the third part of the understanding we require in order to support troubled children and young people – that is, how resilience can provide a pathway to their wellbeing.

Chapter 21: Understanding resilience

Resilience has been described as a *"universal capacity which allows a person, group or community to prevent, minimise or overcome damaging effects of adversity"* (Newman, 2004).[171] It is not just about reforming but about the possibility of growth.

Life is not and never has been problem-free. We are usually only aware of problems when we fail to cope. Such problems may increase or decrease our motivation to try again and/or learn the necessary skills for success. Some challenges, however, arepotentially toxic in how they can affect development.

Expert View

"Resilience is shaped and built by experiences, opportunities and relationships – what could be termed the 'social determinants' of resilience."

Matilda Allen[172]

Resilience has become a very popular concept, often linked closely to wellbeing. So, to ask the question again, how exactly does resilience differ from wellbeing?

Wellbeing is primarily concerned with having the necessary skills and qualities to function successfully in whichever society you are born into.

Resilience is concerned with those skills and qualities that enable a child or young person to cope with adversity. The child or young person manages positively those challenges that could have been expected to have a negative impact on them. Historically, the study of resilience evolved through researchers and practitioners trying to understand why some children and young people were beaten by adversity while others seemed to survive despite it.

This chapter and those that follow will spend some time making it clear that, although wellbeing is good for all, there will be some children and young people who need a deeper understanding, with interventions more focused on adverse life experiences.

---

171 Newman T (2004) *What Works In Building Resilience?* London: Jessica Kingsley Publishers.
172 Allen M (2014) *Building Children And Young People's Resilience In Schools.* Public Health England.

Wellbeing is a relative concept, in that different societies define it differently. An interesting approach is to think of what children and young people would look like if they possessed wellbeing. What skills and personal qualities would they have? What would their families be like and the schools they attend? For the moment let's stay with the skills and qualities a child or young person with wellbeing would have in most Western societies. They might be:

- Emotionally literate
- Good self-esteem
- Believe they could change
- Ability to problem-solve   .
- Good relationship skills

Resilience is focused on the positive adaptation of children and young people when faced by a threat to their development. Under such conditions, children and young people cope and adapt positively despite the adverse conditions. The two key factors to appreciate are firstly that there is a threat, and secondly that the child or young person will cope.

Here is a frequently used example of a child who overcame some extreme adverse conditions.

> "A five-year old child watched helplessly as his younger brother drowned. In the same year, glaucoma began to darken his world. His family was too poor to provide the medical help that might have saved his sight. His parents died during his teens. Eventually he found himself in a state institution for the blind. As an African-American, he was not permitted to access many activities within the institution, including music. Given the obstacles he faced, one would not have easily predicted that he would someday become a renowned musician."

This man's name was Ray Charles.

A brief history of resilience

To fully appreciate the role that resilience has in supporting the wellbeing of troubled children, we need first to explore in some detail the history of resilience and current thinking on the subject. Research into resilience can be seen to have passed through many phases (O'Dougherty Wright, Masten & Narayan, 2013).[173]

Phase 1

The first wave looked for the factors that seemed to be compatible with resilience. Factors such as good cognitive abilities, self-regulation, self-esteem, good peer relationships, positive outlook on life and having a sense of meaning. This phase was characterised by researchers asking *what* was it that made one individual resilient when faced with adverse experiences and another succumb to problems.

A concern with this approach was that it saw resilience as being an inherent property of the individual. Resilience was something you either had or didn't have. So children and young people who were not resilient 'lacked the right stuff' and by implication were somehow to blame for it.

Phase 2

The second phase turned its attention to *how* questions. What were the underlying processes that resulted in resilience? The focus was on how different factors linked to each other. How did factors within the child or young person interact with those in the family to result in a negative or positive outcome? This is summed up by Wyman (2003), who wrote: *"Resilience reflects a diverse set of processes that alter children's transactions with adverse life conditions to reduce negative effects and promote mastery of normative developmental tasks."*[174]

This approach argued that within all children and young people there are systems that serve to adapt and protect the individual on their developmental pathway. Examples of these systems are attachment to secure relationship closeness and self-regulatory systems to control emotions. Questions asked now were less about why a child or young person was resilient, but more about the connections between them and their context. Two children or young people in an abusive family do not necessarily experience the same level of abuse; also how each reacts to the abuse will differ. In addition, how children experience such adverse experiences will depend on age. The meaning of sexual abuse to a very young child is different to a teenager in

173 O'Dougherty Wright M, Masten A & Narayan A (2014) Resilience Processes In Development: Four Waves. In Goldstein S & Brooks RB (Eds.) *Handbook Of Resilience In Children* (pp. 15–37). New York: Springer.

174 Wyman P (2003) Cited in O'Dougherty, Wright M, Masten A & Narayan A (2014) Resilience Processes In Development: Four Waves (pp.15–37). In Goldstein S & Brooks RB (Eds.) *Handbook Of Resilience In Children*. New York: Springer.

that they do not yet fully understand it. The impact is more severe when they are older as they now have an understanding of betrayal and humiliation.

Phase 3

This phase took existing knowledge and focused on developing experiments to promote positive adaptation and prevent problems in at-risk children and young people. This phase was dominated by theory-driven intervention designs, using experiments and randomised control. The norm was for multifaceted intervention programmes. These aimed to promote resilience development in children and young people, achieved through reducing the adverse risks and exposure to adversity or through building resources and/or nurturing relationships.

Phase 4

Current research accepts that adaptation occurs at many different levels that interact with each other. Areas studied include genes, neurobiology, brain development, behaviour and context. This approach believes that development is the result of probabilistic epigenesis – that is, the environment that a child or young person lives in can trigger certain genetic information to be active. Research has shown a correlation between socioeconomically disadvantaged adolescents and their blood pressure, excess fat and high levels of the stress hormone cortisol (Hamblin, 2015).[175] Understanding resilience has come a long way. We now understand that resilient children and young people are not simply born that way, but rather genetic and environmental factors interact to protect them from adverse effects.

Making sense of probabilistic epigenesis is no easy task. We know that there are numerous factors that combine to provide a child or young person with resilience. With so many factors, the number of potential combinations is almost limitless. An analogy can help. Let's imagine that every factor affecting a young person is a coloured ball. There are balls for temperament, housing, parental mental health and so on. Now imagine a roulette wheel. Each ball is spun on the wheel, and the number that it falls on becomes part of a code for a unique outcome. The outcome may be positive or negative - the young person may succumb to the adverse experiences, or they may become resilient. Biological, psychological and environmental factors are all at work in a complex and ongoing process of constant multi-directional interactions.

---

175 Hamblin J (2015) *The Paradox Of Effort: A Medical Case Against Too Much Self-Control.* Available at: https://www.theatlantic.com/health/archive/2015/07/the-health-cost-of-upward-mobility/398486/ [last accessed 4 February 2021]

Adverse experiences and development

The genetic side of this complex relationship is still in its early days; we do know much about the effects that the social and physical environment can have on development, for better or worse. As we are concerned with the adverse effects of life experiences on development, here is some evidence as to how an adverse environment can impact on a child or young person.

- Using Functional Magnetic Resonance Imaging (fMRI) children and young people from lower-income families have been found to have ten per cent less brain grey matter. Grey matter contains neural cells, dendrites and synapses, which are essential for cognition, information processing and self-control. The differences in brain volume increased over the time children and young people were exposed to differing income households (Hanson, Hair & Shen, 2013).[176]

- Unsurprisingly, children exposed to trauma and violence have been found to have higher activation in the amygdala. This area is central to survival instincts and strong emotions such as fear. Traumatised children tend to be more reactive to situations and are less able to be still and calm (Palombo et al, 2015).[177] Teicher et al (2004) found that victims of trauma, abuse and early stress had a smaller corpus callosum.[178] This is the bundle of fibres linking the left and right brain hemispheres. This reduces the capacity to communicate or cooperate.

The danger with early research into resilience was its overfocus on proximal factors, in which the children and young people and the family became the main areas of study. As a result, increased inequality was ignored, as was poverty and the degradation of communities. Macro-social issues could be ignored and the status quo maintained. Such research complemented a prevailing neoliberal approach to social issues. Neoliberalism believes in free-market trade. It essentially blames the poor for being poor, believing that they lack aspirations and are work-shy.

It is only the fourth phase of resilience research that seeks to give a much deeper and wider analysis of the nature of adverse childhood experiences and those processes that give rise to resilience.

176 Hanson J, Hair N & Shen D (2013) Family poverty affects the rate of human infant brain growth. *PLoS One* 8(12): e80954.

177 Palombo S, Mariotti V, Iofrida C, Pellegrini S (2015) Genes and aggressive behavior: epigenetic mechanisms underlying individual susceptibility to aversive environments. *Front Behav Neurosci* 12: 17.

178 Teicher M, Dumont N, Ito Y, Vaituzis C, Giedd J, Andersen S (2004) Childhood neglect is associated with reduced corpus callosum area. *Biol Psychiatry* 56(2): 80–85.

Measuring resilience

Resilience is not like other psychological constructs; it is not a thing in itself, but an outcome. A definition shared by many researchers is that:

"resilience refers to positive outcomes, adaptation or the attainment of developmental milestones or competencies in the face of significant risk, adversity, or stress."
(Naglieri, LeBuffe & Ross, 2014).[179]

Measuring resilience is no easy challenge. The quote above highlights two essential aspects. First, there needs to have been some degree of risk or adversity. Clearly, events such as war and abuse qualify for this - these are acute events that cause extreme distress. At the same time, though, there can be children and young people coping with chronic stress – for example, frequent school changes, poor-quality childcare or even harsh discipline at home. All these acute and chronic conditions would meet the criteria for adversity.

The risk factors that children and young people face fall at many levels. The community could be a dangerous one with few after-school programmes or one with many resources and good role models. The family could be a risk factor through violence and poor parenting practices, or it could be positive in its care and support. And then there are the risk factors within children and young people themselves - for example is their temperament flexible or feisty?

---

179 Naglieri J, LeBuffe P & Ross K (2013) Measuring Resilience In Children: From Theory To Practice. In Goldstein S & Brooks RB (Eds.) *Handbook of Resilience In Children* (pp. 39–55). New York: Springer.

How to help – measuring resilience

☞ Resilience is the outcome of the complex interaction of many variables, so to measure the many risk or protective factors is a considerable challenge. At present the solution has been to measure what are known as 'within-child factors'. The following are examples of tests that satisfy some of the necessary criteria for test reliability and validity. Namely, they are readily available, are norm-referenced, come with a manual and are specifically designed for use with children and young people.

- **Devereux Early Childhood Assessment (two to five years)** – This test assesses three areas central to resilience: initiative, self-control and attachment. Children who score low on these could be at risk of developing social, emotional and mental health problems.

- **Resiliency Scales for Children and Adolescents (nine to eighteen years)** – This test assesses personal qualities and vulnerabilities linked to resilience. It uses a five-point scale on questions. It has three global scales for senses of mastery, relatedness, and emotional reactivity.[180]

---

180 Daniel B & Wassel S (2002) *Assessing And Promoting Resilience In Vulnerable Children 1: The Early Years*. London: Jessica Kingsley Publishers.

Chapter 22: What can be done to increase resilience?

"The resilience of the human organism is even more amazing than its vulnerability."
(Klein, 1944)[181]

There are many ways in which we can support children and young people who face, or have faced, adverse circumstances. Children and young people do not cope with adverse conditions by 'pulling themselves up by their own bootstraps'. Instead their resilience emerges, as has been consistently argued, through the complex interaction of within-child factors such as family, school and community. The areas to be considered to support at-risk children and young people are therefore always specific to the individual.

Children and young people who displayed behaviours that were considered by adults to be either inappropriate or concerning have been understood and classified in many ways. The terms used are in their own way a record of changing ideas and attitudes. Words such as 'retarded', 'cretin', 'imbecile', 'moronic' and 'maladjusted' have all been used as respectable terms to describe the misfortunes of troubled children. Today the classification, diagnosis and treatment of childhood mental disorders is such a wide field that to do justice to wellbeing for each condition is beyond the scope of this book. This chapter will therefore focus on children and young people who have either externalising or internalising disorders. First, we need to define these.

> ## Key Point
>
> *Resilience emerges through the complex interaction of within-child factors such as family, school and community.*

Externalising disorders – These behaviours are typically socially negative, disrupting and disturbing and affect the environment and those within it – usually parents, teachers and peers. They are readily visible to observers. The common disorders frequently diagnosed are:

- Attention Deficit Hyperactivity Disorder (ADHD)
- Oppositional Defiance Disorder (ODD)
- Conduct Disorder (CD)
- Pathological Demand Avoidance Disorder (PDA)

181 Klein M (1994) Cited in Hall L (2015) *Coaching In Times Of Crisis And Transformation.* London: Kogan Page Limited.

While there are many areas of concern, a common problem for children and young people facing externalising disorders is their lack of self-control. As we have seen, the ability to control their behaviour develops as one of a child's executive functioning skill, as their prefrontal cortex develops connections through maturation combined with parental care. It is considered a protective factor as it enables a child or young person to stop, think and choose, which is the core skill for making good decisions. Because of its importance, we will return to self-control with practical suggestions for development.

Internalising disorders – These disorders are less readily observable and include such conditions as anxiety and depression. Often the symptoms cause internal distress (also called intropunitive) that is self-harming. Being less observable, these symptoms are more difficult to detect in the very young who have less developed verbal skills or emotional awareness of their internal states. The commonest ones are:

- Anxiety
- Depression
- Selective mutism

As with externalising disorders, there are many difficulties that children and young people face with internalising disorders; however, one that is common to all is a poor sense of worth. To engage with any suggested interventions, they need to feel that they are worth it and that they are of value in and of themselves. The development of self-esteem is therefore a key consideration.

Whether a child will develop externalising or internalising behaviours in response to the stresses they have experienced will be influenced by the factors already detailed. It is now widely agreed that doctors and other professionals are more likely to diagnose girls with internalising mood disorders such as anxiety and depression, and boys with externalising disorders such as attention deficit hyperactivity disorder (ADHD).

Causes of externalising disorders

There are many causes of externalising disorders, including:

- **Biological** – Children and young people who have a mentally ill parent are four times more likely to develop an illness themselves. The inherited temperamental disposition of the children and young people may also predispose them to certain types of disorders. One child may be more prone to a fear reaction (internalised disorder) when stressed, whereas a sibling may become frustrated and angry (externalised disorder).

- **Gender (socialisation)** – Girls are taught to think, feel and behave differently to boys. Boys more frequently respond to adverse experiences with outward behaviour whereas girls more often turn inward. This is often expressed as *boys explode, girls implode.* However, these are only general patterns. To know whether any particular boy or girl follows it, the individual needs to be studied.

- **Environmental** – Growing up in a home where there is inconsistent parenting can impair a child or young person in learning to self-regulate their own behaviour.

How to support children and young people who have an externalising disorder – self-control

Also referred to as self-regulation, self-control is the process by which the mind *"has control of functions, states, and inner processes"* (Ylvisaker & Feeney, 2009).[182] It allows a child or young person to inhibit an automatic response and assess past behaviours before making a decision about how best to respond.

A plausible reason for children or young people struggling with self-control is that they lack the skill – or they have the skill but it is not an automatic part of their repertoire when they become distressed. Like any skill, if it already exists weakly it can be strengthened and if it doesn't exist it can be taught.

With regard to adolescents, the media view this as a time when children and young people lack self-control; they are, as Bell and McBride (2010) put it, *"all gasoline, no brakes, and no steering wheel."*[183] More detailed studies have found that *"when there is no emotional information present, adolescents function as well if not better than adults"* (Hare et al, 2008).[184] However, when there is emotional information and adolescents are requested to make decisions in the heat of the moment their performance is worse. It seems then, that adolescents have difficulties in showing restraint when faced with heated situations, but in cool situations they can be as rational

182 Ylvisaker M & Feeney T (2009) Apprenticeship in self-regulation: Supports and interventions for individuals with self-regulatory impairments. *Developmental Neurorehabil* 12: 370–79.
183 Bell CC, McBride DF (2010) Affect regulation and prevention of risky behaviours. *JAMA* 304(5): 565–66.
184 Hare T, Tottenham N, Galvan A, Voss HU, Glover G & Casey B (2008) Biological substrates of emotional reactivity and regulation in adolescence during an emotional go-nogo task. *Biol Psychiatry* 63(10): 927–34.

as adults. This tension between being rational and impulsive can vary between individuals, and it can be developed (Casey & Caudle, 2013).[185]

 ## How to help – self-control

☞ A starting point in deciding how to improve self-control is to observe how and what children and young people with good self-control do. The processes they use are:

- Self-monitoring
- Self-monitoring plus reinforcement
- Self-reinforcement
- Self-management

(Reid et al, 2005)[186]

These four processes are believed to collectively underpin self-control.

☞ The following programme outline is based on the research of Norris (2016).[187]

- **Self-monitoring** – To develop self-control, it is important for the child or young person to first agree on a target behaviour to improve. Then they must agree how they will record the frequency with which it occurs.

- **Self-monitoring plus reinforcement** – This builds on the previous step but includes a reward that the child or young person receives for maintaining the behaviour assessment phase.

- **Self-reinforcement** – This time the reward is agreed with the child or young person for meeting an agreed degree of improvement. Involvement means taking responsibility for their behaviour.

185 Casey BJ & Caudle K (2013) The teenage brain: self control. *Curr Dir Psychol Sci* 22(2): 82–87.

186 Reid R, Trout AL & Schartz M (2005) Self-regulation interventions for children with attention deficit/hyperactivity disorder. *Except Child* 71: 361–77.

187 Norris LA (2016) *Self-Regulation Strategies For Students With Disruptive Behaviour Disorders.* Accessed at: https://repository.stcloudstate.edu/cgi/viewcontent.cgi?referer=&httpsredir=1&art icle=1024&context=sped_etds [last accessed at 16 February 2021]

- **Self-management** – Now the child or young person monitors their progress with a significant adult. Agreed criteria are needed for improvement. If both parties agree that improvement has been made then the child or young person again has an agreed reward.

Using approaches such as these has assisted children or young people who are classified as having disruptive behavioural disorders of childhood and as a result poor self-control. Additional user-friendly ideas include:

- **In class** – Secret signals that remind the child or young person what they are expected to do.

- **Aide memoir of rules** – A list of in-class rules to remind the children and young people of behavioural expectations, possibly with positive and negative consequences.

- **Post-it on desk** – With key messages, such as 'Hand up!' and 'Do not shout out!'

- **At home** – Rewards for not interrupting. A point system for not interrupting when a specific task is going on – for example, when an adult is on the phone.

- **Incentives** – A point system for every time in the week a child or young person does not interrupt and shows self-control. An agreed reward for a set number of points.

Causes of internalising disorders

Although children and young people with externalising disorders clearly disrupt others as well as their own learning, internalising disorders also have specific implications. The educational performance of children and young people with internalising disorders will be hindered through a lack of attention and confidence to new learning challenges. They are also more at risk for psychopathological disorders and even suicide (Pine et al, 1998).[188]

Some of the key indicators for children and young people experiencing such disorders are being depressed most of the day, loss of interest in normal activities, a change in weight, insomnia, tiredness, loss of self-

---

188 Pine D, Cohen P & Gurley D (1998) The risk for early-adulthood anxiety and depressive disorders in adolescents with anxiety and depressive disorders. *Arch Gen Psychiatry* 55: 56–64.

worth, lack of concentration, and physical symptoms with no apparent physical cause. Causes of internalising disorders include:

■ **Biological** – Some children are born with an innate temperament of behavioural inhibition. This means they have a strong emotional reactions to novelties and are over-sensitive to unfamiliar situations and will withdraw. Children who are behaviourally inhibited are more likely to develop anxiety-type disorders. This predisposition links with family and environmental risk factors.

■ **Cognitive** – Many children have a behavioural inhibition that predisposes them to such difficulties as anxiety and depression. They have a cognitive bias towards negativity. This is important as it is in childhood that most adult anxiety disorders begin. The depressed child will see the glass as being half empty and the anxious child is likely to see the empty box as somewhere a spider could lurk. Both anxious and depressed children likely to interpret ambiguous information in a negative way.

How to support children and young people who have an internalising disorder – challenging thoughts

There are several ways to change the unhelpful thinking styles that are associated with internalising disorders in children and young people.

Attention Bias Modification Treatment, which involves the use of sophisticated equipment to safely expose children or young people to threatening and non-threatening stimuli in order to teach them to pay attention to certain stimuli and ignore others.

Cognitive restructuring, which involves the identification and labelling of distorted and maladaptive thoughts, such as jumping to conclusions, emotional reasoning and over-generalisation. The distorted thinking patterns are challenged and rebutted.

How to help – challenging unhelpful thoughts

☞ **The hot cross bun model**

Cognitive-behavioural therapy (CBT) has become a very well-researched treatment for internalising disorders such as anxiety and depression. It fits well here as the key aim is to change the way a child or young person is thinking.

If a child or young person can learn that it is their thoughts that are the main cause of their difficulties, then the hot cross bun model can be a tool to help them restructure the way they think. It is the negative thought habits that result in them feeling anxious or depressed. So, if the thoughts can be changed, the negative feelings should also change.

A well-presented workbook of how to use CBT on anxiety and depression is *Cognitive Behavioural Therapy Skills Training Workbook.*[189] It both explains the hot cross bun model in detail and provides questions to guide a child or young person towards developing a more positive thinking style. Examples of positive and negative thoughts are presented below.

Negative thought example:

---

189 Hertfordshire Partnership University NHS Foundation Trust (2016) *Cognitive Behavioural Therapy Skills Training Workbook.* Available at: https://www.hpft.nhs.uk/media/1655/wellbeing-team-cbt-workshop-booklet-2016.pdf [last accessed 4 February 2021]

Positive thought example:

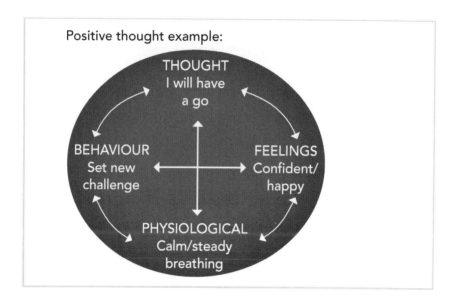

Chapter 23: Building the skills for school success

We know that there is a link between a child or young person who faces adverse experiences and school failure. However, we also know that having adverse childhood experiences does not and cannot offer a prognosis as to the outcome for any specific individual. As Jaime Escalante tells his students: *"You do not enter the future – you create the future. The future is created through hard work."*[190]

Key Point

Many troubled children will enter school lacking in school-ready skills. Without these skills they are already at a disadvantage compared with their peers.

We know that many troubled children will enter school lacking in school-ready skills. Without these skills they are already at a disadvantage compared with their peers. So a useful line of enquiry is: *What are the variables that can explain why one student succeeds, despite their circumstances, while others succumb?*

Core skills needed for school success include:

- Social competence
- Problem-solving
- Autonomy
- Positive thinking
- Emotional regulation
- Belonging
- Consequential learning
- Friendships

Many troubled children and young people need to be taught appropriate skills to cope with the demands they face in school. For example, McLaughlin (2012) argues that these children or young people need first to learn how to manage their intense emotions before they can master higher-order skills such as conflict-management.[111]

---

190 Escalante J (1990) *The Jaime Escalante Math Program*. Available at: https://files.eric.ed.gov/fulltext/ED345942.pdf [last accessed 4 February 2021]

In many primary schools there will be a small number of children who are clearly troubled. Staff know and understand the difficulties and challenges these children face. The school has had these children assessed and a range of support has been put in place. Typically, the support involves:

Nurture group support – Where the children are socialised in small groups to learn social interaction skills.

Play therapy – A psychodynamic approach, usually delivered on a one-to-one basis, which enables children to explore unresolved emotional conflicts.

In addition, the children receive the support of an extra adult (teaching assistant, or TA) in their class. Usually the children who have a range of diagnosed difficulties, including attachment, ADHD, autistic spectrum condition, communication and learning difficulties, receive this support several times each week. Despite this, when the children are in their mainstream class they are extremely volatile with frequent emotional outbursts combined with running out of class. The result is that the TA's role becomes more custodial; they retrieve them when they run and calm them when they cry. For the TA this can become a very thankless daily routine. Often the children enjoy running off, knowing that the TA will come for them.

> ## Key Point
>
> *Adult energy and time should be focused on increasing positive behaviours, not decreasing negative ones.*

To amend this routine, the TA needs to find time to engage with the children. This means that in addition to 'policing' the children, the TAs have a set of meaningful tasks that they are working on to 'support' the children.

It is worth noting that troubled children often habituate to negative feedback. When they misbehave it is as if they know that this will trigger a response in the adult. Without knowing it, every time an adult reacts to a child's inappropriate behaviour, the child is controlling the adult.

For school staff the need is for their energy to be spent on positive behaviours for the child. The aim of the staff is to increase their behavioural repertoire. If a child fights frequently then the adult needs to have a plan of how to respond to this, but more importantly they should look for opportunities to praise the child for not fighting. Adult energy and time should be focused on increasing positive behaviours, not decreasing negative ones.

How to help – supporting troubled children in the classroom

BounceAbility is a flexible programme that provides the TA or other support worker with constructive tasks to work on when supporting troubled children. The aim of BounceAbility is to provide a readily accessible toolbox of activities to carry out with a troubled child. It is designed with primary-age children in mind. It also has the intention of developing a positive relationship between the child or young person and the adult.

Included are eight tools. Each one is briefly explained followed by examples of the techniques that a TA could use to teach, strengthen or develop the skill. It is presented in four stages.

☞ Stage 1: Assessment

First, there is a need to obtain some basic data on the child or young person. To achieve this, the following questionnaire is to be completed by someone who knows the child or young person well. Score each question out of ten.

Social competence

Can the pupil get along with other children?

1	2	3	4	5	6	7	8	9	10

Can they make requests politely?

1	2	3	4	5	6	7	8	9	10

Can they accept other children's feelings?

1	2	3	4	5	6	7	8	9	10

Problem-solving

Can they work with other children on a problem?

1	2	3	4	5	6	7	8	9	10

Can they think of different solutions when stuck?

1	2	3	4	5	6	7	8	9	10

Can they ask for help appropriately?

1	2	3	4	5	6	7	8	9	10

Autonomy

Can they take the lead sometimes?

1	2	3	4	5	6	7	8	9	10

Can they make choices?

1	2	3	4	5	6	7	8	9	10

Can they stand up for themselves?

1	2	3	4	5	6	7	8	9	10

Positive thinking

Can they readily recall happy memories?

1	2	3	4	5	6	7	8	9	10

Can they say two thinks that they enjoy doing?

1	2	3	4	5	6	7	8	9	10

Can they say two things they like about themselves?

1	2	3	4	5	6	7	8	9	10

Emotional regulation

Can they accept being reprimanded?

| 1 | 2 | 3 | 4 | 5 | 6 | 7 | 8 | 9 | 10 |

Can they express anger appropriately?

| 1 | 2 | 3 | 4 | 5 | 6 | 7 | 8 | 9 | 10 |

Can they recognise and name different feelings?

| 1 | 2 | 3 | 4 | 5 | 6 | 7 | 8 | 9 | 10 |

Belonging

Can they display a positive attitude to school?

| 1 | 2 | 3 | 4 | 5 | 6 | 7 | 8 | 9 | 10 |

Can they play an active part in school activities, etc?

| 1 | 2 | 3 | 4 | 5 | 6 | 7 | 8 | 9 | 10 |

Do they willingly attend school?

| 1 | 2 | 3 | 4 | 5 | 6 | 7 | 8 | 9 | 10 |

Consequential learning

Can they understand how their behaviour affects others?

| 1 | 2 | 3 | 4 | 5 | 6 | 7 | 8 | 9 | 10 |

Can they think through the consequences of their actions?

| 1 | 2 | 3 | 4 | 5 | 6 | 7 | 8 | 9 | 10 |

Can they accept responsibility for what they do?

| 1 | 2 | 3 | 4 | 5 | 6 | 7 | 8 | 9 | 10 |

Friendships

Can they express friendliness appropriately?

1	2	3	4	5	6	7	8	9	10

Can they show interest in other people?

1	2	3	4	5	6	7	8	9	10

Can they actively maintain a relationship?

1	2	3	4	5	6	7	8	9	10

☞ Stage 2 - Scoring

Now add together the total of the three questions under each subheading, and divide it by three to reach a final score for that dimension. Transfer these scores to the Wheel of Change below. This is a 'Radar Graph', so the nearer to the centre the score the greater the need for development.

Wheel of change

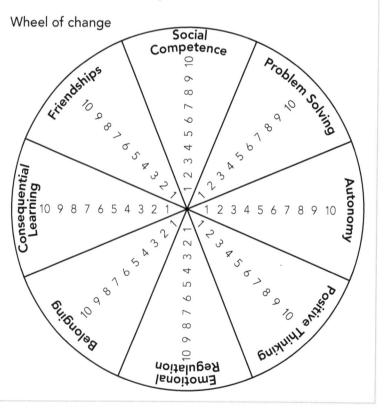

Stage 3 - Targeting

A decision is then made as to which specific skill is to be worked on. It is often preferable to choose a skill where some success can be expected, rather than the most difficult one. Nothing breeds success like success!

Chapter 24: The core skills in depth

Following on from the previous chapter, the Bounceability approach enables children and support workers (usually their TA) to work together to identify specific skills to develop. We have seen that there are eight core skills needed for school success:

- Social competence
- Problem-solving
- Autonomy
- Positive thinking
- Emotional regulation
- Belonging
- Consequential learning
- Friendships

In this chapter, we will examine these skills in more depth and look at practical ways to help children and young people develop them.

Social competence

Competence is a child or young person's belief in being able to set tasks and succeed. They will have an 'I can do it' attitude. This can often be seen in the toddler years when a child will refuse to be helped and insist that 'I can do it myself'. Being competent is about having mastered a skill to a level of proficiency. Children or young people who lack a sense of competency can suffer 'learned helplessness'. That is, they do not believe that they have the skills to effect any change in their life. They can have a victim mentality, which can be the result of many failures leading to feelings of incompetency.

  How to help – social competence

☞ An excellent way to promote competence is to identify a specific skill that the child or young person has mastered, and then provide them with an opportunity to teach or show it to their peers. In addition to this:

- Find opportunities for the child or young person to carry out specific tasks. It may take them longer and it may be done less well, but it shows adult faith and it promotes a sense of competency through sharing tasks.
- Social competence involves having good interaction skills. Involve children or young people in working together to achieve a shared goal that can only be achieved through cooperation, or use games that involve sharing and turn-taking.

Problem-solving

Children and young people are natural problem-solvers. As a species we rely more on our ability to solve problems than any other animal. Much of an animal's behaviour is hardwired into them; they do not have to learn how to fly, swim or burrow. The human infant relies on learning a language and, with support from adults, utilising this language to learn new skills. From being able to use a knife and fork, to solving mathematical problems, we rely on language and adult support. Some ways to promote problem-solving are as follows.

 How to help – problem-solving

☞ You can help with problem-solving skills by talking out loud when you are solving a problem. Identify the problem, then say it out loud. Work out some possible solutions to address the problem. Discuss the pros and cons of each one. Then pick a solution and test it out.

- **Problem:**
  You find that you are often on your own at playtime.

- **Possible solutions:**
  Ask if you can stay in and miss playtimes.
  Pro: Avoids the problem.
  Con: It doesn't help you make friends.

  Ask to join in with a game.
  Pro: Shows initiative.
  Con: You may be rejected.

  Ask an adult to help you find someone to play with.
  Pro: Adult will help and it is safe.
  Con: The other children may tease you for asking for help.

  Pick a solution and test it out.

Other ways to promote problem-solving are role play and the problem-solving ladder. Role play can develop thinking and problem-solving skills - you can role play playground disputes, or being a leader or follower in a group, and explore feelings and solutions to common issues. The problem-solving ladder (illustrated below) teaches children and young people that their choices can help them solve a problem or make a situation worse.

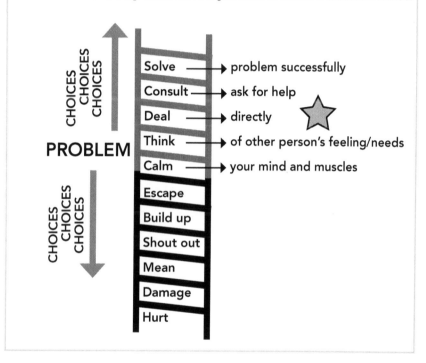

Autonomy

Being able to make choices and decisions freely without being controlled by others gives any child or young person a feeling of personal autonomy. When we are told to do something – for example, 'you must' or 'you should' – there is a natural inborn tendency to refuse to comply because one's personal autonomy is being taken away.

 ## How to help – autonomy

 Sign up – Joining any school or community organisation will promote autonomy through providing opportunities for the child or young person to have an influence on some aspect of their environment.

 Ask me – Teachers, parents and carers giving choices to a child or young person, or actively involving them in decision-making, can help to build their personal autonomy.

 1-2-3 then me – A child or young person is set a task. They think about it for one minute, discuss it with a peer for two minutes and then have three minutes to plan what they intend to do. Only then can they ask for assistance.

Positive thinking

Children as young as five understand the basic principles of positive thinking, i.e. that what you think can affect how you feel. The mind is biased towards expecting bad things to happen because we more readily remember past unhappy events than happy ones. If a child persistently learns to see the threats in situations, they are likely to develop a negative mindset. Children who are more optimistic are less likely to develop depression later in life.

A cautionary note: While positive thinking is an essential skill for all children and young people, there are still key skills that are needed to tackle the challenges they face. As the old saying goes: *"When the going is tough and the path is rough, thinking you can isn't always enough."*

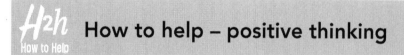 **How to help – positive thinking**

☞ **Teach and practise positive thoughts**

- One thing I like about myself is...
- I feel good when...
- People can rely on me to...
- A recent success was when I...
- A skill I have recently learned is...
- A favourite memory I have is...

☞ **Help the child or young person find words that give them a positive feeling**

Strong	Helpful	Kind
Determined	Clever	Playful
Supportive	Wise	Prepared
Funny	Cheerful	Dependable
Imaginative		

☞ **Find the positive in everything**

Transition has the potential to adversely impact children and young people in a variety of ways, especially those who are already vulnerable.

- When things don't work out as planned, help the children and young people find something good from the experience. *"It rained on our picnic, but it didn't spoil it because..."*
- Think differently when things go wrong: *"Was it a problem or an inconvenience?"*
- Reinterpret past events: *"Remember you didn't want to join the gym club? Just look at how much you love it now!"*

Emotional regulation

As we have seen, self-regulation (or self-control) means that a child or young person is able to manage their own thoughts, feelings and behaviours to reach a goal. It is when a child or young person is able to have impulse control over a short-term desire to enable a longer-term goal to be achieved. A child or young person who can self-regulate is able to focus their attention and ignore distractions. This is a school-ready skill.

How to help – emotional regulation

☞ The Vygotskian Way (for young children)

Adult: "I will show you a picture of an animal, we will all say what the animal is doing, and then we will do the same."

As an example, the adult shows a picture of a rabbit. Everyone says what the animal is doing, i.e. running. Everyone runs on the spot.

For a frog it might be jumping, and for a bear it might be sleeping.

Next, the adult shows the picture silently and the children now give the command to themselves aloud: "Run!", "Jump!", "Sleep!"

Finally, the adult now says: "You will only do what the animal is doing if I say 'please'."

The self-regulated child or young person will be able to make choices between competing options. For young children, self-regulation can be fostered on a daily basis, providing opportunities to make choices. Would you like a glass of milk or water? Shall we play in the garden or go to the park? Remember any game that involves waiting is helping the child to self-regulate.

Belonging

Belonging means that a child or young person has a secure relationship with peers and/or adults. This means that their needs are met, they are kept safe and they will be helped if needed. Having a sense of belonging means that children or young people learn through experience how to be warm, caring, consistent, predictable and open to understand other people's needs.

H²h How to help – belonging

☞ **Familiarity** – Whether at home or school, routines and rituals allow for related experiences to become familiar – for example, having a break and a snack at the same time or special one-to-one time for reading or listening to stories.

☞ **Special time** – This can be when the adult and the child or young person share in an activity that they both enjoy: painting, drawing or building, etc. The activity is the means to an end. Spending time with each other is a way of saying 'I enjoy being with you'.

☞ **PACEful approaches** – For children with attachment issues, the ideas of Dan Hughes (2018) are worth exploring.[191] His model uses **PACE:**

▪ **Playfulness** – "*When children laugh and giggle, they become less defensive and more reflective. Playfulness can help keep it all in perspective... It can also defuse a difficult or tense situation when the parent has a touch of playfulness in his or her discipline.*"

▪ **Acceptance** – Unconditionally accepting a child makes them feel secure, safe and loved. "*Actively communicating to the child that you accept the wishes, feelings, thoughts, urges, motives and perceptions that are underneath the outward behaviour. It is about accepting, without judgment or evaluation, their inner life.*"

▪ **Curiosity** – Without judgement children become aware of their inner life. "*Curiosity involves a quiet, accepting tone that conveys a simple desire to understand the child: what do you think was going on? What do you think that was about?*"

---

191 Hughes D (2018) *Dan Hughes' PACE Model.* Available at: https://share.nelincs.gov.uk/wp-content/uploads/2018/08/Dan-Hughes-PACE-model.pdf [last accessed 4 February 2021]

> ■ **Empathy** – A sense of compassion for the child and their feelings. *"The adult will stay with the child emotionally, providing comfort and support... The adult is also communicating strength, love and commitment, with confidence that sharing the child's distress will not be too much. Together they will get through it."*

Consequential learning

Consequential learning means that a child or young person makes decisions based on knowing the consequences that will result from different choices. For example, a child learns that if they leave their toys out at night they will get wet and possibly damaged – there is a logical/natural consequence to their actions. In social life children and young people learn that they if they are unkind to friends then they are likely to lose them.

 ## How to help – consequential learning

☞ **The Thinking Test** – When about to make a decision, a child or young person is encouraged to answer three brief questions:
■ Why would I want to do this?
■ Are there any negative outcomes if I do this?
■ Are there more rewards than risks in doing this?

☞ **Reflective learning** – When a child or young person makes a behavioural mistake, take time to turn it into a learning opportunity. Ask them what they did and what was the consequence. How do they think they could make amends and what could they do differently next time?

☞ **Practise 'if-then' thinking** – Ask the child or young person to think through different scenarios.
■ If you accidentally broke a friend's pen, then what would happen?
■ If you couldn't afford the cinema ticket for a favourite film, what then?
■ If your friend didn't ask you to their party, what then?

Friendships

Children and young people's friendships have different characteristics at different stages of development. In the early years, children have friends with whom they share imaginative play. In the middle years gender separation is common and the focus is on shared norms and personal preferences. By adolescence, friendship depends on self-disclosure and mutual affection. A common issue across all stages is that having friends during transition times is especially important.

H²h How to help – friendships

☞ **Circle of friends** – This is a way of supporting vulnerable children and young people through peer support. A group of volunteers forms a support network around a child or young person who is experiencing social difficulties. The group meets with the individual to maintain a positive supportive relationship, and also works to problem-solve any issues that arise.

☞ **Sharing play** – Any relationship is built on sharing ideas, activities and resources. Encourage young children to play for short periods where you show them how to share, take turns, etc.

☞ **Show and tell** – Having good social skills is important if children and young people are to develop friendships. Such skills as sharing, cooperating and listening are core friendship skills. While most will learn through observation, some children or young people will need such skills explained to them. A simple model is to *tell* them what the skill is. *Show* them examples of the skill. Let them practise the skill. Then give them feedback for their progress. Remember to break any skill down into smaller parts to help ensure success. A useful reference is *Kid Skills* by Ben Furman. [192]

---

192 Furman B (2003) *Kid Skills*. Available at: https://www.kidsskillsacademy.com/course/kidsskills-for-parents/ [last accessed 4 February 2021]

Part 6:
Complex difficulties and disadvantage

Chapter 25: Children with complex difficulties

This chapter is concerned with children and young people who face additional challenges to those everyday ones all children face. There are many children and young people who have a range of additional needs; these include learning, sensory, physical, emotional and behavioural difficulties.

Key Point

There is a need to ensure that children and young people with profound and multiple challenges are as able to achieve their individual potential as any other children or young people.

Children and young people with such challenges are more at risk of mental health problems than those who do not - research shows that some twenty-five to forty per cent of people with learning disabilities have mental health problems (NICE, 2016).[193] This makes their wellbeing all the more important to include in a resource such as this. For children and young people with additional needs, the medical model has dominated with its emphasis on fixing defects. There is a need to use newer approaches such as positive psychology to ensure that children and young people with profound and multiple challenges are as able to achieve their individual potential as any other children or young people.

If there is a particular challenge in applying the principles of wellbeing to children or young people with SEND, then the group that challenges the principles most are those with Complex Learning Difficulties and Disabilities (CLDD). This group of children and young people, in addition to having learning difficulties, have other significant difficulties such as physical disabilities, sensory impairment or a severe medical condition. Establishing a clear definition of CLDD is no easy task. Porter and Down (2002) described such children with complex needs as:[194]

"... a wide and varied group of learners... including pupils who do not simply require a differentiated curriculum or teaching at a slower pace, but who, at times, require further adaptation to teaching if they are to make progress."

---

193 NICE (2016) *Mental Health Problems In People With Learning Disabilities: Prevention, Assessment And Management.* Available at: https://www.nice.org.uk/guidance/ng54 [last accessed 4 February 2021]

194 Porter J & Down R (2002) *Pupils With Complex Learning Difficulties: Promoting Learning Using Visual Materials And Methods.* Tamworth: NASEN.

At home and in school, these children and young people will require a high level of adult support for their learning and personal care. Some may communicate with gesture, eye pointing or symbols, or using simple language.

Children with CLDD will typically:

- Use a range of communicating strategies including augmented approaches and assisted technologies.
- Have conditions that co-exist and which overlap and interlock resulting in an atypical and uneven profile.
- Have a range of layered needs: mental health, social, behavioural, emotional, physical, medical, sensory, communication or cognitive.

The wellbeing of this group is of particular concern because of they are recognised as having a high degree of mental health problems. A key conclusion reached by a CLDD Research Project (2011) was as follows:[195]

> *"Mental health is the most pervasive and co-occurring need to compound and complicate children's special educational needs and disabilities. In recognition of this, the project has developed supporting information for schools. We recommend that schools consider creating a 'Wellbeing Team' to promote emotional wellbeing in all children and young people and build emotional resilience in those with Complex Learning Difficulties and Disabilities."*

There is a growing number of children and young people with CLDD owing to medical and social challenges. For example, advances in medical science mean that today eighty per cent of children born at twenty-six weeks or less will survive; however, more than fifty per cent of these will have severe and complex disabilities (Marlow et al, 2005).[196] Children with Foetal Alcohol Spectrum Disorders (FASD) are recognised as a group who may have learning difficulties ranging from mild to profound.

---

195 Specialist Schools And Academies Trust (2011) *The Complex Learning Difficulties And Disabilities Research Project Developing Pathways To Personalised Learning*. Available at: https://files.eric.ed.gov/fulltext/ED525543.pdf [last accessed 4 February 2021]

196 Marlow N, Wolke D, Bracewell M & Samara M (2005) Neurologic and developmental disability at six years of age after extremely preterm birth. *N Engl J Med* 352(1): 9–19.

The complexity of conditions experienced by children and young people can be seen in a case reported by Blackburn (2010), who cited a child who was diagnosed with all of the following difficulties:[197]

- Foetal alcohol syndrome
- Autistic spectrum disorder
- Reactive attachment disorder
- Attention deficit hyperactivity disorder
- Sensory integration disorder

So far it has been implicitly assumed that the children and young people we have been concerned with are essentially 'normal' or 'neurotypical'. Yet we know there are many children and young people who are not neurotypical. To omit these from a book on wellbeing would be an omission too far, and unjustifiable. This book is aimed at all children and young people, not just those who fit a set of criteria.

In the account that follows you may find yourself agreeing with some ideas and not with others. Whichever it is, understanding how we can promote wellbeing for these children and young people will strengthen our broader understanding of the key processes involved.

Being publicly owned

When children and young people have a visible physical disability they become public property or, as Pearson (2019) puts it: *"You lose your anonymity, and become public property."*[198] That is, you have to endure being looked at every time you venture out. As a disabled child or young person they have no choice but to cope with the fact that every look from every passerby confirms that they are different from others. This becomes a chronic stress for the individual, something that is inescapable and has to be coped with.

---

197 Blackburn CM, Spencer NJ, Read JM (2010) Prevalence of childhood disability and the characteristics and circumstances of disabled children in the UK: secondary analysis of the Family Resources Survey. *BMC Pediatr* 10: 21.

198 Pearson A (2019) *Eugenics: Science's Greatest Scandal: Series 1 Episode 2.* Available at: https://www.bbc.co.uk/programmes/m00095jf [last accessed 16 February 2021]

A shared humanity with common needs – knowing me, knowing you

The only person you will ever have a real chance to get to know and understand is yourself. When we observe other people we make an assumption of what kind of person they are from their behaviour and language. Yet we can never directly experience the world as they do. When we take a personality test we are put into the boxes that the maker of that particular test believes to be relevant – but they are their boxes, not ours. Are you really an introvert or an extravert? Surely we are too complex to be summarised and pigeon-holed by well-meaning psychologists.

We are each reflections of what it is to be human. At the surface, we are all very different and unique; we each have different tastes in music, food and so on. But because we are all built on the same human blueprint, we have similarities that are common to us all. We all need food, shelter and warmth, but beyond these biological needs there also psychological ones:

- To be safe and secure
- To be accepted and valued
- To relate with others
- To be competent
- To have some autonomy

Central to achieving wellbeing for children and young people with SEND, Bailey (2012) believes that autonomy, competence and relatedness are essential for a sense of wellbeing.[199] Gail Bailey has written extensively on the issues of wellbeing for children and young people with visual impairments, and many of her practical suggestions are equally relevant for children and young people with CLDD.

So, in a way we all share the same needs, although how we achieve them may be different. This is especially true for children and young people with CLDD. Before we consider wellbeing for children and young people in this diverse group, we need to explore the use of labels and the medicalisation of children and young people with such challenges. This is necessary as it throws light on the extent of the challenge.

---

199 Bailey G (2012) *Emotional Well-Being For Children With Special Educational Needs And Disabilities*. London: Sage Publications Ltd.

There are arguments for and against labels: Is it helpful to describe children and young people as having CLDD? The truest answer is *yes and no.*

Yes. It does give some general idea as to the challenges that an individual is facing. They will have a learning disability (increasingly known as an intellectual disability) and will find household tasks more difficult. They will need additional support in these areas of their life. It is helpful to understand that children and young people with CLDD have specific needs that will call for particular initiatives to meet these needs.

Mencap believes that people with learning disabilities face inequalities in every area of life. In 2010 a report by Professor Jim Mansell highlighted the struggle that families of children and young people with profound and multiple learning disabilities had to receive the services and support needed. His report, *Raising our Sights*, argued that this group of people faced discrimination, prejudice and low expectations.[200] Reports continue to support this view. The fact that the services that provide for children and young people with profound and multiple difficulties have been under-resourced for so long means that change is more likely if the challenge is made as a group rather than individuals.

No. "*Every time you label me you dehumanise me*" (Kierkegaard). The only way to know another person is to get to know them. We are all unique. The danger is that we respond to the label and not the individual. So the extreme position would say that there is no such thing as an autistic child, a child with Down's syndrome or a CLDD child – there are simply children with a range of individual strengths, qualities and needs.

The danger of this homogenisation happening with children and young people with CLDD is somewhat less serious, as we shall consider later. Children with CLDD require an intensive, highly personalised learning curriculum. This means that for learning to occur, the child needs to be known and understood. Porter and Down (2002) explain that if these children and young people are to achieve their potential, then they will require educational approaches that go beyond differentiation.[194]

---

200 Mansell J (2010) *Raising Our Sights: Mencap.* Accessed at:https://www.mencap.org.uk/advice-and-support/profound-and-multiple-learning-disabilities-pmld/raising-our-sights-guides [last accessed 16 February 2021]

Chapter 26: The disability paradox

The search for meaning and the need to understand *why* a child or young person has to face and endure the challenges associated with both severe physical and mental conditions is a human trait.

For there to be no reason is both distressing and frustrating, and so often for a parent or carer there is no rational explanation to make sense of what has happened. The questioning of professionals involved rarely results in the sort of answer that parents and carers want.

There is no *why* to explain the unforeseen consequences when numerous random factors collide. When people say *"It was meant to happen, it was fate"*, this is a normal attempt to make some sense of what seems meaningless and unjustifiable. But *fate* implies that there was some purpose, some intention of the consequence happening. We cannot infer intention from consequences that were the result of random events. It would be like asking a lottery winner *"Why did you win?"*

Key Point

No medical explanation can ever fully explain how any syndrome will present itself in an individual, because individuals will always respond in unique ways.

While some factors play a significant role, they are rarely the full story – that is, such factors are not entirely independent but instead partly independent. A neurological cause will be influenced by family factors and the unique personality of the individual will always play an important role. So no medical explanation can ever fully explain how any syndrome will present itself in an individual, because individuals will always respond in unique ways. And as we shall see later, other factors will also affect how well a child or young person will cope with their CLDDs.

Promoting value

The question 'Can life be meaningful for children and young people who face such multiple challenges?' shows both prejudice and a lack of insight and understanding. Without entering into any religious justifications, the following points are relevant:

- We are each ends in our own right; we are not means to an end. Nobody should have to justify their existence, no matter what the circumstances of their birth. You cannot give expectations or duties to someone who played no informed part in what was being decided for them by others.

- We can only understand and appreciate the world through the senses and understandings we have. We cannot imagine how the world may appear to others unlike us. We can use metaphors of what we think it might be like to not have some of our senses, but these are attempts to bridge a gap to make sense of what we cannot understand.

- There are many different ways of knowing and being, and we should not be so egocentric as to believe that our measure of things is the only one. Children and young people with CLDD do not not need language to experience the wind on their face, views of forests or or to feel valued by having an adult just sit and enjoy being with them.

- Children and young people who face multiple challenges have the same rights as any of us, no more and definitely no less. We all have the right of freedom of access, so if appropriate resources, facilities and aids are not provided, you are denying that individual their right.

"The thing is that we only really celebrate disability when there's a skill involved. Take the Paralympics, incredible as they are, they're all about strength, courage and bravery. All I really wanted to do was to celebrate the smallness of it all, of just being in the world without justification. There's joy in the little things… and humour and laughter."[201]

This is a quote from the stand-up comedian John Williams. In one of his shows he talks about his son who has autism. Often the value of who we are is dependent on what we can give to society. So education is seen as being an investment in the future, as the children and young people of today will be the wage-earners and taxpayers of tomorrow. For children and young people with CLDD this is difficult, so what can they give to society? If we can resolve this, we can begin to challenge a social norm that currently disables rather than enables children and young people with CLDD.

The disability paradox

To make sense of this we need first to consider the 'disability paradox'. Neurotypical people (that is, people with a typical brain) believe that people with a disability, whether physical or mental, are living an undesirable and unhappy life. However, the paradox is that a significant number of people

---

201 Williams J (2016) *My Son's Not Rainman: One Autistic Boy, A Million Adventures.* London, Michael O'Mara

with disabilities believe that they have a very good quality of life. There are several aspects to this problem that need exploring. First, the human brain is biased to notice anything different from the usual. So, for example, if in a line of fences there is one at the wrong angle, we are drawn to that one. Similarly, when we see someone who has some physical difference then we are drawn to look twice. We *project* ourselves onto that person.

How would we feel if we couldn't, see, walk, talk or hear? The thought is both terrifying and unimaginable. So we assume that anyone with some functional impairment must be living a less than happy life. As a result we offer pity, not empathy. We can empathise with a friend who has lost their job, because we can more easily imagine being in that situation. But we cannot imagine the unimaginable. We cannot empathise with someone so very different from us.

Key Point

The paradox is that people with disabilities report having the same or an even better quality of life than able bodied, neurotypical people.

We can, though, empathise with people with a functional impairment when they strive to overcome their impairment or show remarkable degrees of bravery. These are the dominant norms we value in our society (Nussbaum, 2011).[202] So when we see people competing in the Paralympics, we see them escaping their condition and overcoming adversity. These are traits we know and understand and therefore we can empathise.

So where is the paradox? We show pity to everyday disability and we empathise on occasions. The paradox is that people with disabilities do not spend their days wallowing in self-pity, wishing they were not disabled. Studies show that despite their apparently negative situation, people with disabilities report having the same or an even better quality of life than able bodied, neurotypical people.

The reason for this is twofold. First, the person with the disability can see all the things they *can* do, rather than what they can't. The normal perceiver can only see and imagine all they couldn't do if it was them. And secondly, there is 'hedonic adaptation'. This is the tendency for humans to always return to a state of relatively stable happiness despite major positive or negative events or life changes (Lyubomirsky, 2012).[203]

202 Nussbaum MC (2011) *Creating Capabilities: The Human Development Approach.* Cambridge, MA: Belknap Press.

203 Lyubomirsky S (2012) *Hedonic Adaptation To Positive And Negative Experiences.* Available at: http://sonjalyubomirsky.com/files/2012/09/Lyubomirsky-2011.pdf) [last accessed last accessed 4 February 2021]

To summarise, from a social perspective, people with disabilities are judged by the norms that are valid for those with no disability. So people with a disability can be doubly disabled – once by the limitations of their condition and once through either failing to meet or not adopting the social expectations of the able-bodied community.

The argument put forward above has far-reaaching implications. In fact, we are now faced with some critical questions as to how children and young people with CLDD are educated. Is it fair to assume that they can learn the same curriculum as neurotypical children and young people and that they can learn in the same way, despite having medical deficits?

We should consider the ideas of Imray and Colley (2017), who present a strong argument that, although we have high ideals for children and young people with CLDD, we do in fact fail them.[204]

The aim to deliver the same curriculum to all children and young people in the same setting was the Holy Grail of the inclusion agenda. This was how a socially inclusive society was to be achieved. The National Curriculum (NC) was introduced by the Education Reform Act of 1988 and implemented in 1989, and it was intended for all neurotypical children and young people aged between five and sixteen. However, the NC was clearly not applicable for children and young people with CLDD.

Expert View

"A person's ability to communicate is not dependent on their being able to master certain skills, it is dependent on our ability to listen and communicate responsively."

Jo Grace (The Sensory Projects)

To bridge the gap for children and young people aged five to sixteen with special educational needs (SEN), performance scales (P scales) were developed. These were to apply to children and young people with SEN who could not access the NC, but could be said to be working towards it. Children and young people considered to have profound and multiple learning difficulties would usually be operating around P1 to P3, and those with severe learning difficulties between P4 and P8. Using this approach, inclusionists could at least argue that all children and young people were broadly under the same education umbrella.

---

204 Imray P & Colley A (2017) *Inclusion Is Dead: Long Live Inclusion*. London: Routledge.

Chapter 27: Abilities and capabilities

The *Capability Approach* was originally developed by Indian economist and philosopher Amartya Sen in the 1980s.[205] He argued that we need to look critically at the way societies value their citizens. In America, the philosopher Martha Nussbaum has shown that this model has important implications for our understanding and valuing children and young people with CLDD.

Influenced by Sen, her model sees each person as being an end in themselves, and not a means to an end. For Nussbaum, people with CLDD are judged on the same criteria as everyone else, resulting in a social injustice. There are two key areas. In reasoning terms, people are valued if they can make rational choices and behave in ways that make sense to other people. In economic terms, is it mutually advantageous to invest in this person? Will they become employable and able to pay their way in society?

How can we deal briefly with these arguments? First, as Nussbaum (2011) says: *"We all, more or less have the same sort of reason."*[202] The way 'normal' people reason is not inherently more or less reliable that the way someone with learning difficulties reasons. It is only conceived differently. Our history is full of examples of flawed reasoning by supposedly rational thinkers. There are many different ways of knowing and reasoning. We cannot exclude those with learning difficulties from the right to have as good a life as we would wish for ourselves.

Second, as long as society holds a contract of mutual advantage between itself and its citizens, those with learning difficulties will be undervalued. If the value of a society's members is always based on the values and experiences of the majority, then – even with the best will in the world – there will be minority groups such as those with CLDD who are excluded and marginalised.

---

205 Sen A (2012) *Sen's Capability Approach.* Available at: https://iep.utm.edu/sen-cap/ [last accessed 4 February 2021]

When these two criteria are applied to children and young people with CLDD, they will clearly fall short. This can help to explain why they are a marginal group in our society. We do not understand them and they are unable to pay their own way.

The *capabilities* model challenges these values. What are capabilities? They are more than abilities. Abilities are what we are can do – '*I have the ability to read*' means '*I can read*'. But '*I have the capability to read*' means that '*given the right support I can learn to read*'.

Essentially:

■ Ability is what you can do
■ Capability is what you could do

So how does this apply to children with CLDD?

It is argued that children and young people with CLDD learn differently from neurotypical children (Imray & Hinchcliffe, 2014) and therefore need to be taught differently. Also, is what is being taught appropriate and relevant?[206] If it is not within the range of possibility for children and young people with CLDD to be successful within the National Curriculum, then we need to question whether should they be taught this curriculum.

Some of the main characteristics of children and young people with learning difficulties are:

■ Difficulty remembering
■ Problems paying attention
■ Difficulties with concepts relating to time
■ Organisational problems

This level of learning ability is most clearly understood when we consider standard developmental milestones for these children and young people, irrespective of age. These are:

---

206 Imray P & Hinchcliffe V (2014) *Curricula For Teaching Children And Young People With Severe Or Profound And Multiple Learning Difficulties: Practical Strategies For Educational Professionals*. Abingdon, Oxfordshire: Routledge/Taylor & Francis Group.

- Notices stimuli
- Object permanence
- Contingency awareness
- Initiates actions to achieve desired results
- Makes choices
- Learns by imitation

These milestones occur for neurotypical children in the first eighteen months of life. They fall into Piaget's sensorimotor stage, which was his first stage of child development. Furthermore, brain studies are finding that the neural pathways in pre-term babies may not be only damaged, but also incomplete (Champion, 2005).[207] The argument that these children and young people can be taught using the same pedagogy and following the same curriculum as neurotypical children essentially means that we continue to give them access to a system that is unsuitable for them (Wedell, 1995).[208]

With the fast-changing techniques in neuroimaging it is feasible that, in the near future, we will be able to identify neural markers or biomarkers to detect learning difficulties in infancy and consequently change their developmental learning trajectory through early interventions (Goswami, 2008).[209]

Expert View

"It is widely accepted that to personalise learning will involve some innovation. We do not have a system for engaging in innovation in education."

David Hargreaves

The idea that the National Curriculum is right for every learner is at the heart of inclusion. For inclusionists, learners may be at different points on the curriculum, but they are all on the same one. But the fact that a curriculum is suitable for the many does not justify it being taught to the few that it isn't suitable for. So, what is the alternative?

---

207 Champion PR (2005) The At-Risk Infant – Approaches To Intervention: The Champion Centre Model. In Carpenter B & Egerton J (Eds.) *Early Childhood Intervention: International Perspectives, National Initiatives And Regional Practice* (pp. 39–52). Coventry: West Midlands SEN Regional Partnership.

208 Wedell K (1995) Making inclusive education ordinary. *Br J Spec Educ* 22(3): 100–04.

209 Goswami U (2008) *Learning Difficulties: Future Challenges, Mental Capital And Well-Being Project*. London: Government Office for Science.

Personalised learning through engagement

As Hargreaves (2006) said, schools need to *"transform their responses to the learner from the largely standardised to the profoundly personalised".*[210]

Before considering wellbeing for children with CLDD it is first worth appreciating the vulnerability of this group, especially as having SEN is the greatest predictor for worsening mental health in children (Department for Education, 2011).[211] Research suggests that children and young people with CLDD are often more isolated from their peers, as the following statistics show:

- Thirty-three per cent of children with learning disabilities find it harder than average to make friends
- Twenty-five per cent find it difficult to make friends
- Fourteen per cent have no friends

In addition, there are important differences between children and young people with and without learning disabilities that can increase their risk of mental health issues. Children and young people with learning disabilities are significantly more likely to be exposed to poverty and social exclusion through circumstances:

- Forty-seven per cent are living in poverty compared to thirty per cent of all children.
- In thirty per cent of households, neither parent is in employment, compared to fourteen per cent of households with children without learning disabilities.
- Thirty per cent of children with learning disabilities live in a single-parent household.

We know with evidence that children and young people with learning disabilities are at much greater risk of having mental health problems than children who do not have learning disabilities. But in addition to the problems risks associated with their disability they are also poorer, live in less advantageous family circumstances and have fewer friends; all of which are known to be associated with an increased risk of mental health problems.

---

210 Hargreaves D (2006) A New Shape For Schooling? In Carpenter B (2010) *Children With Complex Learning Difficulties.* London: SSAT.

211 Department for Education (2011) *Support And Aspiration: A New Approach To Special Educational Needs And Disability – A Consultation.* Norwich: The Stationery Office.

Wellbeing is just as important as a proactive intervention for children and young people with CLDD as for any other children. The important proviso needs to be that to support any child or young person, we need to know them as an individual; or, as Nussbaum (2011) puts it: *"What is each person able to do and to be?"*[202]

Wellbeing for children with complex difficulties

The ideas that follow are general and apply to everyone to some degree, but not to any one person entirely.

A working definition of wellbeing for the purpose of this section might be taken from the Health and Advisory Service (1995), which describes it *"as including, satisfying personal relationships and being able to play and learn appropriate to their age and ability".*[212]

In less prosaic language, wellbeing is really concerned with a person's quality of life and how happy they are, at home as well as in school. Relevant here is the important message from Lyons and Cassebohm (2010): *"The life satisfaction of children with Profound and Multiple Learning Difficulties (PMLD) can be discerned."*[213] They stress that contributions should be taken seriously from family and carers as to the wellbeing of their children. Family and carers know their children well enough to know their likes and dislikes, what makes them happy and what makes them sad.

School staff know what good mental health looks like for any child or young person, and are able to respond to indicators of changes in physical or mental health. For children and young people with limited movement, and those who are wheelchair users, it is important that a 24-hour postural care management plan is in place with input from physiotherapy and occupational therapy at all stages.

---

212 Health Advisory Service (1995) *Together We Stand: Child And Adolescent Mental Health Services.* London: HMSO.

213 Lyons G & Cassebohm M (2010) *Student Wellbeing For Those With Profound Intellectual And Multiple Disabilities: Same, Same But Different?* Available at: https://www.researchgate.net/publication/277061620_Student_wellbeing_for_those_with_profound_intellectual_and_multiple_disabilities_Same_same_but_different [last accessed 4 February 2021]

H2h How to help – wellbeing for children with complex difficulties

☞ **The foundation** stone for working to develop wellbeing in children and young people with CLDD is always to remember that, while each of us may face very different challenges, we are all essentially the same. We all need to feel valued, safe, competent and able to have some fun. Children and young people with CLDD are no different.

☞ A key element in wellbeing for children and young people with CLDD is **engagement with learning**. Adults can ensure that a learner with CLDD is engaging with their curriculum via a user-friendly approach developed by Carpenter (2015)[214]. The approach breaks a learner's engagement down into seven learning components:

- Awareness
- Initiation
- Persistence
- Anticipation
- Discovery
- Investigation
- Curiosity

Through observing a child or young person on each of these components, the adult is able to produce an engagement profile. This then provides information for staff to focus on areas to improve, strengthen and develop, enabling a child or young person with CLDD to more fully and successfully engage with learning. This can become a cornerstone that enhances the senses of wellbeing for any child or young person.

---

214 Carpenter B (2015) *Engaging Learners With Complex Learning Difficulties And Disabilities: A Resource Book For Teachers And Teaching Assistants.* Abingdon, Oxfordshire: Routledge.

There are six major **dimensions of wellbeing** for children and young people with CLDD. It is not a definitive list, and the focus will always vary depending on what is thought to be important for a given individual at a given time, but it is a helpful overview of areas to explore and develop when seeking to evaluate and build the wellbeing of children and young people with CLDD. Examples will be given for each dimension, but each could easily have a chapter in its own right.

- **Friendship** – At the heart of everyone's identity is their relationship with other people. Who we are is to a large part defined by the people we have meaningful relationships with. Every attempt to develop or strengthen friendships for children or young people with CLDD will enhance their sense of wellbeing. Circles of Support is one such example.

- **Competency** – Some children and young people may acquire competency in certain areas while having difficulties in others. Recognising and recording examples of skills a child or young person has will reinforce a sense of personal competency.

- **Control** – Opportunities should be created for children and young people to make choices. These choices should of course be dependent upon their cognitive ability and communication skills.

- **Value** – When adults spend time with children and young people with CLDD they are communicating to them that they are valued. No one has to justify their being in the world and we are all social animals hardwired to attach to our primary carers and enjoy the company of others. So sharing time together, for no extrinsic reason, conveys a sense of being valued.

- **Sensory and Physical** – Music and dance have been found to support children and young people with CLDD. While there may be obvious limitations for some individuals, dance involves factors that are good for a sense of wellbeing - including exercise, music that is typically uplifting and energising, and working with other people.

- **Fun** – When we have fun together it strengthens a bond between us. Laughing at the same time shows that we inhabit the same world and we see things the same way.

Chapter 28: The impact of poverty

We have seen that wellbeing has become something of a Holy Grail. Having looked at the different key factors that play a role in determining a child or young person's wellbeing, there is one final factor that it would be remiss not to consider. This is the disadvantage that many children and young people experience on account of living in poverty, and how this affects their wellbeing. This chapter is not intended to be any kind of political polemic against present or past governments. Often the expression bandied around is that we are on a 'level playing field'. This assumes that all children who come to school are equal, yet the evidence suggests that this is far from true.

> **Key Point**
>
> *Any notions that human traits such as intelligence differ by social class or race are known to be wrong.*

Perhaps it is valid to begin by establishing firmly that any notions that human traits such as intelligence differ by social class or race are known to be wrong. Historically, the early 20th century saw the growth of eugenics as a scientific explanation, seeking to demonstrate that such differences did exist within and between populations. Populations could, it was argued, be improved through selective breeding for those traits that were valued. The generally held view by founders of this approach, such as Francis Galton, was essentially that those living in poverty were poor because they were innately less able than others who were more successful in life.

This view that society should and could engineer the best adults was so pervasive that it shaped the 1944 Education Act in the UK, which had all children sit an exam to determine whether they were university material or more appropriately destined to be labourers. This test has been shown to be culturally biased in that middle-class children, on account of their background experiences, are more suited to pass the test than those from different socioeconomic or cultural backgrounds.

The lengths that supporters of views of this kind would go to has been found to be unscrupulous and deceitful. An example here is the work of Sir Cyril Burt, who claimed that by studying twins who were raised in different social conditions he could prove it was nature that determined a child's intelligence, rather than nurture. His work was found to be fraudulent because his case stories were discovered to be fictitious (Burt, 1981).[215]

Evidence shows that, no matter where in the world one looks, neonates progress in their mother's womb at the same rate. And as we have mentioned in earlier chapters, up until the age of two, all children – providing their mothers have a reasonable standard of living (food, medical care, etc.) – achieve the same developmental milestones, irrespective of race, religion or culture. The way to improve any population is therefore not to filter it, but simply to ensure that all expectant mothers are well cared for.

Today there are government initiatives that would sit well with some eugenicists. The introduction of a two-child limit to Child Tax Credit and Universal Credit will have more effect on families with low incomes by limiting the size of their family, whereas those who are on higher incomes will have more children. Isn't this eugenics by the backdoor?

Expert View

"Poor maternal psychological wellbeing explains around half of the socioeconomic disparity in behavioural and emotional problems, and the effect is strongest for children in poverty."

Haroon Chowdry & Tom McBride[216]

From an educational perspective, one could fairly expect well-off countries to enhance the wellbeing and future prospects of their children and young people through education. Education could be legitimately seen as a way out of poverty, a way to make a society more equal and enhance the wellbeing of all through increased social mobility. However, a study on behalf of the Joseph Rowntree Foundation found that:

"Those young people who live in conditions of relative poverty, however defined, are more likely to attain lower educational outcomes than young people living in relative affluence. Conversely those achieving low educational outcomes are also more likely to then experience poverty."

(Raffo et al, 2006)[217]

---

215 Burt C (1981) In Gould SJ (1996) *The Mismeasure Of Man*. London: Norton WW & Co Ltd.

216 Chowdry H & McBride T (2017) *Disadvantage, Behaviour and Cognitive Outcomes: Longitudinal Analysis from Age 5 to 16*. Early Intervention Foundation.

217 Raffo C, Dyson A, Gunter H, Jones L, Kalambouka A & Hall D (2006) Education and poverty: mapping the terrain and making the links to educational policy. *Int J Incl Educ* 13(4): 341–58.

How prevalent is poverty?

Four million children live in poverty, according to the Children's Society. That is nine in every average classroom. Fifty-three per cent of children in poverty are under five years old.

In America, some 12.8 million lived in poverty in 2017; that is, one in five children. Of these, roughly one in twelve lived in extreme poverty, which is defined as an annual income of less than half the poverty level ($35 a day for a family of four). The number of children under five living in poverty was 3.9 million – 1.8 million of whom were living in extreme poverty.[218]

We are not short of evidence suggesting that a link between poverty and negative wellbeing in children and young people is a risk of mental ill health. To take just one example, in her 2013 annual report on public mental health, England's then Chief Medical Officer Dame Sally Davies identified that children and young people living in disadvantaged socio-economic conditions were at increased risk of mental illness.[219]

Key Point

We are not short of evidence suggesting that a link between poverty and negative wellbeing in children and young people is a risk of mental ill health.

In fact, children and young people aged eleven to sixteen are three times more likely to have severe mental health problems if they live in the bottom fifth of family income when compared with children and young people living in the top fifth. Their health is also more likely to be compromised owing to their mothers' poor nutrition, exposure to stress, and poor working conditions, as well as limited access to poorer-quality public services. Children with lower socioeconomic status have poorer cognitive performance across areas that include language function and cognitive control (attention, planning and decision-making).

218 Children's Defense Fund (2018) *Child Poverty In America 2017: National Analysis*. Available at: https://www.childrensdefense.org/wp-content/uploads/2018/09/Child-Poverty-in-America-2017-National-Fact-Sheet.pdf [last accessed 4 February 2021]

219 UK Government (2013) *Annual Report of the Chief Medical Officer 2013 Public Mental Health Priorities: Investing in the Evidence*. Available at: https://assets.publishing.service.gov.uk/government/uploads/system/uploads/attachment_data/file/413196/CMO_web_doc.pdf) [last accessed 4 February 2021]

Studying poverty in any society can take place at many levels:

- Micro: The individual
- Meso: Immediate social context
- Macro: Social structures, notions of power and inequality

We will be concerned here primarily with the micro level. A report by the Children's Society concluded that children and young people living in poverty have:

- Poorer physical health
- More mental health problems
- Lower achievement at school
- A poorer sense of wellbeing

The result can be a child or young person who believes they are a failure and has a very negative view about their future.

There is no single factor in poverty that can explain why this is. It is like a cocktail effect. Several negative features of poverty such as poor housing or being in debt can put parents and carers into a negative downward spiral from which is is very hard to escape.

How poverty impacts the individual

Living in poverty is at its most damaging when an individual is young and the key developmental processes are taking place. We will consider briefly the effects of disadvantage across four broad areas:

- Brain development
- Emotional and social development
- Acute vs chronic stressors
- Cognitive difficulties

Brain development – Poverty can actually affect neurological growth, which impedes the executive functioning of the prefrontal cortex, where decision-making and self-control is thought to take place. This fact has profound implications for how we think about society, and in particular the cyclical nature of poverty. Put simply, a key reason why many of those who grow up in poverty fail to break free of it may be that their brains simply are not given the opportunity to develop the capacity to do so. They are physically changed, and limited, by their background.

Expert View

"Surveys have shown that a common view about why poor people are poor is that they don't try hard enough. But neurons don't deserve blame or credit. They just behave according to the laws of the natural world."

Martha J. Farah[220]

In an American study (Hanson et al, 2013), children from high-, medium- and low-income families had MRI scans between the ages of five months and four years.[176] The children from the lower-income families had ten per cent lower volumes of grey matter, which is essential for cognitive functioning.

Emotional and social development – There seem to be two kinds of emotions: primary and secondary. Primary ones are innate and universal. Ekman (2004), a major researcher in this area, believes that emotions such as joy, anger, surprise, disgust and fear are dependent on 'hard-wired' neural networks in the limbic system, particularly the amygdala.[59] Secondary or social emotions such as embarrassment, gratitude, forgiveness and cooperation, however, are learned through interaction with others, a process where cognition is intrinsically related.

Children from lower socioeconomic families tend to spend more time watching TV, which is not the best way to learn about emotions and social behaviour. The impact of such experiences can be seen in the behaviours observed in nursery and early learning settings. These include:

■ Acting-out behaviours

■ Impatience and impulsivity

■ Gaps in politeness and social skills

■ Limited range of behavioural responses

■ Inappropriate emotional responses

■ Less empathy

220 Farah M quoted in Sleek S (2015) *How Poverty Affects the Brain and Behaviour.* Association for Psychological Science, August 31 2015.

Acute vs chronic stressors – Chronic stress is when a child experiences negative events continuously over long periods of time. Under such circumstances the child's brain cells do not make connections with others. Acute stress is short-lived but more traumatic for the developing infant.

Cognitive difficulties – These are delays and difficulties in the following cognitive areas:

■ Executive skills

■ Language acquisition

■ Reading

■ Poor background knowledge

'The Matthew Effect'

The various aspects of human development in childhood do not happen independently of each other: they are interconnected. So if a child is exposed to sustained stresses, this will hamper brain development but it is also likely to lead to poor cognitive and emotional development. Similarly, poor emotional development due to a lack of varied stimuli is likely to delay other skills. Teachers report how poverty is affecting their pupils' learning, in that pupils come to school tired, hungry, angry and confused (Weale, 2019).[221] In their research, Wilkinson and Pickett (2018) found that wellbeing was affected by a level of equality – in other words, the greater the inequality, the less wellbeing was reported for children.[222]

There is a clear message here. Wellbeing is important for all children. But there are many who have more specific needs in relation to wellbeing. Therefore, to only address wellbeing in a single, undifferentiated way would be to support the 'The Matthew Effect'

> *"For whosoever hath, to him shall be given, and he shall have more abundance: but whosoever hath not, from him shall be taken away even that he hath."* Matthew 25: 14–29

---

221 Weale S (2019) *Mental Health Of Pupils Is 'At Crisis Point', Teachers Warn.* Available at: https://www.theguardian.com/society/2019/apr/17/mental-health-young-people-england-crisis-point-teacher-school-leader-survey [last accessed 4 February 2021]

222 Wilkinson R & Pickett K (2018). *The Inner Level.* Allen Lane: UK.

Part 7: Conclusion

Chapter 29: Summary

This chapter recaps on the many factors covered in this book that relate to wellbeing and resilience. Given the global pandemic, the wellbeing and mental health of children and young people has become more important than ever before. Understanding the issues involved enables those involved in shaping a young person's experiences, both at home and at school, to provide more effective support. Simple solutions do not exist; however, with deeper understanding interventions can be chosen carefully rather than in a piecemeal fashion. If we are predicting an increase in mental health problems, then we should be able to prepare for it.

Defining wellbeing

There are many key terms that relate and link to each other in this area, and sometimes they are used interchangeably. Having a clearer idea as to the meaning of each one is important if a deeper understanding is to be achieved and obfuscation avoided. An important starting point is to appreciate the similarities and differences between 'wellbeing' and 'mental health'. Essentially, with wellbeing, whether a child or young person has a little or a lot is a matter of degree; with mental health conditions the difference is more clear-cut. For example, while degrees of difference do of course exist, one either has an issue with social anxiety or one does not.

> ### Key Point
> *If we are predicting an increase in mental health problems, then we should be able to prepare for it.*

Furthermore, wellbeing is a relative concept that depends greatly on when and where it is being considered. Wellbeing in the 1920s was not the same as wellbeing in the 1970s, and the post-war 'baby boomers' had very different notions of quality of life to those which will be experienced by children born post-pandemic. Each generation also has its own ideas of how best to parent and educate its young people. Nor is wellbeing the same for children and young people living in affluence compared to those who live in poverty or on welfare benefits.

Developing wellbeing

Throughout this book, the aim has been to show that increasing the wellbeing and resilience of children and young people, while it is always a noble aim, needs to be based on an understanding of core issues. Of particular importance is how stress interferes with development. When children are in a safe context where they experience care and nurture in abundance, the negative effect of any stress is mitigated. This is where children gradually learn emotional self-control, and with it the ability to manage stress in a positive way. When young people are not given an opportunity to learn emotional self-control, stress can spiral out of control with long-term negative consequences for wellbeing.

What works for improving wellbeing

Schools are under constant pressure to show academic progress, and they are expected to do the same with wellbeing. Yet they are faced with a plethora of resources that purport to achieve success in this area. In order to make informed decisions, an understanding of 'evidence-based practice' and the best questions to put to any resource will provide an invaluable touchstone for making good choices. With that said, there are times when a rigid adherence to a scientific approach results in narrow thinking that is not appropriate when studying wellbeing and young people. For example, how children and young people facing the same challenges manage their wellbeing can vary profoundly. To understand this is to understand that when you meet a child with autism, that is exactly what you have met – an individual child with autism. Over generalising from one child with autism to another shows blinkered thinking.

Measuring outcomes

Linked to 'what works' is the question of whether wellbeing can be measured so that progress can be shown. This is a complex matter. Questions need to be answered such as who is seeking the information and for what purpose – measuring what, and for whom,

Key Point

Measuring what, and for whom, are important considerations where wellbeing is concerned.

are important considerations where wellbeing is concerned. Is the measurement to benefit society or the individual? How wellbeing is defined will also make a difference. Is it a property of individuals, or is it in the relationships an individual has with their context? It is only through an awareness of these issues that valid measurements can be obtained and used.

Address the sail as well as the leak

Scientific work on wellbeing was largely overlooked until 1998, when a new form of psychology was developed that went beyond the traditional aim of fixing problems. For Positive Psychologists, just removing the problem was not the answer. The idea was not just to move people from -5 to zero, but to move them from zero to + 5; in other words, to help them maximise their potential and flourish. A simple metaphor makes this clearer. If a sailing boat has a leak, the leak must be fixed. However, it is the sails that enable the boat to move forward. Positive Psychology is concerned with people's sails. How can they be supported in achieving their goals, their ambitions? An old criticism of psychology is that it spends time tracing people's lives into their past, while people are living their lives into the future. So with respect to wellbeing and resilience, Positive Psychology focuses on the strengths that children and young people have. It looks at ways of building their positive emotions.

Positive emotions matter

We seem to readily accept that negative emotions such as fear, anxiety and anger serve an evolutionary function. They enabled our ancestors to survive life in the jungle or the wilderness, where predators were a real threat. Becoming quickly frightened and running away from strange movements or sounds meant that you lived to tell the tale. 'Fight or flight' is the default position triggered in us by unusual and sudden changes in our environment. So such emotions became, over time, hard wired in us. But what of positive emotions? Joy, curiosity and fun also lead us to behave in certain ways. They lead us to engage with our world. To approach new challenges with a sense of excitement and positive anticipation. Whether at home or in school, feeling safe and loved and having a sense of belonging are the emotions children need in order to thrive and grow.

Signature strengths

If we are to help children and young people achieve a sense of wellbeing, then knowing their existing strengths – especially as they relate to wellbeing, and to moderating psychological distress – is just as important, if not more so, as knowing about any deficits or weaknesses. Signature or character strengths are the tools we all need to become the best that we can, and the essential means by which children and young people can achieve their personal potential. And importantly they can be fostered and strengthened. Knowledge of these strengths, for parents and teachers, means that activities can be engaged with that serve a purpose over and above their apparent goal.

The complexities of development

An understanding of how children develop and grow is essential for any programme that aims to enhance wellbeing. While we are more aware of the many factors that play a role in development, how exactly they interact is still not well understood. The same mixture of factors can have debilitating effects in one child but not in another. We see this when we look at twin studies. The same environment, apparently, does not produce identical children, despite identical genes. What is needed is a broader perspective, one that acknowledges the complexity of the process while offering constructive suggestions for our project of wellbeing and resilience.

Building blocks for wellbeing

Emotionally, children depend on adults to gradually learn how to experience and manage a wide range of feelings. Every child must complete set 'tasks' as they develop which grow in complexity. However, the building blocks for later tasks depend upon earlier ones being completed successfully. If not, they will have a negative ripple effect on a child's later development. For example, the child who is deprived of attention in infancy can become an adolescent who needs a lot of attention. Both home and school will be well aware if they contain such an individual. An appreciation of the tasks and challenges associated with different developmental stages will alert adults as to how best to create an environment that supports young people in mastering them. In line with this thinking, more and more schools today are looking at relationships and attachment, and aiming to understand and support children with behavioural problems, rather than simply seeking to manage behaviour.

A mind of their own

Cognitive neuropsychology has enabled us to understand how the human brain enables complex thinking processes to take place. Through learning a language, children gradually become able to monitor and manage their behaviour. We are the only animal with the ability to think about yesterday and plan tomorrow. Language frees us from being bound, as most animals are, to the here and now. So while it is usual for children to make behavioural mistakes before the age of three, after this the acquisition of language allows most of them to improve control of their behaviour. The two-year-old's classic supermarket tantrum becomes the five-year-old's deferred gratification. Such abilities are linked to the development of skills known as executive functioning, located in the frontal cortex, but they also depend on healthy interaction with adults.

The teenage years

Today we have considerable insight into the changes that occur during the teenage years. We understand how the brain goes through a period of reconfiguration that can make adolescents more emotionally volatile. Studies suggest that the brain is not fully developed until young adulthood, that is 24 or 25 years, and during this long period of development family stress can increase. Parents find can find it hard to accept that they are now sharing their home with another adult, not a child, and parenting styles that were once appropriate now sometimes cause more problems than they solve.

Self-care for parents and carers

When exploring the wellbeing and resilience of children and young people, it would be naive to ignore the adults who care for them at home. With the increased pressures placed on parents and carers by the COVID-19 pandemic, self-care becomes all the more important. The old adage "you can't give it away if you haven't got it" applies here. For parents and carers, making time to look after their own emotional and physical wellbeing is essential. This can include reviewing a day for what went well, engaging in a form of physical exercise and staying in touch with family and friends.

A sense of belonging

Research shows that the more pupils feel that they belong to their school, the fewer behavioural problems occur and the greater their overall academic performance. Linked to this is the issue of peer friendships. The one thing young people miss when not in school (as during a pandemic) is contact

Key Point

The more pupils feel that they belong to their school, the greater their overall performance.

with their peers. For adolescents it is being accepted and valued by their peers that matters most. Relying on social media for contact is a poor substitute. Measures of a pupil's sense of belonging to their school and class can provide useful information regarding their wellbeing.

Rethinking behaviour management

Policies that rely on rewards and sanctions to ensure order are now regarded as less and less effective. When data on the use of sanctions is examined, some interesting facts emerge. In mainstream schools a small minority of students often receive the most sanctions – in other words, the same students are punished for not changing their behaviour. This clearly suggests that something is wrong with the model, and that we should understand why and look for alternatives. Sadly, some young people have habituated to the 'stick'; if something happens frequently enough it becomes the norm, and punishment is what they have come to expect. Also there are many children and young people who have social, emotional and mental health problems that contribute to their breaking behavioural rules. Is it fair that they should be punished? Alternative policies that employ restorative practices can produce changes in behaviour in a more effective and compassionate way.

The challenge of the future

It is not uncommon for major life transitions to cause stress in children and young people. Changing schools is an obvious example. Knowing that this is likely to happen enables good practices to be put in place in advance. This is especially important for those who are known to be susceptible to issues of anxiety at such times.

The burden of the past

The mental health difficulties that many children and young people face are not caused from within, but from their past experiences. Many children are troubled because they had too much of what they did not need, and not enough of what they did need. When behaviour is a cause for concern it is best to describe the behaviour as problematic, rather than saying that the child is the problem. The behaviour is best seen as a form of communication. If adults can act as 'behavioural detectives' then they will be better placed to find more positive ways forward. So asking questions like "what has happened to this child?" or "what problem does this child think they have, for their behaviour to make sense?" are likely to be good starting points for an approach based on support rather than punishment.

Becoming resilient through bounceability

Our understanding of resilience has moved a long way from thinking that you either have it or you don't. We now realise that contextual factors contribute as much as temperamental ones. As a result, we can measure resilience and strengthen those 'within child' factors that we know are vital for it, such as self-control. Being able to bounce back from challenges depends on a combination of skills – skills which are evidence-based, and capable of being learned by children and young people.

Wellbeing for all children

All children have the same basic human needs – to be valued, loved and cared for. And they need challenges, and to have some control in their lives. Children who face complex and multiple challenges have the same right as any other child to wellbeing. It is only when the majority understand the similarities they share with these children, rather than the differences between them, that we move closer to being an inclusive society. The 'disability paradox' could usefully be included in every school pastoral curriculum. We should all be valued as 'ends in ourselves' and not just in terms of our potential economic value to society.

To those that have...

We cannot naively believe that wellbeing is equally available to every child and young person. Social inequalities can make achieving wellbeing much harder, but at the same time more important, for some who struggle to obtain basic essentials of food, shelter and warmth. The impact of deprivation on children can be profound. It negatively affects all aspects of their development, and it must be at the forefront of our minds when we are looking to improve wellbeing and resilience in our children and young people, whether at home or in school.

Chapter 30: A last word to parents and carers

Parenting is a deeply moving and satisfying experience, yet at times it can also be frustrating and confusing. Babies do not come with an instruction manual. It is perhaps only when we become grandparents that we have the wisdom and experience to help us understand how best to meet children's needs. For many of us who do not have the benefit of grandparents close by, the Internet, social media and books such as this one must try to fill the knowledge gap.

There is no one parenting style that is ideal for everyone. What is effective at one age may not be useful later. What works well for one child may not work for their siblings. Treating our children as if they were all the same would be wrong. So how can we be consistent and ensure fairness on such shifting sands? Being true to our principles but flexible in what we do is the answer.

When we really engage with a child about how he or she learns, it becomes clear that some factors are internal to the child (for instance a preference for reading, or listening, or 'hands-on' learning), but there are also many important factors that relate to the environment. Where possible, changes should be made that will enable the child to focus, concentrate and produce his or her best work.

Key Point

We show them daily that they are valued. We support their friendships and stimulate their minds. Parents and carers are wellbeing practitioners.

It is important to know that building wellbeing and resilience is a natural process within any family. You are not required to read books to have high levels of wellbeing and resilience. We all teach our children core self-care skills. Through encouragement we help them to accept failures, learn from mistakes and try again. This is the stuff of resilience. We show them daily that they are valued. We support their friendships and stimulate their minds with games. Parents and carers are wellbeing practitioners. There can be times when we feel unsure if we are on the right track. We hear so much about children's wellbeing and mental health that we question ourselves: "Am I doing it correctly?" At such times, resources such as this book can help allay unnecessary fears and anxieties. It will probably confirm most of what you are already doing. It may suggest new ideas, or you may find a technique that is helpful. Sometimes, an idea might not work for you 'off the peg' but you can quickly adapt it.

On the other hand, there may be times when for unknown reasons a child seems not to be thriving. Perhaps they focus too readily on what they can't do and appear to develop a negative outlook on life. While there is no obvious problem, you just 'know' that their wellbeing is at risk. At such times, a resource such as this can provide a way forward. Perhaps it will put into words some of your fears, offer reassurance and provide a range of practical ideas and resources to address your concerns.

Our aim is to be 'good enough' parents and carers. Our young people are works in progress. They have yet to master many skills. Our commitment is to be there for them, and to offer support and encouragement. The future wellbeing and resilience of our children can be developed. Tomorrow belongs to those who prepare for it today.

Chapter 31: A last word to teachers and schools

The wellbeing and resilience of children and young people in some form has always been the concern of teachers, and the ethos that today's senior management teams seek to promote in schools is typically one of mutual respect between adults and learners.

However, the changes of the past that shaped the educational system that we know today have not always been conducive to individual wellbeing. The drive for better and better academic results has marginalised some learners. Students who, for a range of different reasons, could not keep pace and meet the required levels of progress and achievement became less desirable.

This meant that some schools found themselves being expected to take in more and more at risk children and young people. Indeed, we know that for a combination of reasons the number of children with social, emotional and mental health issues in any class is rising. Teachers and support staff are increasingly seen as frontline workers with respect to wellbeing and mental health issues.

The increase in whole school approaches to wellbeing is a reflection of the invaluable role that schools play in the broader development on children and young people's wellbeing and resilience. These approaches see the value of a universal strategy so that all children can benefit, and

Key Point

The uncertain times we live in make education more important than ever before for the future success of our children and young people.

such a model has many advantages. No children or young people are omitted or overlooked; programmes can be cheaper to deliver, and the risk of stigma for children is reduced as everyone is governed by the same principles and policies. A drawback, which in the right circumstances can justify a more targeted approach, is that the staff involved in delivering wellbeing and resilience programmes are not specialists, and at risk children might benefit from more intensive forms of support. Often a combination of these two philosophies can prove to be the most appropriate way forward.

Overall, it is abundantly clear that schools, teachers and support staff make a significant contribution to the levels of wellbeing and resilience of all children. For at risk and vulnerable learners, they can make all the difference. Fundamentally, there are two ways to increase wellbeing in the classroom. It can be successfully 'taught' as a curriculum activity. It can also be 'caught', through young people seeing staff show care and compassion to each other. Successful schools do both.

The uncertain times we live in make education in all its forms more important than ever before for the future success of our children and young people. As ever schools must be in the vanguard, strengthening and supporting the wellbeing and resilience of all learners.

Index of *How to Help* advice

References

Albee GW, Bond LA & Cook Monsey TV (1992) *Improving Children's Lives: Global Perspectives On Prevention*. Thousand Oaks, CA: Sage.

Allen KA & Bowles T (2012) Belonging as a guiding principle in the education of adolescents. *Aust J Educ Dev Psychol* 12: 108–19.

Arsenio W, Gold J & Adam E (2006) Children's Conceptions And Displays Of Moral Emotions. In Killen M & Smetana J (Eds.) *Handbook Of Moral Development* (pp. 581–609). Mahwah, NJ: Lawrence Erlbaum Associates.

Arslan G & Duru E (2017) Initial development and validation of the school belongingness scale. *Child Ind Res* 10(4): 1,043–58.

Bailey G (2012) *Emotional Well-Being For Children With Special Educational Needs And Disabilities*. London: Sage Publications Ltd.

Barkley RA & Murphy KR (2006) *Attention-Deficit Hyperactivity Disorder: A Clinical Workbook* (3rd ed.). New York: Guilford Press.

Bates J, Pettit G, Keiley M, Laird R & Dodge K (2007) Predicting the developmental course of mother-reported monitoring across childhood and adolescence from early proactive parenting, child temperament, and parents' worries. *J Fam Psychol* 21(2): 206–17.

Batmanghelidjh C (2007) *Shattered Lives: Children Who Live With Courage And Dignity*. London: Jessica Kingsley Publishers.

Ben-Arieh A & Frones I (2011) Taxonomy for child well-being indicators: A framework for the analysis of the well-being of children. *Childhood* 18(4): 460–76.

Bell CC, McBride DF (2010) Affect regulation and prevention of risky behaviours. *JAMA* 304(5): 565–66.

Belsky J & Pluess M (2009) The nature (and nurture) of human plasticity in early development. *Perspect Psychol Sci* 4(4): 345–41.

Biesta G (2007) Why 'What Works' won't work: Evidence-based practice and the democratic deficit in educational research. *Educ Theory* 57(1):1–22.

Blackburn CM, Spencer NJ, Read JM (2010) Prevalence of childhood disability and the characteristics and circumstances of disabled children in the UK: secondary analysis of the Family Resources Survey. *BMC Pediatr* 10: 21.

Blakemore SJ (2018) *Inventing Ourselves: The Secret Life of the Teenage Brain*. London: Doubleday.

Borkowski JG & Burke JE (1996) Theories, Models And Measurements Of Executive Functioning: An Information Processing Perspective. In Lyon GR & Krasnegor NA (Eds.) *Attention, Memory and Executive Function* (pp. 235–62). Baltimore, MD: Paul H. Brookes Publishing Co.

Bornstein MH, Jager J & Steinberg LD (2013) Adolescents, Parents, Friends/Peers: A Relationships Model. In Weiner I, Lerner RM, Easterbrooks MA & Mistry J (Eds.) *Handbook Of Psychology, Vol 6: Developmental Psychology* (2nd ed., pp. 393–434). New York, NY: Wiley.

Bornstein M, Davidson L, Keyes CLM & Moore KA (2012) *Well-Being: Positive Development Across The Life Course*. Mahwah, NJ: Lawrence Erlbaum Associates.

Bowlby J (1998) *Separation: Anxiety And Anger: Attachment And Loss (Volume 2)*. New York, NY: Pimlico.

Brassai L, Piko BF & Steger MF (2011) Meaning in life: is it a protective factor for adolescents' psychological health? *Int J Behav Med* 18: 44–51.

Briefel R (1999) *Universal-Free School Breakfast Program Evaluation Design Project: Review Of Literature On Breakfast And Learning*. Princeton, MJ: Mathematica Policy Research.

Bronfenbrenner U (1979) *The Ecology Of Human Development.* Cambridge, MA: Harvard University Press.

Brown E, Khan L & Parsonage M (2012) *A Chance To Change: Delivering Effective Parenting Programmes To Transform Lives.* London: Centre for Mental Health.

Bruner J (1996) *The Culture Of Education.* Cambridge, MA: Harvard University Press.

Bryan T & Bryan J (1991) Positive mood and math performance. *J Learn Disabil* 24(8): 490–94.

Burt C (1981) In Gould SJ (1996) *The Mismeasure Of Man.* London: Norton WW & Co Ltd.

Cairns K (2001) The Effects Of Trauma On Childhood Learning. In Jackson S (Ed.) *Nobody Ever Told Us School Mattered: Raising The Attainments Of Children In Public Care.* London: British Association for Adoption and Fostering (BAAF).

Caldji C, Tannenbaum B, Sharma S, Francis D, Plotsky P & Meaney M (1998) Maternal care during infancy regulates the development of neural systems mediating the expression of fearfulness in the rat. *Proc Natl Acad Sci USA* 95(9): 5,335–40.

Cameron RJ & Maginn C (2009) *Achieving Positive Outcomes For Children In Care.* London: SAGE.

Carr A (1999) *Handbook Of Child And Adolescent Clinical Psychology: A Contextual Approach.* London: Routledge.

Carpenter B (2015) *Engaging Learners With Complex Learning Difficulties And Disabilities: A Resource Book For Teachers And Teaching Assistants.* Abingdon, Oxfordshire: Routledge.

Casey BJ & Caudle K (2013) The teenage brain: self control. *Curr Dir Psychol Sci* 22(2): 82–87.

Casey B (1994) In Howe A & Richards V (Eds.) (2011) *Bridging The Transition From Primary To Secondary School.* Oxford: Routledge.

Champion PR (2005) The At-Risk Infant – Approaches To Intervention: The Champion Centre Model. In Carpenter B & Egerton J (Eds.) *Early Childhood Intervention: International Perspectives, National Initiatives And Regional Practice* (pp. 39–52). Coventry: West Midlands SEN Regional Partnership.

Children's Defense Fund (2018) *Child Poverty In America 2017: National Analysis.* Available at: https://www.childrensdefense.org/wp-content/uploads/2018/09/Child-Poverty-in-America-2017-National-Fact-Sheet.pdf [last accessed 4 February 2021]

Children's Society (2019) *The Good Childhood Report 2019.* Available at: https://www.understandingsociety.ac.uk/research/publications/525853 [last accessed 16 February 2021]

Clark AC, Martinez MM, Mize-Nelson J, Wiebe SA & Espy K (2014) Children's Self-Regulation And Executive Control: Critical for Later Years. In Landry SH & Cooper CL (Eds.) *Wellbeing: A Complete Reference Guide, Volume 1: Wellbeing in Children and Families.* Hoboken, NJ: Wiley-Blackwell.

Clarke J (1998a) *Growing Up Again: Helping Ourselves, Helping Our Children.* Seattle, WA: Parenting Press.

Claxton G (2018) *The Learning Power Approach.* Carmarthen: Crown House Publishing.

Cohen S, Doyle WJ, Skomere DP, Fireman P, Gwaltney JM & Newsom JT (1995). State and trait negative affect as predictors of objective and subjective symptoms of respiratory viral infections. *J Pers Soc Psychol* 68(1): 159–69.

Coleman J & Hagell A (2007) *Adolescent Risk And Resilience: Against The Odds.* Chichester, West Sussex: John Wiley & Sons, Ltd.

Coleman J & Hendry L (1999) *The Nature Of Adolescence.* London: Routledge.

Cooper-Kahn J & Dietzel L (2008) *Late, Lost And Unprepared.* Bethesda, USA: Woodbine House Incs.

Connor JM (2012) Physical Activity And Well-Being. In Bornstein M, Davidson L, Keyes C & Moore C (Eds.) *Well-Being Positive Development Across The Life Course.* New York: Psychology Press.

Colley D & Cooper P (2017) *Attachment and Emotional Development in the Classroom: Theory and Practice*. London: Jessica Kingsley Publishing.

Craig-Martin M (2015) *On Being An Artist*. UK: Art/Books.

Creasey G, Jarvis P & Knapcik E (2009) A measure to assess student–instructor relationships. *IJ-SoTL* (2): 14.

Csikszentmihalyi M (1990) *Flow: The Psychology Of Optimal Experience*. New York, NY: Harper and Row.

Daniel B & Wassel S (2002) *Assessing And Promoting Resilience In Vulnerable Children 1: The Early Years*. London: Jessica Kingsley Publishers.

Davis N (2017) *Self-Harm Among Girls Aged 13 To 16 Rose By 68% In Three Years, UK Study Finds*. Available at: https://www.theguardian.com/society/2017/oct/18/self-harm-girls-aged-13-to-16-rose-68pc-three-years [last accessed 4 February 2021]

De Bellis M, Hooper S, Spratt E, Woolley D (2001) Neuropsychological findings in childhood neglect and their relationships to pediatric PTSD. *J Int Neuropsychol Soc* 15(6): 868–78.

Department for Education (2011) *Support And Aspiration: A New Approach To Special Educational Needs And Disability – A Consultation*. Norwich: The Stationery Office.

Department for Education (2014) *The Impact Of Pupil Behaviour And Wellbeing On Educational Outcomes*. Available at: https://www.gov.uk/government/publications/the-impact-of-pupil-behaviour-and-wellbeing-on-educational-outcomes [last accessed 15 February 2021]

Department for Education (2016) *Behaviour And Discipline In Schools: Advice For Headteachers And School Staff*. Available at https://assets.publishing.service.gov.uk/government/uploads/system/uploads/attachment_data/file/488034/Behaviour_and_Discipline_in_Schools_-_A_guide_for_headteachers_and_School_Staff.pdf [last accessed 4 February 2021]

Department for Education (2017) *Permanent And Fixed Period Exclusions In England: 2015 To 2016*. Available at: https://assets.publishing.service.gov.uk/government/uploads/system/uploads/attachment_data/file/645075/SFR35_2017_text.pdf [last accessed 4 February 2021]

Department for Education (2018) *Mental Health And Behaviour In Schools*. Available at: https://assets.publishing.service.gov.uk/government/uploads/system/uploads/attachment_data/file/755135/Mental_health_and_behaviour_in_schools__.pdf [last accessed 4 February 2021]

DeCharms R (1968) *Personal Causation: The Internal Affective Determinants Of Behavior*. New York: Academic Press.

Denckla MB (1996) A Theory And Model Of Executive Function: A Neuropsychological Perspective. In Lyon GR & Krasnegor NA (Eds.) *Attention, Memory and Executive Function* (pp. 263–78). Baltimore, MD: Paul H. Brookes Publishing Co.

Devon N (2019) *Archie Tragedy Tells Us We Can't Blame Tech For Mental Ill Health*. Available at: https://www.pressreader.com/uk/tes-times-education-supplement/20190201/page/8 [last accessed at 4 February 2021]

Devereux Advanced Behavioral Health Center for Resilient Children (2021) *Devereux Early Childhood Assessment (DECA) Preschool Program, Second Edition*. Available at: https://centerforresilientchildren.org/preschool/assessments-resources/the-devereux-early-childhood-assessment-preschool-program-second-edition/ [accessed 4 February 2021]

Dix P (2017) *When The Adults Change, Everything Changes*. Wales: Independent Thinking Press.

Dogra C, Warner-Gale F & Parkin A (2018) *A Multidisciplinary Handbook Of Child And Adolescent Mental Health*. London: Jessica Kingsley Publishers.

Doll B & Lyon M (1998) Risk and resilience: implications for the practice of school psychology. *Sch Psychol Rev* 27(3): 348–63.

Doll B (2014) Enhancing Resilience In The Classroom. In Goldstein S & Brooks RB (Eds.) *Handbook Of Resilience In Children*. London: Springer.

Dweck CS & Leggett EL (1988) A social-cognitive approach to motivation and personality. *Psychol Rev* 95(2): 256–73.

Ein-Dor T (2014) Facing danger: How do people behave in times of need? The case of adult attachment styles. *Front Psychol* 5: Article 1,452.

Ekman P (2004) *Emotions Revealed: Understanding Faces And Feelings.* St Ives, UK: Phoenix Paper Ball.

Eliot L (1999) *What's Going On In There?: How The Brain And Mind Develop In The First Five Years Of Life.* New York, NY: Bantam Books.

Elkind D (2009) In Scarlett W, Chin Ponte I and Singh J (2009) *Approaches To Behavior And Classroom Management: Integrating Discipline And Care.* Newbury Park, CA: Sage.

Elton Report (1989) *Discipline In Schools: Committee Of Enquiry Report.* London: Her Majesty's Stationery Office.

Erikson EH (1993) *Childhood And Society.* New York, NY: Norton.

Escalante J (1990) *The Jaime Escalante Math Program.* Available at: https://files.eric.ed.gov/fulltext/ED345942.pdf [last accessed 4 February 2021]

Faber A & Mazlish E (2012) *How To Talk So Kids Will Listen And Listen So Kids Will Talk.* London: Templar Publishing.

Fagot BI (1997) Attachment, parenting, and peer interactions off toddler children. *Dev Psychol* 33(3): 489–99.

Fassbender C, Murphy K, Foxe J & Wylie J (2004) A topography of executive functions and their interactions revealed by functional Magnetic Resonance Imaging. *Brain Res Cogn Brain Res* 20(2): 132–43.

Fear RM (2017) *Systematic Desensitisation For Panic And Phobia.* Oxford: Karnac Books Ltd.

Felitti V, Anda F, Nordenberg D, Williamson D, Spitz A, Edwards V, Koss M & Marks J (1998) Relationship of childhood abuse and household dysfunction to many of the leading causes of death in adults: the adverse childhood experiences (ACE) Study. *Am J Prev Med* 20(2): 245–58.

Foege WH (2003) Foreword. In Bornstein MH, Davidson L, Keyes CLM, Moore KA (Eds.) (2012) *Well-Being: Positive Development Across The Life Course.* Mahwah, NJ: Lawrence Erlbaum Associates.

Ford G (2006) *The New Contented Little Baby Book.* London: Vermilion.

Fonagy P (2014) *What Works For Whom?: A Critical Review Of Treatments For Children And Adolescents.* New York, NY: Guilford Press.

Frances P (2013) *Coin Metaphor* (E Berne). Available at: http://understandingta.blogspot.com/2013/06/transactional-analysis-in-psychotherapy_15.html [last accessed 4 February 2021]

Frankl V (2004) *Man's Search For Meaning.* London: Rider.

Fredrickson B (2001) The role of positive emotions in positive psychology. *Am Psychol* 56(3): 218–26.

Fredrickson B (2004) The broaden-and-build theory of positive emotions. *Philos Trans R Soc London B Biol Sci* 359(1449): 1,367–78.

Fredrickson B & Branigan C (2005) Positive emotions broaden the scope of attention and thought-action repertoires. *Cogn Emot* 19(3): 313–32.

Frick P & Cornell AH (2007) The moderating effects of parenting styles in the association between behavioral inhibition and parent-reported guilt and empathy in preschool children. *J Clin Child Adolesc Psychol* 36(3): 305–18.

Furlong M, Gilman R & Huebner E (2014) *Handbook Of Positive Psychology In Schools.* Abingdon, Oxfordshire: Routledge.

Furman B (2003) *Kid Skills.* Available at: https://www.kidsskillsacademy.com/course/kidsskills-for-parents/ [last accessed 4 February 2021]

Galton M, Gray J & Ruddock J (1999) *The Impact Of School Transitions And Transfers On Pupil Progress And Attainment.* Research Report RR131. Nottingham: DfEE.

Garcia C (2015) *How Poverty Affects the Brain And Behaviour.* Available at: https://www. psychologicalscience.org/observer/how-poverty-affects-the-brain-and-behavior [last 16 February 2021]

Gilman R (2001) The relationship between life satisfaction, social interest, and frequency of extracurricular activities in adolescent students. *J Youth Adolesc* 30: 749–67.

Gimp Monkeys (2012) *Gimp Monkeys.* Available at: https://www.tetongravity.com/video/ski/ Gimp-Monkeys-1796173 [last accessed 4 February 2021]

Giedd JA, Snell JW, Lange N, Rajapakse JC, Casey BJ, Kozuch PL (1996) Quantitative magnetic resonance imaging of human brain development: Ages 4–18. *Cereb Cortex* 6(4): 551–60.

Goleman D (2005) *Emotional Intelligence.* London: Bloomsbury Publishing.

Goldstein S & Brooks RB (2014) *Handbook Of Resilience in Children.* London: Springer.

Goodenow C (1993) The psychological sense of school membership among adolescents: Scalke development and educational correlates. *Psychol Sch* 30: 79–90.

Goodenow C & Grady KE (1993) The relationship of school belonging and friends' values to academic motivation among urban adolescent students. *J Exp Educ* 62(1): 60–71.

Goswami U (2008) *Learning Difficulties: Future Challenges, Mental Capital And Well-Being Project.* London: Government Office for Science.

Gowing A (2019) Peer–peer relationships: A key factor in enhancing school connectedness and belonging. *Educ Child Psychol* 36(2): 64–77.

Graham S & Harris KR (1996) Addressing Problems In Attention, Memory And Executive Functioning: An Example From Self-Regulated Strategy Development. In Lyon GR & Krasnegor A (Eds.) *Attention, Memory And Executive Function* (pp. 263–79). Baltimore, MD: Brookes.

Greene D, Lepper MR & Nisbett RE (1973) Undermining children's intrinsic interest with extrinsic reward: A test of the "overjustification" hypothesis. *J Pers Soc Psychol* 28(1): 129–37.

Grusec, J, Saritas D & Daniel E (2014) The Nature of Effective Parenting: Some Current Perspectives. In Landry SH & Cooper CL (Eds.) *Wellbeing In Children And Families* (Vol 1, pp. 157–77). Hoboken, NJ: Wiley-Blackwell.

Hagenaars M, Stins J & Roelofs K (2011) Aversive life events enhance human freezing responses. *J Exp Psychol* 141(1): 98–105.

Hamblin J (2015) *The Paradox Of Effort: A Medical Case Against Too Much Self-Control.* Available at: https://www.theatlantic.com/health/archive/2015/07/the-health-cost-of-upward-mobility/398486/ [last accessed 4 February 2021]

Hanson J, Hair N & Shen D (2013) Family poverty affects the rate of human infant brain growth. *PLoS One* 8(12): e80954.

Hare T, Tottenham N, Galvan A, Voss HU, Glover G & Casey B (2008) Biological substrates of emotional reactivity and regulation in adolescence during an emotional go-nogo task. *Biol Psychiatry* 63(10): 927–34.

Hargreaves DH (1996) *Teaching As A Research Based Profession: Possibilities And Prospects.* London: Teacher Training Agency.

Hargreaves D (2006) A New Shape For Schooling? In Carpenter B (2010) *Children With Complex Learning Difficulties.* London: SSAT.

Health Advisory Service (1995) *Together We Stand: Child And Adolescent Mental Health Services.* London: HMSO.

Hertfordshire Partnership University NHS Foundation Trust (2016) *Cognitive Behavioural Therapy Skills Training Workbook.* Available at: https://www.hpft.nhs.uk/media/1655/wellbeing-team-cbt-workshop-booklet-2016.pdf [last accessed 4 February 2021]

Howard-Jones P (2014) Neuroscience and education: myths and messages. *Nat Rev Neurosci* 15: 817–24.

Howe A (2010) Managing Primary – Secondary Transfer. In Howe A & Richards V (Eds.) *Building Transition From Primary To Secondary School* (p. 158). Abingdon, Oxfordshire: Routledge/Taylor & Francis Group.

Hughes D (2018) *Dan Hughes' PACE Model.* Available at: https://share.nelincs.gov.uk/wp-content/uploads/2018/08/Dan-Hughes-PACE-model.pdf [last accessed 4 February 2021]

Imray P & Colley A (2017) *Inclusion Is Dead: Long Live Inclusion.* London: Routledge.

Imray P & Hinchcliffe V (2014) *Curricula For Teaching Children And Young People With Severe Or Profound And Multiple Learning Difficulties: Practical Strategies For Educational Professionals.* Abingdon, Oxfordshire: Routledge/Taylor & Francis Group.

Inhelder B & Piaget J (1958) *The Growth Of Logical Thinking: From Childhood To Adolescence.* New York, NY: Basic Books.

Joseph Rowntree Foundation (2016) *Creating Anti-Poverty Childcare System.* Available at: https://www.jrf.org.uk/report/creating-anti-poverty-childcare-system [last accessed 4 February 2021]

Karpov Y (2014) *Vygotsky For Educators.* New York, NY: Cambridge University Press.

Kay L (2019) *School Readiness, Governance And Early Years Ability Grouping.* Available at: https://journals.sagepub.com/doi/abs/10.1177/1463949119863128 [last accessed 4 February 2021]

Kelly G & Lernihan U (1974). Kinship Care As A Route to Permanent Placement. In Iwaniec D (Ed.) (2006) *The Child's Journey Through Care: Placement Stability, Care Planning, And Achieving Permanency* (pp. 99–112). Hoboken, NJ: Wiley-Blackwell.

Klein M (1994) Cited in Hall L (2015) *Coaching In Times Of Crisis And Transformation.* London: Kogan Page Limited.

Kochanska G (1997) Multipole pathways to conscience for children with different temperaments: From toddlerhood to age 5. *Dev Psychol* 33: 228–40.

Kohn A (1999) *Punished By Rewards.* New York, NY: Houghton Mifflin Company.

Krumwiede A (2014) *Attachment Theory According To John Bowlby And Mary Ainsworth.* Norderstedt, Germany: Open Publishing.

Kumpulainen K, Rasanen E, Henttonen I & Almqvist F (1998) Bullying and psychiatric symptoms among elementary school aged children. *Child Abuse Negl* 22: 705–17.

Kvernbekk T (2017) *Evidence-Based Educational Practice.* Available at: https://oxfordre.com/education/view/10.1093/acrefore/9780190264093.001.0001/acrefore-9780190264093-e-187 [last accessed 4 February 2021]

Ladd G (2005) *Children's Peer Relations And Social Competence: A Century Of Progress.* New Haven, CT: Yale University Press.

Ladd G, Kochenderfer-Ladd B & Sechler C (2014) Classroom Peer Relations As A Context For Social And Scholastic Development. In Landry S & Cooper CL (Eds.) *Wellbeing In Children And Families* (pp. 243–70). Oxford: John Wiley & Sons, Ltd.

Ladd G, Kochendefer-Ladd B, Visconti K & Ettekal I (2012) *Children's Classroom Peer Relationships And Social Competence As Resources For Learning And Achievement At School.* Charlotte, NC: Information Age Publishing.

Landsford J (2012) Boys' and girls' relational and physical aggression in nine countries. *Aggress Behav* 38(4): 298–308.

Lengua L (2008) *Anxiousness, Frustration, And Effortful Control As Moderators Of The Relation Between Parenting And Adjustment In Middle-Childhood.* Available at: https://onlinelibrary.wiley.com/doi/abs/10.1111/j.1467-9507.2007.00438.x [last accessed 4 February 2021]

Lyons G & Cassebohm M (2010) *Student Wellbeing For Those With Profound Intellectual And Multiple Disabilities: Same, Same But Different?* Available at: https://www.researchgate.net/

publication/277061620_Student_wellbeing_for_those_with_profound_intellectual_and_multiple_ disabilities_Same_same_but_different [last accessed 4 February 2021]

Lyubomirsky S (2012) *Hedonic Adaptation To Positive And Negative Experiences.* Available at: http://sonjalyubomirsky.com/files/2012/09/Lyubomirsky-2011.pdf) [last accessed last accessed 4 February 2021]

Marcia J (1966) *Identity Development Theory.* Available at: https://courses.lumenlearning.com/ adolescent/chapter/identity-development-theory/ [last accessed 4 February 2021]

Matsumoto D (2000) *Culture And Psychology: People Around The World* (2nd ed.). Belmont, CA: Wadsworth/Thomson Learning.

Mace R (2019) *All Together Now: Why Schools Should Foster A Sense Of Belonging.* Available at: https://www.tes.com/magazine/article/why-schools-should-foster-sense-of-belonging [last accessed 4 February 2021]

Marlow N, Wolke D, Bracewell M & Samara M (2005) Neurologic and developmental disability at six years of age after extremely preterm birth. *N Engl J Med* 352(1): 9–19.

Maslow A (1971) *The Farther Reaches Of Human Nature.* New York, NY: Viking Press.

Masten AS & Coatsworth JD (1998) The development of competence in favourable and unfavourable environments: Lessons from research on successful children. *Am Psychol* 56: 227–38.

McAtee EC (1999) *Investigation Of Deficits In Higher Level Executive Functioning As A Prerequisite For Adult Basic Education Intervention, Final Report, Fiscal Year 1998–1999.* Edinboro, PA: Northwest Tri County Intermediate Unit.

McLaughlin K, Greif Green J, Gruber M, Sampson N, Zaslavsky A, Kessler R (2012) Childhood adversities and first onset of psychiatric disorders in a national sample of US adolescents. *Arch Gen Psychiatry* 69(11): 1,151–60.

Mellor A (2019) Cited in Hazell W. A Matter Of Life And Death. *Times Education Supplement* 15 March 2019. Available at: https://www.kuleuven.be/thomas/algemeen/obed/item/5/44618/ [last accessed 4 February 2021]

Midgen T, Theodoratou T, Newbury K & Leonard M (2019) 'School for Everyone': An exploration of children and young people's perceptions of belonging. *Educ Child Psychol* 36(2).

Mischel W (2015) *The Marshmallow Test: Understanding Self-Control And How To Master It.* Ealing, London: Corgi Imprint.

Morewood G (2017) *For Pupils With SEND, Exclusion Is The Road To Nowhere.* Available at: https://blog.optimus-education.com/pupils-send-exclusion-road-nowhere [last accessed 4 February 2021]

Morraine P (2012) *Everyday Executive Functions.* London: Jessica Kingsley Publishers.

Morris I (2015) *Teaching Happiness And Well-Being in Schools: Learning To Ride Elephants.* London: Continuum.

Nadeau M, Nolin P, Chartrand C (2013) Behavioral and emotional profiles of neglected children. *J Child Adolesc Trauma* 6: 11–24.

Naglieri J, LeBuffe P & Ross K (2013) Measuring Resilience In Children: From Theory To Practice. In Goldstein S & Brooks RB (Eds.) *Handbook of Resilience In Children* (pp. 39–55). New York: Springer.

Neckerman K (2004) *Social Inequality.* New York, NY: Russell Sage Foundation.

Newman T (2004) *What Works In Building Resilience?* London: Jessica Kingsley Publishers.

New Economics Foundation (2009) *A Guide to Measuring Children's Well-Being.* Available at: https://neweconomics.org/2009/09/guide-measuring-childrens-wellbeing [last accessed 4 February 2021]

NICE (2016) *Mental Health Problems In People With Learning Disabilities: Prevention, Assessment And Management.* Available at: https://www.nice.org.uk/guidance/ng54 [last accessed 4 February 2021]

Norris LA (2016) *Self-Regulation Strategies For Students With Disruptive Behaviour Disorders.* Available at: https://repository.stcloudstate.edu/cgi/viewcontent.cgi?referer = &httpsredir = 1&article = 1024&context = sped_etds [last accessed at 16 February 2021]

Nuffield Foundation (2009) *Changing Adolescence Programme Briefing Paper.* Available at: https://www.nuffieldfoundation.org/wp-content/uploads/2019/12/Changing-Adolescence_Social-trends-and-mental-health_introducing-the-main-findings.pdf [last accessed 15 February 2021]

Nussbaum MC (2011) *Creating Capabilities: The Human Development Approach.* Cambridge, MA: Belknap Press.

O'Brien J (2016) *Why Are So Many SEN Pupils Excluded From School?* The *Guardian*, 27 October 2016. Available at: https://www.theguardian.com/teacher-network/2016/oct/27/why-are-so-many-sen-pupils-excluded-from-school-because-we-are-failing-them [last accessed 4 February 2021]

O'Dougherty Wright M, Masten A & Narayan A (2014) Resilience Processes In Development: Four Waves. In Goldstein S & Brooks RB (Eds.) *Handbook Of Resilience In Children* (pp. 15–37). New York: Springer.

Olweus D (1978) *Aggression In The Schools. Bullies And Whipping Boys.* Washington, DC: Hemisphere, Wiley.

Organisation for Economic Co-operation and Development (2013) *OECD: Your Better Life Index.* Available at: http://stats.oecd.org/Index.aspx?DataSetCode = BLI Index website: http://www.oecdbetterlifeindex.org/ [last accessed 15 February 2021]

Palombo S, Mariotti V, Iofrida C, Pellegrini S (2015) Genes and aggressive behavior: epigenetic mechanisms underlying individual susceptibility to aversive environments. *Front Behav Neurosci* 12: 17.

Parada R (2019) Assessing perceived school support, rule acceptance and attachment: evaluation of the psychometric properties of the School Belonging Scale (SBS). *Educ Child Psychol* 36(2): 106–16.

Parr C (2019) Cortisol: Not The Baddie You Might Have Thought. *Times Educational Supplement*, 8 March 2019. Available at: https://www.pressreader.com/uk/tes-times-education-supplement/20201120/page/92 [last accessed 4 February 2021]

Patty WL & Johnson LS (1953) *Personality And Adjustment* (p. 277). New York, NY: McGraw-Hill.

Payne S (2013) The physical activity profile of active children in England. *Int J Behav Nutr* 10: 136.

Prince-Embury S (2006) *Resiliency Scales For Children And Adolescents* (9–18). Available at: https://www.pearsonclinical.co.uk/Psychology/ChildMentalHealth/ChildPsychopathology/ResiliencyScalesforChildrenandAdolescents/ResiliencyScalesforChildrenandAdolescents.aspx [last accessed 4 February 2021]

Pearce C (2016) *A Short Introduction To Attachment And Attachment Disorder.* London: Jessica Kingsley Publications.

Pearson A (2019) *Eugenics: Science's Greatest Scandal: Series 1 Episode 2.* Available at: https://www.bbc.co.uk/programmes/m00095jf [last accessed 16 February 2021]

Pennington BF, Bennetto L, McAleer O & Roberts RJ (1996) Executive Functions And Working Memory: Theoretical And Measurement Issues. In Lyon GR & Krasnegor NA (Eds.) *Attention, Memory and Executive Function* (pp. 327–48). Baltimore, MD: Paul H. Brookes Publishing Co.

Peterson C, Park N & Sweeney P (2008) Group well-being: morale from a positive psychology perspective. *Appl Psychol* 57(1): 19–36.

Pine D, Cohen P & Gurley D (1998) The risk for early-adulthood anxiety and depressive disorders in adolescents with anxiety and depressive disorders. *Arch Gen Psychiatry* 55: 56–64.

Pollard L & Rosenberg M (2012) The Strengths-Based Approach To Child Well-Being. In Bornstein M, Davidson L, Keyes C & Moore K (Eds.) *Well-Being: Positive Development Across The Life Course* (p. 14). Mahwah, NJ: Lawrence Erlbaum Associates.

Porter J & Down R (2002) *Pupils With Complex Learning Difficulties: Promoting Learning Using Visual Materials And Methods*. Tamworth: NASEN.

Posner MI & Rothbart MK (2007) Research on attention networks as a model for the integration of psychological science. *Annu Rev Psychol* 58:1–23.

Price BH, Daffner KR, Stowe RM & Mesulam MM (1990) The compartmental learning disabilities of early frontal lobe damage. *Brain* 113: 1,383–93.

Public Health England (2015) *Measuring Mental Wellbeing In Children And Young People*. Available at: https://assets.publishing.service.gov.uk/government/uploads/system/uploads/attachment_data/file/768983/Measuring_mental_wellbeing_in_children_and_young_people.pdf [last accessed 4 February 2021]

Quinn M & Quinn T (2000) *What Can The Parent Of A Teenager Do?* Newry: Family Caring Trust.

Raffo C, Dyson A, Gunter H, Hall D, Jones L, Lalmbouka A (2009) Education and poverty: mapping the terrain and making the links to educational policy. *Int J Incl Educ* 13(4): 341–58.

Rashid T, Anjum A, Lennox C & Quinlan D (2015) *Assessment Of Character Strengths In Children And Adolescents*. Available at: https://www.researchgate.net/publication/281765645_Assessment_of_Character_Strengths_in_Children_and_Adolescents [last accessed 4 February 2021]

Reid R, Trout AL & Schartz M (2005) Self-regulation interventions for children with attention deficit/hyperactivity disorder. *Except Child* 71: 361–77.

Resnick M (2005) Some Reflections On Designing Construction Kits For Kids. In John Gray (Ed.) *The Supportive School* (p. 21). Newcastle: Cambridge Scholars.

Rosenberg M (2001) *Extending Self-Esteem*. Cambridge: Cambridge University Press.

Rutter MJ & Smith DJ (1995) *Psychosocial Disorders In Young People: Time Trends And Their Causes*. Chichester, West Sussex: John Wiley & Sons, Ltd.

Salovey P, Rothman AJ, Detweiler JB & Steward WT (2000) Emotional states and physical health. *Am Psychol* 55: 110–21.

Schaffer R (1996) *Social Development*. Oxford: Blackwell.

Schmidt Neven R (2010) *Core Principles Of Assessment And Therapeutic Communication With Children, Parents And Families: Towards The Promotion Of Child And Family Wellbeing*. Abingdon, Oxfordshire: Routledge.

Seligman MEP (2002) Positive Psychology, Positive Prevention And Positive Therapy. In Snyder CR & Lopez SJ (Eds.) *Handbook Of Positive Psychology* (pp. 3–7). New York, NY: Oxford University Press.

Seligman MEP & Csikszentmihalyi M (2000) Positive Psychology: An Introduction. *Am Psychol* 55(1): 5–14.

Seligman M (2011) *Flourish: A New Understanding Of Happiness And Well-Being – And How To Achieve Them: A New Understanding Of Happiness And Wellbeing: The Practical... Psychology To Make You Happier And Healthier*. London: Nicholas Brealey Publishing.

Sen A (2012) *Sen's Capability Approach*. Available at: https://iep.utm.edu/sen-cap/ [last accessed 4 February 2021]

Shayer M & Adey P (1981) *Towards A Science Of Science Teaching*. London: Helnemann.

Sheel A (2016) Sex differences in the physiology of exercise: an integrative perspective. *Exp Psychol* 101(2): 211–12.

Skinner BF (2011) *About Behaviourism*. New York: Knopf Doubleday Publishing.

Slaten C (2019) *Students With A Greater Sense Of Family And School Belonging Are Less Likely To Become Bullies.* Available at: https://education.missouri.edu/2019/07/students-with-a-greater-sense-of-family-and-school-belonging-are-less-likely-to-become-bullies/ [last accessed 4 February 2021]

Slavin RE (2002) Evidence-based education policies: Transforming educational practice and research. *Educ Res* 31: 15–21.

Sleek S (2015) *How Poverty Affects The Brain And Behaviour.* Available at: https://www.psychologicalscience.org/observer/how-poverty-affects-the-brain-and-behavior [last accessed 16 February 2021]

Southam-Gerow MA (2016) *Emotion Regulation In Children and Adolescents.* London: The Guilford Press.

Specialist Schools And Academies Trust (2011) *The Complex Learning Difficulties And Disabilities Research Project Developing Pathways To Personalised Learning.* Available at: https://files.eric.ed.gov/fulltext/ED525543.pdf [last accessed 4 February 2021]

Spock B (2018) *Dr. Spock's Baby And Child Care.* London: Pocket Books.

Sroufe L(1990) An Organisational Perspective On The Self. In Cicchetti D & Beeghly M (Eds.) *Transitions From Infancy To Childhood: The Self* (pp. 281–307). Chicago: University of Chicago Press.

Stack S (2015) Learning outcomes in an online vs traditional course. *IJ-SoTL* 9(1): 1–18.

Steger M (2009) Meaning In Life. In Lopez SJ & Snyder CR (Eds.) *The Oxford Handbook Of Positive Psychology.* Oxford: Oxford University Press.

Strand S, Fletcher J (2014) *A Quantitative Longitudinal Analysis Of Exclusions From English Secondary Schools.* Oxford: University of Oxford.

Sykes E, Bell J & Vidal Rodeiro C (2016) *Birthdate Effects: A Review Of The Literature From 1990 On.* Available at: https://www.cambridgeassessment.org.uk/images/109784-birthdate-effects-a-review-of-the-literature-from-1990-on.pdf [last accessed 4 February 2021]

Teicher M, Dumont N, Ito Y, Vaituzis C, Giedd J, Andersen S (2004) Childhood neglect is associated with reduced corpus callosum area. *Biol Psychiatry* 56(2): 80–85.

Thompson AH, Barnsley RH & Dyck RJ (1999) A new factor in youth suicide: The relative age effect. *Can J Psychiatry* 44(1): 82–85.

Tokic A & Pecnik N (2010) Parental behaviours related to adolescents' self-disclosure: Adolescents' views. *J Soc Pers Relat* 28: 201–22.

Toffler A (1984) *Future Shock.* New York, NY: Random House.

Department for Education (2017) *Transforming Children And Young People's Mental Health Provision: A Green Paper.* Available at: https://assets.publishing.service.gov.uk/government/uploads/system/uploads/attachment_data/file/664855/Transforming_children_and_young_people_s_mental_health_provision.pdf [last accessed 4 February 2021]

Truss E (2016) Cited in Nagel P (Ed.) *Mental Health Matters* (p.8). London: Bloomsbury.

Twenge JM (2019) The Sad State Of Happiness And The Role Of Digital Media. In Helliwell JF, Layard R & Sachs JD (Eds.) *World Happiness Report 2019.* Available at: https://worldhappiness.report/ed/2019/the-sad-state-of-happiness-in-the-united-states-and-the-role-of-digital-media/ [accessed 4 February 2021]

UK Government (2010) *Equality Act 2010.* Available at: https://www.legislation.gov.uk/ukpga/2010/15/contents [last accessed 4 February 2021]

UK Government (2013) *Annual Report of the Chief Medical Officer 2013 Public Mental Health Priorities: Investing in the Evidence.* Available at: https://assets.publishing.service.gov.uk/government/uploads/system/uploads/attachment_data/file/413196/CMO_web_doc.pdf) [last accessed 4 February 2021]

UNICEF (2007) *An Overview Of Child Wellbeing In Rich Countries.* Available at: https://www.unicef.org/media/files/ChildPovertyReport.pdf [last accessed 4 February 2021]

UNICEF (2012) *School Readiness: A Conceptual Framework*. Available at: https://www.unicef.org/earlychildhood/files/Child2Child_ConceptualFramework_FINAL(1).pdf [last accessed 4 February 2021]

van Ijzendoorn MH, Dijkstra J & Bus AG (1995) Attachment, intelligence and language: A meta-analysis. *Soc Dev* 4: 115–28.

van Woerden H (2018) *The Annual Report Of The Director Of Public Health*. Available at: https://www.nhshighland.scot.nhs.uk/Publications/Documents/DPH-Annual-Report-2018_(web-version).pdf [last accessed 4 February 2021]

Vygotsky L (1986) *Thought And Language*. Cambridge, MA: Massachusetts Institute of Technology Press.

Weale S (2019) *Mental Health Of Pupils Is 'At Crisis Point', Teachers Warn*. Available at: https://www.theguardian.com/society/2019/apr/17/mental-health-young-people-england-crisis-point-teacher-school-leader-survey [last accessed 4 February 2021]

Wedell K (1995) Making inclusive education ordinary. *Br J Spec Educ* 22(3): 100–04.

Weisner T (1984) Ecocultural Niches Of Middle Childhood. In Collins W (Ed.) *Development During Middle Childhood: The Years From Six To Twelve* (pp. 335–69). Washington, DC: National Academy of Sciences.

Werner P (1994) *Building Children And Young People's Resilience In Schools*. Available at: https://assets.publishing.service.gov.uk/government/uploads/system/uploads/attachment_data/file/355766/Review2_Resilience_in_schools_health_inequalities.pdf [available at 16 February 2021]

Wilkins B, Boman P & Mergler A (2015) *Positive Psychological Strengths And School Engagement In Primary School Children*. Available at: https://www.cogentoa.com/article/10.1080/233118 6X.2015.1095680 [last accessed 4 February 2021]

Wilkinson R & Pickett K (2018). *The Inner Level*. Allen Lane: UK.

Wilkinson R & Pickett K (2010). *The Spirit Level*. London: Penguin.

Wilkinson-Lee AM, Zhang Q, Nuno VL & Wilhelm MS (2011) Adolescent emotional distress: The role of family obligations and school connectedness. *J Youth Adolesc* 40(2): 221–30.

Woolard J (2010) *Psychology For The Classroom: Behaviourism*. Oxon: Routledge.

World Happiness Report (2019) *Chapter 2: Changing World Happiness*. Available at: https://worldhappiness.report/ed/2019/changing-world-happiness/ [last accessed 4 February 2021]

Wyman P (2003) Cited in O'Dougherty, Wright M, Masten A & Narayan A (2014) Resilience Processes In Development: Four Waves (pp.15–37). In Goldstein S & Brooks RB (Eds.) *Handbook Of Resilience In Children*. New York: Springer.

Young Minds (2016) *Young Minds Annual Report 2015–2016*. Available at: https://youngminds.org.uk/media/1233/youngminds-annual-report-15-16-final.pdf [last accessed at 4 February 2021]

Ylvisaker M & Feeney T (2009) Apprenticeship in self-regulation: Supports and interventions for individuals with self-regulatory impairments. *Developmental Neurorehabil* 12: 370–79.

H²h
How to Help

To keep up to date with the *How to Help* series, bookmark:

www.pavpub.com/howtohelp